System Administration Ethics

Ten Commandments for Security and Compliance in a Modern Cyber World

Igor Ljubuncic
Tom Litterer

Apress®

System Administration Ethics: Ten Commandments for Security and Compliance in a Modern Cyber World

Igor Ljubuncic
London, UK

Tom Litterer
Portland, OR, USA

ISBN-13 (pbk): 978-1-4842-4987-1
https://doi.org/10.1007/978-1-4842-4988-8

ISBN-13 (electronic): 978-1-4842-4988-8

Managing Director, Apress Media LLC: Welmoed Spahr
Acquisitions Editor: Natalie Pao
Development Editor: James Markham
Coordinating Editor: Jessica Vakili

Cover designed by eStudioCalamar

Cover image designed by Freepik (www.freepik.com)

Distributed to the book trade worldwide by Springer Science+Business Media New York, 233 Spring Street, 6th Floor, New York, NY 10013. Phone 1-800-SPRINGER, fax (201) 348-4505, e-mail orders-ny@springer-sbm.com, or visit www.springeronline.com. Apress Media, LLC is a California LLC and the sole member (owner) is Springer Science + Business Media Finance Inc (SSBM Finance Inc). SSBM Finance Inc is a **Delaware** corporation.

For information on translations, please e-mail rights@apress.com, or visit http://www.apress.com/rights-permissions.

Apress titles may be purchased in bulk for academic, corporate, or promotional use. eBook versions and licenses are also available for most titles. For more information, reference our Print and eBook Bulk Sales web page at http://www.apress.com/bulk-sales.

Any source code or other supplementary material referenced by the author in this book is available to readers on GitHub via the book's product page, located at www.apress.com/978-1-4842-4987-1. For more detailed information, please visit http://www.apress.com/source-code.

Printed on acid-free paper

Table of Contents

About the Authors

Igor Ljubuncic is a physicist by vocation and a Linux geek by profession. Igor comes with many years of experience in the hi-tech industry, including medical, high-performance computing (HPC), data center, cloud, and hosting fields, with emphasis on complex problem solving and the scientific method. To date, Igor's portfolio includes 15 patents, 16 books, several open-source projects, numerous articles published in leading journals and magazines, and presentations at prestigious international conferences like LinuxCon, CloudOpen, OpenStack days, IEEE events, and others. In his free time, Igor writes car reviews and fantasy novels and manages his award-winning blog, dedoimedo.com.

Tom Litterer is a business leader and a future-focused thinker with three decades of experience in the industry. Tom spent the first 6 years of his career as a UNIX system administrator, transitioning from novice to expert. He has since managed each of the key areas within Information Technology (IT), including help desk, site operations, high-performance computing (HPC) services, identity and access management, lab operations, internal cloud deployment, engineering tools, and licensing. He was also the global manager of Intel's HPC servers and storage chip design environment. Tom is currently the associate director of Data Center and Cloud Infrastructure at Portland State University (PSU), Oregon, USA. In this role, he is responsible for all Linux, Windows, virtualization, storage, backup, and HPC services in local data centers as well as the university's cloud infrastructure.

About the Technical Reviewer

Jesse Smith is a Canadian open-source programmer and system administrator. When he's not fixing code and updating servers, he scribbles articles for the distrowatch.com web site. On the odd occasion he steps away from the computer, he likes to garden, play *HeroQuest* with friends, go for walks by the water, and feed ducks.

Acknowledgments

We would like to thank Alison Nimura, Ryan M. Bass, and many others at Portland State University (pdx.edu) who contributed to the crafting of The Ten Commandments of System Administration Ethics; Jake Litterer and Cathy Litterer for much of the chapter editing; and Jesse Smith of DistroWatch (`distrowatch.com`) for providing technical editing services; a special shout-out to the thousands of Dedoimedo (`dedoimedo.com`) followers who have supported Igor's musings, including his many books. Most importantly, this book would have never been completed without the loving support, encouragement, and tolerance of overseas video calls and obscure ethical conversations from our wives, Irena Ljubuncic and Tracy Litterer.

Preface

Ethics is a tricky word. For most people, if they ever stop to think about it, ethics evokes the idea of an orchard somewhere in Ancient Greece, with philosophers sitting in the shade of fig trees, debating the meaning of life and the implication of free will. It rarely evokes the floor plan of an IT building, with bewildered engineers and system administrators discussing their work in philosophical terms.

If only it were that simple.

When we started our technical careers, we didn't think much about any moral implications of our actions. Sure, we watched the corporate training videos, and we knew that we shouldn't bribe government employees or try to use our business credit card to buy ourselves decking for a vacation house in the mountains. But there was no mention of how simple, innocent things like a misconfigured server or a wrong data access permission could have profound, long-lasting ethical implications.

That awareness came later. Much later. After mistakes had been made.

After a few decades of hard experience being guided by our moral compass and some lucky trial and error, the book on system administration ethics was born in an instant. Once the idea germinated, it was a walk in the park. Literally.

During a chance meeting halfway around the world, walking across a beautiful botanical garden, we started our conversation about ethics. We spoke about how we wanted to help the current and future generations of system administrators, data center technicians, engineers, and programmers by providing a book of guidelines and principles that will help them make the right ethical choices, regardless of the technology and the situation they are faced with. We wanted to help new system administrators understand that technological abstraction is not a moral abstraction and that every choice we make has important, meaningful, even life-changing implications.

But guidelines and principles are not...strong enough for the harsh technological climate we live in. No, we need something bigger. We need dos and don'ts. We need commandments.

This book has twelve parts: the introduction; ten chapters, each discussing a different ethical area (ten chapters, ten commandments); and the epilogue (a section for managers).

However, rather than just instructing readers what to do, we provide example stories. We begin each of the twelve parts with a story that follows the life of a system administrator encountering ethical issues through his first few months of employment. We get to see and experience the work dilemma and problems through the eyes of an IT person facing the challenges of the modern, hectic world of technology. After that, each chapter provides an in-depth discussion of the ethical area, the dos and the don'ts.

Our desire is to teach the reader the ten commandments of system administration ethics that are applicable to any technology scenario, today or tomorrow. Finally, we do have one hope, too; that you will enjoy reading this book as much as we did writing it.

—Igor and Tom,
July 2019

Prologue: In the Beginning …

"There will be an investigation," Alex said, staring down at his phone, thumbing up whatever he was half-reading.

"What?" Daniel said.

"Yeah, there's going to be an investigation," Alex said, raising his eyes.

"How do you know that?" Belinda asked.

"Well, why do you think Mike called in this meeting? It's gotta do with the data breach last week," Alex plodded on, oozing smug confidence.

"Who told you that?" Belinda insisted.

"So? What's that got to do with us?" Gopal interjected. He tried to sound defiant, but he actually sounded worried.

Alex shrugged, typing on his phone.

The team had gathered outside the Lotus meeting room on the second floor, waiting for the guys inside to wrap their session. Someone was gesturing wildly at a whiteboard full of blue rectangles and illegible text. A few of the participants were listening. Most were busy staring at their email clients on their laptops.

To Wendell, the dynamics of his new team were still a bit strange. He had joined the company only 2 months earlier – and what a 2 months had it been. Lots of online training, most of it rather refreshing; awesome cafeteria; and, of course, the actual work. Fun stuff.

Until the breach last week anyway.

Mike showed up 6 minutes late and knocked impatiently on the glass door, and that concluded the previous meeting, which was passionately running over. With terse smiles and half-murmured apologies, the occupants left. Wendell stepped in last and sat in the corner, close to the AC vents. He liked the place, but he always felt it was too hot for his taste.

Mike looked flustered. Well, if Alex's web of rumors rang true, Mike had just come back from a 2-hour meeting with the chief operating officer and corporate legal, discussing the weekend fiasco. Officially, the discovered security hole had been plugged on Saturday morning, but the fallout ripples seemed to spread and intensify.

"I want to talk to you about the data breach," Mike said without much preamble. He was trying to hook up the HDMI cable into his laptop – and failing. It was always the other way around.

"It's a conspiracy," Henry said. "There's a whole organization behind cables and connectivity." Wendell wasn't really sure what to think of Henry. Older than the rest of the team, with gray hair and laid-back style, he seemed to be coasting to an early, safe retirement. And he always had a joke.

Belinda rolled her eyes. There were a few half-hearted chuckles in the group.

"Also, guys, we won't have the team event on Friday."

The chuckling stopped. "Why not?" Alex bristled.

Mike did not look pleased, but his usual patience was gone. "Because of the breach, Alex! The management staff had a meeting, and we decided we need to focus on operational excellence right now."

"It's not our fault those storage guys screwed things up," Jacob said.

"Not the storage guys," Caesar piped in, almost forcefully. "The database guys."

Gopal sniffed. "I'm sure it was caused by the team that likes to put all those color stickers on room walls."

Alex blinked, hard, back to reading something on his phone.

Mike switched to the external display, and a beginning of what looked like a long presentation was showing up. "Guys, listen now. Let's not blamestorm. Let's brainstorm. We're in this together, and it's not who did what. What's important is that we understand what happened and what we need do from here on. The way it looks like right now is there's gonna be an investigation and it will be on all of the news feeds."

Ethics in the Digital World

Sounds familiar, does it not?

If you've worked in the Information Technology (IT) industry in the past two decades, you must have heard, seen, witnessed, or even been involved, directly or indirectly, in an incident of this kind. Major outages, significant customer impact, data breaches, and data loss are an all too common phenomenon in the modern digital world.

And they involve more than just the technological aspect of "what might have gone wrong."

When you think about the modern digital world, you envision minimalistic offices, shiny, buzzing data centers, movie-like control centers and ops rooms full of serious-faced engineers and technicians, loud but productive meetings of intelligent minds, gadgets everywhere, and, of course, stylish cafeterias and game rooms where the hard-working, overstressed IT folks can relax.

You rarely associate the word ethics with this mental image.

One of the first and the most familiar lists of ethics, specifying good vs. evil, is the Judeo-Christian Ten Commandments. Moral philosophy goes back to Ancient Greece, where it first defined what we associate with societal ethics nowadays: the concepts of good and bad, right and wrong. The question of morality arose way before we used advanced technology in such a pervasive way as we do in the beginning of the 21st century. Through most of human history, ethics were associated with crime, justice, and politics. Science and engineering were domains of their own. Later, the field of medicine and medical practice became the first scientific pursuit to encompass the notion of ethical and moral conduct within the Hippocratic Oath.

As life becomes more digital, niche practices that were once the playground of nerds, hobbyists, and technology pioneers are now becoming essential, inseparable pieces of human life. Even people, especially system administrators, who have no interest in privacy or security are being exposed to ethical questions, almost on a daily basis. Our constant interaction with hardware and software pushes technology right into the field of ethics. And yet, for most people, computers remain wondrous, detached, and, above all, conscience-free objects.

It is not a surprise that people would fail to ascribe an ethical dimension to the world of information technology. It is a cold world. A world of certainties. Ones and zeros. Machines have no moral dilemmas. They do what they are told.

When you look at software code and algorithms, it is very easy to forget that the written instructions are a manifestation of their *human* creators, the engineers and programmers who code the logic. But somewhere along the way, things get lost in the translation from intention to instruction, and with it, the moral boundaries get blurred.

On its own, the problem would not be serious if information technology remained what it was 30 years ago. Today, our lives depend on computers. A server goes down, and trains are forced to stop their journeys. A service goes down, and hospital monitors cease functioning. We lose access to the Internet, we cannot do our financial transactions, businesses are forced to halt their operations.

Oh, and our personal data gets stolen.

It is easy to just blame technology, but we must not forget that behind any machine instruction, there is a human governing the process. Someone made decisions, invested in mechanisms, defined the logic, or even actively manipulated data.

Why Should I Care?

As it happens, you might be that human.

The world of technology can be broadly separated into two: those who run and administer the digital infrastructure and those who use it. As a *user*, you are rarely exposed to the decision-making that goes on behind the scenes. As an *administrator*, your choices – governed by your moral compass – impact the lives of thousands, maybe millions out there.

Not a problem, you might say. You will just behave *ethically*. You will make sure to make the right choices all the time. Problem solved.

Well, it is not quite as simple as that.

The first issue is that we all have different moral compasses – different upbringing, different education, different culture, different social and religious values, different skills, different *emotions*, and perhaps even different intelligence. No two persons are the same, nor are the circumstances that shape their lives identical. It is impossible to expect everyone to have the exact same reasoning when they do things.

The second issue is that people often believe they are *right* when they do things. We do not like making bad choices; so we convince ourselves, given the evidence, preconceptions, misconceptions, and beliefs that we have, that we are doing the right thing. Making an ethical transgression, so to speak, may not be deliberate. In fact, few people go out of their way to cause harm and malice. Most of the time, we accidentally, inadvertently make mistakes, and we are not even aware of them.

The third issue is, our actions are never isolated, especially when we work as part of a team. Indeed, pick any job in the IT industry, and you will find yourself interacting with people, whether you want it or not.

Then, companies have policies and values, too.

Established businesses often have well-worded manifestos that broadly define, usually in legal terms, what the employees are expected to do and, quite as importantly, what not to do. Sometimes, such policies are framed into codes of conduct. Sometimes, they also have a more humane side so people can identify with them, and they are known as company values.

These policies can help people adjust to their environment, so that they work effectively with others. However, regardless of what they are called, the policies and values usually revolve around the human dimension. They rarely mention technology.

In recent years, IT security and compliance have come under spotlight, and these security guidelines sometimes touch on specific policies or the usage of technology in the office. The Health Insurance Portability and Accountability Act (HIPAA),[1] enacted by the US Congress in 1996, and the EU General Data Protection Regulation (GDPR),[2] made in 2016 and implemented in early 2018, are great examples of complex legislation with significant impact on the technological landscape. Both have been designed to address the changes and challenges in the digital world, and yet, they only satisfy the legal side of the equation. System administrators are expected to uphold such laws and regulations, but they are not told how to do this – and often, even their managers do not have sufficient expertise to provide necessary guidance.

Largely, the world of machines is left to its own devices.

As a system administrator, you will find yourself in a fast-paced, highly layered, complex world of technology; and it may be quite difficult to perceive or understand the potential ethical areas that touch upon your work. How do code commits, version control, and staging servers have anything to do with ethics? Why would a database administrator need to concern themselves with, apart from the purely technological considerations, how many columns or data fields are in the personnel table? Why should someone monitoring server performance in an operations center have to think about anything other than the amount of work at hand?

Moreover, ethics is not something that comes naturally to most techies. On an almost cynical level, one may call it a *soft* area. That's not what techies do.

But then, there may come a day where you are being asked to come into a meeting and explain your actions regarding the data breach from

---

[1] www.gpo.gov/fdsys/search/pagedetails.action?granuleId=CRPT-104hrpt736&
packageId=CRPT-104hrpt736
[2] https://ec.europa.eu/info/law/law-topic/data-protection_en

the previous week. At that point, the question of ethics – *your* ethics – will arise, and you may not even be aware that there ever was such a question.

So what do you do?

We go back to basics.

The Ten Commandments of System Administration Ethics

We believe that technology and ethics are inseparable. We also believe that it is possible to create a universal codex of best ethical practices, regardless of what technology medium you use or the company that employs your skills.

This book breaks down the complex idea of digital ethics into ten major areas. As we go through the book, we will discuss them separately, chapter by chapter. We will also present real-life examples for each of the ethical areas, seen through the eyes of engineers who've experienced how privileged hardware and software access requires ethics. These will be genuine, relatable problems, issues, and questions that we have seen and faced – and you probably have or will soon, too – throughout our careers.

There will, of course, be some overlap. It is virtually impossible to talk about privacy or data security in isolation. In some cases, there will be more than one ethical aspect to our examples, but overall, each chapter will focus on one particular area.

Since this may sound overwhelming, let's start slowly. Let's take a look at the ten commandments of system administration ethics (Figures P-1 and P-2), and then, we will briefly discuss each one of them before we delve deeper.

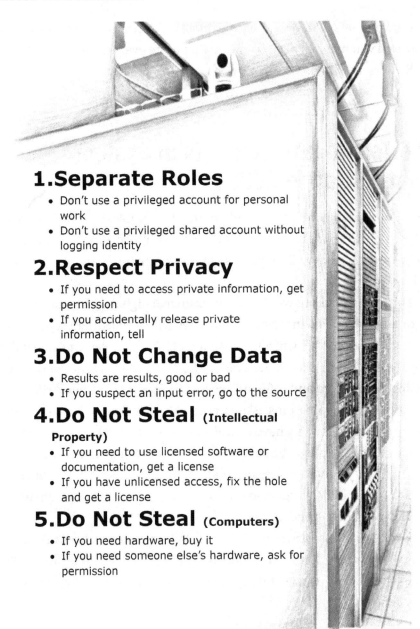

1.Separate Roles

- Don't use a privileged account for personal work
- Don't use a privileged shared account without logging identity

2.Respect Privacy

- If you need to access private information, get permission
- If you accidentally release private information, tell

3.Do Not Change Data

- Results are results, good or bad
- If you suspect an input error, go to the source

4.Do Not Steal (Intellectual Property)

- If you need to use licensed software or documentation, get a license
- If you have unlicensed access, fix the hole and get a license

5.Do Not Steal (Computers)

- If you need hardware, buy it
- If you need someone else's hardware, ask for permission

Figure P-1. *System administration ethics commandments 1–5*

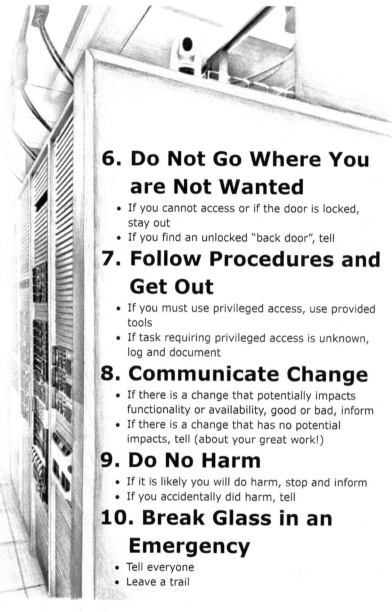

Figure P-2. *System administration ethics commandments 6–10*

Now, let's examine these briefly in slightly more detail.

1. Separate Roles

The modern data center is an almost abstract entity. Sure, it has its physical presence, the rack upon rack of whirring, clicking, beeping servers, mile upon mile of network cables, the powerful A/C systems trying to scoop all the excess heat out, and an odd, forlorn technician wandering through the sterile, chilly aisles. But for most people, data centers are just out there, hidden behind magical cloud interfaces and virtual portals. Moreover, few companies can afford to run their own data centers. Very often, there's an element of physical asset and resource sharing involved, and it is not uncommon for admins and users – sometimes from different business groups and even different organizations – to be logged in on the same server. And that is where friction and conflict – and ethical breaches – may occur.

2. Respect Privacy

As the world grows more global, more open, more accessible, so does our need for privacy. We realize the inevitable dichotomy of our lives in the digital era. We are asked to expose our personal data in order to gain (sometimes useful) functionality that the modern digital wonders and gadgets offer. Each time we put our data out there, we make ourselves vulnerable. People in the positions of *data* power have a moral obligation to safeguard personal information, more so than ever before in human history. Alas, the fine line between what we consider our private world and what the world sees as free for the taking is often blurred.

3. Do Not Change Data

We may argue about our favorite movies, *Star Wars* vs. *Star Trek* (*Star Trek*, of course), the taste in music, or the airspeed of an unladen swallow; but the unquestionable beauty of digital data is that it is discrete, absolute, and true. *"Zeros and ones do not lie."* Or do they?

4. Do Not Steal Intellectual Property

The unprecedented and rather unregulated explosion of the Internet
has taught us that we can have pretty much anything digital for free.
Somewhere, somehow, it can be had. This mentality is so pervasive that we
sometimes forget ourselves, even when we don our work shoes and go into
an office.

5. Do Not Steal Computers

Anonymity and guilt are inversely proportional. The more you have of the
former, the less you have of the latter. In large data centers, with thousands
upon thousands of out-of-warranty hard disks lying about, waiting to
be shipped to a scrap yard, who is going to miss one dusty, barcode-less
metal-and-plastic brick?

6. Do Not Go Where You Are Not Wanted

Curiosity killed the cat. It also made the bored IT engineer wander about
the shiny office buildings, exploring the floors, pulling on door levers, be
they physical or ephemeral.

A day in the life of an IT person will inevitably involve navigating the
world of restricted areas, test data, firewalls, databases full of secrets and
wonders, and helpful colleagues with *just* the right access permissions. The
temptations that exist in the corridors and aisles of the company's office
space carry over into the software world.

7. Follow Procedures (and Get Out)

By nature, engineers have inquisitive personalities. The somewhat childish
streak that fuels innovation in the tech world also makes for a rebellious
streak when it comes to routine work. Following procedures may be

boring, especially if you do not understand or agree with them. After all, the procedures were made by bureaucracy-loving managers, and what do they know about SQL or version control?

8. Communicate Change

"Can't see the forest for the trees" was already a proverb when John Heywood wrote his collection in 1546, a good four centuries before the first digital computer was born. The paradox of the information technology world is that, despite (and maybe because of) the plethora of media, methods and tools we use to exchange data, we still struggle with basic communication. When a typo in an executed software command can cost companies billions or adversely impact the lives of many people, effective, clear, and unequivocal communication becomes paramount.

9. Do No Harm

Rebooting a server shouldn't be a big issue, should it? Deleting a user name entry that no one has accessed in a year is most likely harmless, isn't it? System administrators have an almost whimsical ability to wreak havoc on users, systems, and customers. Such responsibility can have adverse effects: make people either reckless or bashful, quick to make changes, or afraid to make any update. The other side of this coin is that mistakes will happen and harm will be done, regardless of intentions, procedures, preparations, or testing.

10. Break Glass in an Emergency

When things go wrong – and they will – people are often forced to act quickly, without having too much time or opportunity to think their actions through. Insufficient data, pressure, imminent customer impact – they will force our hand into making choices based on less-than-ideal information. Our inhibitions drop, exposing our instincts – and our ethical upbringing – to the elements. Handling emergencies is probably one of the most important exercises in the life of a system administrator. While it may sound trivially excusable to throw caution to the wind, ethics play a critical part in what we do during – and just as importantly after – an emergency situation at work.

Conclusion

At the moment, some of these areas may sound blatantly obvious and others infuriatingly vague. Worry not, we will make sure that each ethical subject is carefully covered, explained, and demonstrated.

Before you read on, we need to request something: it is important for you to put your techie doubts aside. You may be skeptical, just as you were watching the mandatory code of conduct training just a month ago or when leafing through page upon page of monotone legalese that explains when and how you ought to use your credit card while on business trip. You may believe that ethics has no place in the information technology world, or in the best case, it can all be covered with common sense.

We are fully aware of the doubt and resistance – we often had it ourselves at different stages of our careers. But we have also seen how a chain of perfectly sane, logical, and explainable decisions leads to disasters. We also believe that it is possible to marry the concepts of technology and ethics in a quantifiable, fun way. A deterministic way that fits the world of zeros and ones, which do not lie. It does not have to be boring, monotone, or legalese.

Let's begin the journey.

CHAPTER 1

Separate Roles

Wendell thought back to his interactions with each of the team members. Could something they did have contributed to the breach? Maybe his presence triggered events that led to the breach.

The first days at a new workplace are much like visiting a new city. You're a tourist, and most likely in a mild state of shock, preferably a pleasant one. You don't know quite what to do – even if you've done it before – and you're looking for a reputable source of wisdom to help you get around.

For Wendell, the tourist guide was no other than Alex, and he could tell right away that he should tread softly.

"You're lucky," Alex dramatized.

"Oh?"

"Normally, I would wait a few weeks before giving you the access rights, but Mike's keen on getting you on board as quickly as possible, so we're doing the expedited version. You did work with privileged accounts before?"

Wendell nodded.

"All right. So this is how it works. Your standard user is Wendell, and we're going to set up wendell_p now. This will be your *power* user account, and you're going to use it for privileged access. You don't use your ordinary account for that, you use this one."

"Is this a sudo account?" Wendell tried to show some knowledge.

Alex waved impatiently. "It's actually five accounts."

© Igor Ljubuncic, Tom Litterer 2019
I. Ljubuncic and T. Litterer, *System Administration Ethics*,
https://doi.org/10.1007/978-1-4842-4988-8_1

Wendell let out a small laugh. "Five? At my last place, we only used one. Well, two. We had the standard account for pretty much everything, and root when we had to do some admin work on the servers."

Alex blinked. He did not like having his show interrupted, it seemed. "Separate accounts are a smart thing. One, they give you more granularity when it comes to work. Two, they minimize risk. Three, you clearly know what each account does and what it's used for. Now, it's all tied to your user, but it maps to *five* user management systems. First, if you need to work on Windows machines, you're going to have the AD account. Then, there's also high account. This is a privileged account for Windows administration." Alex paused to look at something on his phone screen. "Do you know what privileged access management is?"

Wendell nodded again. "You mean PAM tools?"

"Yes. Good. Because we will need to set you up with SSH access, so you can do remote administration. Now, you SSH with your own account to other systems and then switch to wendell_p there. As a policy, we don't allow the _p users to SSH to other hosts."

"Got it," Wendell said, furiously writing notes down.

Alex swiveled his chair back toward his desk and started typing and running commands, faster than Wendell would have liked, but this was Alex's thing, and he decided not to interrupt.

"Now...the power user account is all good and well, but sometimes, you need proper root." Alex wrote something on a piece of paper. It was an eight-letter string, and Wendell assumed it was a password.

"This is our current root password. Now, normally, you go online to get the password. Let me show you. Here. Go to slash slash accounts; that will redirect to our online password management system. It's called Sesame, and as you can see, it's an ugly thing designed in the past millennium. Here, you log in with your power user. And then click *Request root password*, and it will show the password on the screen for 30 seconds. So if you forget it, or the password rotates, you can always get it this way." Alex raised a finger. "Only with a local IP address. Won't work over the VPN."

Wendell underlined the intranet alias in his notebook. "Understood."

"Excellent. Now let's get some coffee, I'm running on fumes." Without waiting for Wendell to actually respond, Alex bounded off for the coffee area, swinging his old, faded-logo mug like a baton. Along the way, he stopped to exchange a few old and not-so-funny jokes with people sitting at other desks. Wendell didn't really catch the inside meaning of most of it. He believed this was a well-practiced and often repeated ritual.

Once back at Alex's desk, Wendell remembered the first-day-at-work presentation, a seemingly never-ending stream of slides, slogans, and mini interviews with this or that manager. "And what about the VPN access?"

Alex snapped his fingers. "That's *only* going to work from your work laptop. Now, unlike Sesame, which only works inside the company's network, you cannot actually use this one from within the intranet. You have to be on the Internet, like at home or in the coffee shop. But let me show you something neat."

Alex unlocked his phone and launched what looked like a console application, black background and a blinking cursor. "I've set up a special bastion host in the DC that allows me to log in from this device."

Wendell was curious. He also couldn't recall anything about phones being mentioned anywhere for system access. "You SSH to the bastion and then switch to your admin account?"

"Yup. Saves time. When I'm on call at night, and the ops ring me, it's so much easier and faster to just log in on the phone right away and see what's happening. Most of the time, it's just trivial misconfigurations, and I can quickly fix the issues and close the ticket. But if I need to do lots of work, I'll then turn the laptop on, VPN in, and do the full hands on."

Wendell pursed his lips. He found the notion practical, but he was wondering about the security model. He decided not to raise the topic, though.

Alex was typing again. "Since you're new, if you're not sure, it's best to ask. Now, it's a well-known fact, if you do system administration work, you're going to end up making mistakes." Alex stood up, pushing his chair back. "Henry!"

"What's up?"

"How many times have you accidentally rebooted a customer server?"

"Too many," Henry muttered, busy behind his desk.

Alex sat down. "So don't worry about it. But remember. With your power account and root, you can easily cause a severe outage, so double-check your commands; and if you're running a script on multiple hosts, always get someone else to check it before you hit Enter. Anyone in the team will do."

Wendell nodded. "So it doesn't matter who?"

"We all touch pretty much every aspect of administration. Doesn't mean every one of us is an expert on everything, but sometimes, it's necessary. Just the other day I configured Belinda's high account for customer data access. She needed to look at some application logs, because her customer was complaining about performance issues."

Wendell kept on writing in his notebook. It was going to be a long day.

SEPARATE ROLES

*Don't use a privileged account for personal work.

*Don't use a privileged shared account without logging identity.

Why Is Separating Roles Important?

The phrase "With great power comes great responsibility" is widely attributed to Marvel Comics *Amazing Fantasy* #15 back in 1962, way before software-based system administration became an item. But the quote, in one form or another, has been ascribed to Winston Churchill, Voltaire, William Lamb, and perhaps even the Bible.[1] It would seem that, throughout the ages, people understood the moral weight of power.

The leap of faith from government and philosophy to system administration feels rather detached from the implication that the quote carries, especially since the core difference between ordinary users and privileged users in a system is merely in the ID number that their accounts carry.

But it is there.

A position of power allows people to utilize that power and make changes that others cannot do, regardless of their desire or skill. In the IT world, privileged system accounts are the most prevalent interface for system administrators for crossing the boundary from ordinary use, restricted to individuals and their own data, to wider activities that can impact other systems – and in turn other people. When you pause and think about it, the only thing that really stops privileged users from causing all-out mayhem is their judgment.

What do you do if you make a wrong judgment?

You cause damage, of course.

Early on in the software world, engineers realized that they could easily fall prey to their own personal weakness, whims, and honest mistakes and that they needed to create external mechanisms between subjective reasoning and hard data.

As a result, various security mechanisms were designed to create forced separation between common use (everyday work that is unique to each individual, group, or project) and privileged administrative work (maintenance of systems and services that enable people to do their everyday work).

---

[1]https://quoteinvestigator.com/2015/07/23/great-power/

The most common example of separating privileged access from the common user account is the root user (account) in UNIX/Linux systems. With this separation, users of the system can utilize applications and services without having the ability to make changes to the underlying operating system or configuration of the server. But for those who have root access, they have the ability to make pretty much any change in the system, including deleting evidence of their own work (purging system logs, disabling logging, changing permissions, etc.). The root users can really do everything, and in general, there's very little to stop root commands from running.

A major concern of the root account is that *there can be only one* (Highlander fans, rejoice). In other words, if you or I successfully authenticate as the root user, we are both *the* root user. There's no technical differentiation between us, and our commands will be attributed to the same user ID. This makes root an anonymous shared account – the identity of the person logging in is not reliably traceable.

The need to perform administrative tasks – separately from common work – and be able to maintain some level of identification in the system led to the creation of root-like mechanisms (like the popular *sudo* in Linux or *Run As* in Windows functionality), which allow users to temporarily switch from their restricted everyday work to privileged activities and have such work properly logged in the system.

It would appear that all worries and problems of system administration should have been solved by the introduction of root-like tools, wouldn't it?

Well, not quite.

Quite the opposite.

With more people being granted administrative privileges, the IT world created more failure points in its structure. More importantly, none of the tools addresses the fundamental question of ethics. It all comes down to having the right credentials – if you do, you will be allowed access.

Don't Use a Privileged Account for Personal Work

Credentials give you access – but privileged access doesn't inherently include ethical judgment. Since each individual's concept of ethics varies – and it depends on the available data, situation, your mood, your concentration, fatigue, peer pressure, time constraints, and applicable experience – it is important to purposefully minimize the use of privileged access to minimize mistakes. Since it is almost impossible to avoid all mistakes, a healthy and recommended practice is to use privileged access only when absolutely necessary to get the job done, and then to continuously refine processes to minimize the necessity for privileged access use the next time.

Moreover, there are different sets of rules, both technical and business related, for when you use your personal account and when you use a privileged account. For instance, you may decide to delete all the files and folders in your personal account, but doing that with a privileged account would compromise the system and impact all users. In our story, Alex stressed the importance of account separation, and he went through the list of different types of accounts and privileges that existed in their environment, as well as the mechanisms for how to request access to the root account using an intranet portal.

Alex also mentioned the topic of mistakes, and both Henry and he freely admitted to having made them in the course of their work. While one shouldn't be "proud" of their errors, it is important to share them, so that people can develop awareness and learn about the situations and conditions when and where these mistakes happened. For a new employee like Wendell, this should help instill a sense of accountability, a healthy dose of risk-taking, and the understanding that honest mistakes can and will happen.

Now, if we look at it from a different angle, we can also see several shortcomings in the encounter between the two colleagues. Alex wanted to set up Wendell as quickly as possible, which indicates a time constraint that does not necessarily allow all relevant criteria to be met.

However, such "shortcuts" are often dangerous, because they create situations where people with limited knowledge or familiarity with the IT environment are given privileged access. Before granting (and accepting) such access, there should have been some verification of Wendell's understanding of the appropriate use of privileged access within his new position.

Wendell should be comfortable expressing his concerns, whether it relates to his confidence as a system administrator in a brand-new environment or password sharing. He should feel free to interrupt Alex if he needs clarifications, especially since Alex was working quickly and Wendell had to take notes through the lecture and demonstrations.

After all, the purpose of the meeting between Alex and Wendell is to teach the new employee about the procedures and tools used in the company. The only effective outcome is if Wendell has mastered the domain in an effective way. This could also mean documentation on the account management process, a printed cheat sheet, or reference to online training. Alex could have initiated on-the-job training (OJT) by allowing Wendell to type in the commands – and Wendell should have asked the same.

Don't Use a Privileged Shared Account Without Logging Identity

There are several reasons why you'd want to log identity when using a privileged shared account. The obvious answer is information security; if and when something goes wrong, you have a forensic trail.

The less obvious answer is that it reduces suspicion for when things go wrong.

Over the years, the IT industry has developed a strong and often necessary focus on the aspects of security, and many if not all privileged activities are instantly associated with this domain.

A privileged shared account is not a great opportunity to do things without consequences; on the contrary, it needs to be treated with maximum responsibility and accountability. Moreover, work with a privileged shared account should be documented. That way, the IT team has a full log of completed work, and it can associate activities with individuals. Not for the purpose of blame, but to achieve clarity and order and minimize mistakes.

In our story, we have only touched on the root account, but the principle applies to all shared identity accounts, like database or application services. We will touch on these in the coming chapters.

By providing root access, Alex set Wendell up to have no options but to violate the shared account portion of the first commandment (Don't use a privileged shared account without logging identity). Wendell was given access to root but did not receive instructions on the mechanisms to log identity when using it.

Wendell had his reservations, and he should have voiced them to Alex. After all, Wendell did have experience from his previous workplace, and his input could be valuable. If Wendell felt that some of Alex's suggestions were not ideal, could be improved, or potentially introduce risk into the business, he should feel free to say so.

Collaboration among team members is a great way to build trust – and improve the quality of both the work environment and technical tools used. Wendell could raise his suggestions to Alex. If he did not feel comfortable doing that at the spot, he could compile a list and present it at the next team meeting or send an email to the team, to see what they think about his ideas. In the long run, open discussion almost always leads to a refinement of existing procedures.

Furthermore, the use of a personal bastion for on-call work is another transgression. It goes against the eighth commandment (Communicate Change), as Alex created a setup that was not documented as a formal work process, and also the ninth commandment (Do No Harm), since having a privileged "backdoor" access into the network from his phone violates work procedures and allows Alex to cause damage in an unprecedented and unexpected way. We will talk more about these commandments in later chapters.

Processes That Support Ethical Behavior

There are several things that system administration teams can use to facilitate ethical behavior, especially when it comes to privileged access.

Knowledge Transfer

One of the most critical steps in the induction of new employees is an efficient onboarding curriculum, which helps people learn about their roles and responsibilities quickly and without ambiguity.

There was a structured knowledge transfer in Wendell's team. Alex was keen on sharing his experience with the new employee and helping them get on board. Alex went through the different types of accounts and their purpose, and he highlighted important aspects of when and how to use them. He also demonstrated some of the examples, so that Wendell could witness the actual work.

There is some room for improvement, too. For instance, Alex could follow up his verbal explanation with a written document so that Wendell can go back and refer to it, if needed. This can also help clarify any terms or commands that Wendell may have missed.

Wendell listened carefully, asked questions, and took notes. Wendell showed interest in his colleague's teaching, and he requested clarifications when he wasn't entirely sure about a certain topic.

Much like Alex, Wendell can also make the learning session more effective. He could insist on getting all the answers and examples he needs to feel confident in the performance of his duties. He should also be careful not to expose himself to privileged access or allow himself to be exposed by accepting a piece of paper in a "dark alley," which he doesn't need for doing his job. A new employee, like Wendell, should of course be aggressive about learning and doing new things, but also about being ethical and reducing his exposure. He should not make it easy on his teacher.

Work Procedures

Human memory is a remarkable thing – but it can also be fickle, and play tricks on us. We hold vast amounts of knowledge in our heads, but sometimes we need simple clarity, especially when it comes to high-risk work.

The easiest way to ensure work procedures are followed in a predictable, repeatable, and uniform way is to thoroughly document the work processes, so that everyone can refer to the relevant information and be able to do the work just as efficiently and correctly as their colleagues.

This does not remove the need for troubleshooting skills, innovation, or common sense – far from it – but there must be a baseline, a common language that everyone can follow and refer to.

Alex had a complete set of procedures and commands that he could then demonstrate to Wendell. He also went through each account type and explained about their use, their purpose, and scenarios when their use is required, but just as importantly when it is not. A follow-up to the meeting can be a written document.

Wendell understood the importance of following the rules, and he even asked for clarifications when he felt that some of Alex's examples might not fully align with the procedures.

Practice

Work procedures need to be accompanied with hands-on work. This breeds confidence, and allows everyone involved to verify that the lessons are implemented in the right way. Alex took time to show commands. This is quite helpful, because it shows the actual work, and helps build confidence. The session would have been even more effective if Wendell also used the computer and ran those same commands a second time.

Another excellent point in Alex's presentation is to consult one of the team members when running scripts and sensitive commands on multiple hosts. This helps reduce errors and builds rapport.

Behaviors That Deter Ethics

Much like the processes that support ethical behavior, there are certain negative traits that can facilitate the violation of ethics in the workplace. These can manifest on an individual level or team level – or even be part of the wider organizational culture. However, it often starts with an individual.

Overconfidence

Alex is quite sure of himself. His sense of confidence instills a sense of rightness (in his activities), which other people may mistake for ratified work policies. With a new employee like Wendell, it can create a skewed sense of responsibility right from the start. It breeds a wrong type of work culture.

Noncompliance and Mistrust

Alex's behavior also has impact on work procedures. If people do not follow them, this may lead to more mistakes and hence more damage down the road, which will cause strain on the system administrators.

If existing procedures and tools prove inadequate (regardless of how they are used or circumvented) in offering a stable work environment, the company's leadership will probably be forced to implement additional procedures and tools to try to curb future problems and damage. There could be additional implications to such changes, and we will discuss them later on.

As the size and makeup of my system administration team and the customers and servers evolved, the methods I used to change the passwords of shared accounts, primarily the root account, evolved as well. When the team was around five people and supported local servers, initiating the change manually was sufficient. As the team and number of supported servers grew, automation was needed to initiate the regular password change and the secure storing of the password. When centralized service groups needed access to privileged accounts (including the root password), we added the ability to quickly change the password when an employee left the company or moved teams. Twenty-four by seven support from teams around the world created the need to only allow the root password to be "checked out" with a required comment as to why the password was needed. The culture was to then develop processes that did not require the root password for the reason the "checkout" was done.

Changing the root password helps reinforce the culture of reducing the use of shared accounts and increasing the logging of identity when the shared account must be used. Having clear data that shows who knows the root password not only protects the company from a bad actor but it also protects everyone who might have access to the root. The former employee, the new employee, the person halfway around the world – these are the people who get blamed when mistakes or blatant sabotage occurs. Changing the password right after someone leaves and providing the

13

password only when it is needed greatly limits the number of people who need to be part of the discussion when privileged access is identified as what caused a computer environment problem.

In Wendell's story, he immediately became a possible cause of the breach when he received the written root password, even if he never actually used it.

There are several ethical issues related to Alex's work, in addition to the technology and security stack. First and foremost, the use of the on-call bastion host is a violation of the fourth commandment (Do Not Go Where You Are Not Wanted).

Alex should follow the same work guidelines as everyone else when on on-call duty. He should not be making any custom changes to the infrastructure just because he feels like it. Furthermore, we do not know if the bastion host has been configured in a compliant way, whether it's patched or registered in the asset management tool, whether it has security measures, and so on. It acts as an undocumented back door into the environment, and if exploited, it presents a great security risk. No matter how diligent Alex may be, his setup undermines the wider policies and practices. If Alex believes that the entire infrastructure could benefit from a streamlined remote access process, then he should make sure the bastion host idea is ratified by the business as an authorized method of access, which you will learn more about when we discuss the fourth commandment.

Lastly, working in undocumented ways makes systems and services more difficult to maintain and troubleshoot. This is a violation of the seventh commandment (Follow Procedures). Alex should use provided tools, and if the task deviates from the known state, it should be logged and documented. For instance, if Alex's bastion host is compromised, other people might not be aware of its existence, not suspect its role in a potential outage, or not have any way to access it. Moreover, they might not know what to do, as it may have been configured in unusual ways that only the owner understands.

Best Processes and Tools to Support a Culture of Ethics

So far, we have looked at the scenario from two different angles – the conversation as it went and some pointers and clarifications into how it could have been improved. We analyzed this in regard to our first commandment (Separate Roles).

Now, let's assume we're building an IT infrastructure from scratch and we have the luxury of unlimited time and budget and no ghosts of data centers past. We are not burdened by outdated decisions, customer requirements, or legacy systems that cannot be easily changed or updated.

There needs to be a **defined process for account management**. This process needs to be **documented**. Policies, procedures, and tools listed in the documentation need to be revised periodically.

There should be clear separation between privileged administrative work and everyday work, even with people for whom administration is their everyday job. Not all commands and actions require elevated privileges, and as a rule, work should be done with an ordinary account until it is no longer possible. Using a privileged account for simple things such as viewing email or opening a file will taint the account by filling up the log file with clutter or, in the worst case, introducing malware to the account.

There should be at least three levels of privileges – reflected in three separate identities: personal account, privileged user account, and privileged shared account. There is also a very important type of privileged shared account: the administrative account. These should transparently map to different directory services. Changes in the backend should not interfere with how the user logs into systems.

- Personal account – Uniquely associated with an individual, it is the interface for an employee to conduct their work. Work done under a personal account can only affect the person's data. For example, you cannot make changes to permissions or ownership of someone else's files. A personal account should not be used for any work that may affect data owned by other people or functions in the business organization.

- Privileged user account – Also associated with an individual, this account is the interface for an employee to conduct the types of work that require elevated privileges. For example, the employee may use their privileged account to update a database record or access some data in the IT environment that is not accessible to everyone. A privileged user account embodies the principle of need to know. A privileged user account should not be used for any type of personal work; if it can be completed with the personal account, then it should be used first. This is a concept of least privilege.[2]

- Privileged shared account – It is not uniquely associated with an individual. Instead, it is a resource that belongs to teams, groups, business functions, and services. For example, an application server may run under a certain generic user, and employees with the right credentials will be able to switch identity to this privileged shared account in order to administer

---

[2]The idea behind this concept is to complete technical work with the least powerful administrative access available. It minimizes risk and accidental damage due to mistakes.

the application service. Without additional measures (like logging and auditing), the usage of the privileged shared account cannot be traced back to individuals. A privileged shared account should be used for types of work that cannot be done with either the personal or privileged user account. It should not be used for any kind of work that is associated with individual users.

- Administrative account – A special type of privileged shared account is the administrative account. It is different in that it is used specifically for the management of (critical) environment resources that require the highest level of permissions. As such, the misuse of the administrative account can have significant impact on the IT environment. It should be used only for highest-priority work, emergencies, and the types of work that cannot be completed in any other way. It should not be a convenience or a shortcut around bureaucratic obstacles.

All account types must be managed in a consistent manner through some sort of **privileges management** facility (like an online **portal**), following a privileges management set of policies. In general, privileges should be based on several conditions:

- Privileges granted only after successful completion of a verifiable process (like an exam or a certification).

- Privileges are temporary – They must expire after a certain period (e.g., 90 days).

- Privileges must be approved – Upon expiration; there must be a renewal process. It can be identical to the initial privilege granting process or somewhat modified.

- Privileges are granular – Associated with specific work, data, or systems.

- Allocation of privileges must be documented – The process of documentation can be manual, a database, or a database with versioning (all history is kept).

- All changes to allocated privileges must be documented.

Privileged users (if granted permission as mentioned earlier) need to be able to request administrative access in a uniform manner, which does not rely on any manual methods, notes, word of mouth, or similar. The intranet portal that Alex mentioned to Wendell sounds like a reasonable solution – users identify against the portal, and then they can be issued with the administrative password for their immediate use.

However, there must be also a **secondary** backup method that allows system administrators to gain privileged access even if intranet systems are down. This way, they can avoid a deadlock situation where they need administrative access, but they cannot get it because the portal managing the password is not accessible. This will be explained in Chapter 10 (Break Glass in an Emergency).

For privileged shared accounts and administrative account(s), there should be a mechanism of **identity logging** that can map the administrative session and all executed commands to the relevant user. For instance, this can be done by using a wrapper tool that runs the administrative session and writes a journal of commands in parallel. All this is mapped out in Figure 1-1.

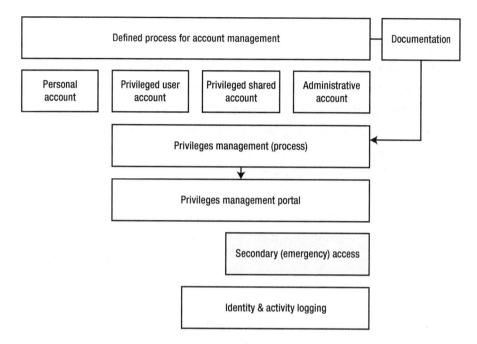

Figure 1-1. *Account management process*

Identity and activity logging is a very important aspect of privileged account use, and its design can have complex ripple effects.

On one hand, the more tools in place, the more visibility there is into potential issues and problems, as well as forensic evidence following outages, breaches, or other work-related mistakes.

On the other, the more security mechanisms that are in place around systems, the more prevalent the notion of *Big Brother* becomes, a maxim conceptualized in George Orwell's novel *1984*.[3] We are all subconsciously tuned to it, and we associate increased security with mistrust and suspicion. One might ask, "Why does the company need to watch after what the employees are doing, are they not trusted?"

---

[3]www.worldcat.org/title/nineteen-eighty-four/oclc/470015866

Indeed, strong security can deter chance crime, but it also creates the sense that everyone is being treated as a potential criminal, which can induce negative emotions at the workplace. It might even encourage people to circumvent security mechanisms, especially if they interfere with work.

Ironically, quite often, identity logging services were introduced into IT environments as a result of less-than-diligent use of privileged accounts and tools, creating chaos and damage with little to no forensic evidence into why and how issues occurred.

And thus, it becomes a self-feeding cycle: If workers embrace security systems and mechanisms (and overcome the idea of mistrust), the less relevant the implemented measures become. Likewise, the more "underground" work is done, the more the company's management may feel the need to introduce tools that offer visibility and structure into everyday administration.

There needs to be a healthy balance between privileged work, identity logging, and trust in the employees. This is where the concepts of audits, alerts, and automation come into play, as they can assist us in building a robust infrastructure based on trust as well as good data trails.

Audits and Alerts

We need to make sure that the tools and checks we put in place remain valid and up to date and that we are able to quickly detect and fix any departure from the desired safe and compliant state.

If you treat every condition we wrote down earlier as an if-then scenario, then it acts as a potential failure point in the system. For example, if a privileged account password needs to be rotated every 90 days, then an alert must be set up for this scenario to maintain compliance.

Our account management infrastructure will only be complete and fully effective if we also have audits and alerts that can warn us that some of the required conditions are being missed, at any one junction on the decision tree (Figure 1-2).

In other words, for every single requirement we created, we also need

- Quantifiable result

- Time-based validation

- Record of completed action (archive and audit)

- Alert on missed action or negative/false result

If a user has been granted elevated privileges, this needs to be audited. If such privileges were granted without the necessary expertise criteria check, the monitoring system will alert. If an account violates any one of the specified conditions, the monitoring system will alert. This allows for a full situational awareness and a resilient environment that does not imperceptibly drift from its intended state (as it often happens in IT businesses).

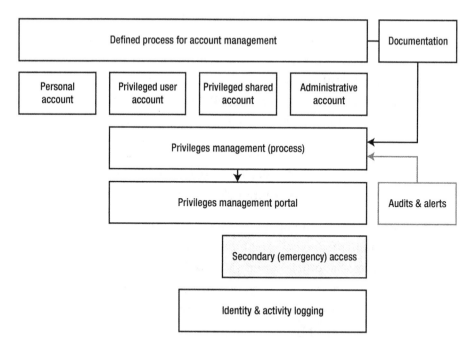

Figure 1-2. *Adding audits and alerts*

Automation

There's still more we can do. **Automation** is an important part of effective system management. Automation reduces workloads, minimizes mistakes, and allows better tracking of completed work. It should be used whenever there's repetitive work involved – whether it's the same command being executed multiple times or the same command running on multiple hosts.

If you can define a work process in a deterministic process – a clear set of if-then conditions with quantifiable results – then you can automate such processes.

There are several examples of automation that can be used, specifically for account management:

- User account creation is fully scripted – After the basic information is provided, the user environment is automatically configured: data quotas, permissions, personal and work folders, etc. In a highly automated environment, the act of being approved for an account will trigger the account creation. Identity and access management tools, such as SailPoint,[4] can be configured to provide full automation across multiple accounts.

- User password management – Various checks are in place to ensure that passwords are managed correctly and in line with the company's policies.

- Environment management – Tools that check every system in the environment for nonstandard accounts or folders, insufficient permissions, inadequate security measures, and more. Such practice can reduce the burden on system administrators and allow clearer focus on ethical issues when they arise.

---

[4]www.sailpoint.com/

The most common way to automate system administration is through the use of configuration management (CM) tools. The concept was born in the 1950s to facilitate inventory management, but it is becoming essential in the IT industry. The deterministic nature of software and the relative homogeneity of systems and services allow for effective use of tools that can mass-deploy or configure the environment.

Typically, there will be a CM server, which stores the configuration templates for different services or systems. Clients (hosts or applications) will contact the server on a predetermined polling frequency and pull these configurations. This ensures commonality, and manual changes are removed. This also facilitates auditing and alerting. Side by side with CM, there are also versioning tools, which help create a history trail of executed work, be they commands or changes to work templates (known as commits).

There is a huge range of CM software. Some of the popular ones include CFEngine,[5] Chef,[6] Puppet,[7] and Ansible;[8] and accordingly their configuration templates are known as recipes or playbooks.

Nowadays, CM has evolved to include various industry methodologies in order to increase the speed of software management lifecycle. Sometimes, it is also used to facilitate software development and system administration, better known through the popular term DevOps.

However, the automation does not have to rely on expensive and complex tools. Do not let operational constraints or requirements that are associated with the use of full-blown configuration management and versioning software deter you.

---

[5]https://cfengine.com/
[6]www.chef.io/chef/
[7]https://puppet.com/
[8]www.ansible.com/

You can create your own automation. You can use BASH or PowerShell scripts to automate user account creation or auditing. You can use scheduled tasks to run a periodic check for noncompliance. You can use a local mail server to send alerts to system administrators if you find discrepancies in the processes or security. Every little effort helps bring in clarity and work quality. This is highlighted in more detail in Figure 1-3.

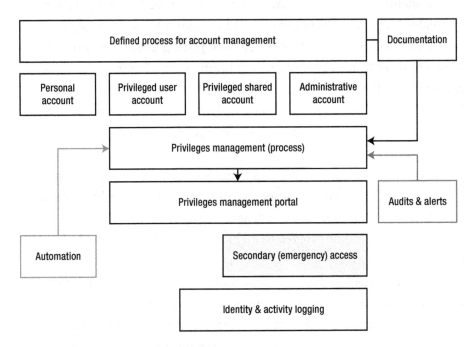

Figure 1-3. *Adding automation*

The importance of these measures is that they introduce structure into work practices and reduce operational noise. In turn, these can help system administrators be more ethical – you do not need to worry about manually making changes to user accounts (which can induce mistakes and strain and "encourage" people to cut corners), you focus on providing a robust and automated infrastructure built on sound ethical principles.

Why Is All This So Important?

The core issue with ethics vs. technology is that it's one big *gray* area. Things are rarely black and white. On the other hand, software is deterministic, and people seek deterministic solutions to technological problems.

This means that companies will invest a lot of effort and money in making perfect solutions from the technology perspective but forget or ignore the *human* equation.

> *Unfortunately, the human side of things cannot be solved with software.*

You Shall Not Pass

Over time, gaining privileged access has become more complex. We know we make mistakes, so we try to make *making mistakes* harder – but not impossible. Sometimes, we assume that mistakes will be inevitable (Design for Failure [DFF] approach), so it's not the question of *if*, it becomes the game of *when* and *how* much – minimizing damage and being able to stop mistakes early and respond quickly.

We also try to keep a trail of our work so that we have enough data to discuss outages and problems after the fact. There is also an assumption that people will be less prone to doing "bad" things if they know they are going to get caught – this is ethics creeping into the world of technology.

To fully understand the importance of ethics vs. technology, let's talk about damage a little bit.

Damage As a Service

Work-related problems manifest in the following ways:

- Case 1: Poor judgment – People make a wrong decision.

- Case 2: Insufficient information – People act based on a limited set of available data.

- Case 3: Lack of procedures and skills – People cause damage due to a combination of ill-defined work procedures and insufficient knowledge in the subject matter.

- Case 4: Deliberate sabotage.

Case 1 cannot be fixed with software – only mitigated. Sometimes, people will even circumvent safety mechanisms in place in order to get the job done, fully convinced that what they are doing is right. Software filters can be used to stop some obvious mistakes (like deleting an entire database or formatting the hard drive) or to slow down the execution of bad commands (deliberate delay for batch tasks running on multiple hosts). Abiding by strict separation of roles and using the least privileges needed to do the job can help minimize damage.

Monitoring and alerts are the mainstay of every system administrator, especially in a large-scale environment – a well-designed solution ensures that you are only responding to the most crucial and valid issues and not spurious errors or false positives. Monitoring alerts are rarely confidential in nature, but sometimes, additional information on the form of context and metadata is required alongside the alerts to enable further troubleshooting.

This additional information can be confidential. In my company, one of the support persons decided to forward the alerts to his personal email ID so that they could be accessed from anywhere.

This was despite a specific policy against doing that. The action was discovered during a security audit, and the person faced disciplinary action.

Case 2 is even harder to fix – because we rely on people making decisions based on a suboptimal set of data. In fact, deliberate "mistakes" may even be encouraged to help learn how to cope with an unknown scenario (you have a server that is currently running customer flows, but due to the server load, you cannot log in and check why). It is important to remember: the more privileges you have, the more careful you need to be. If you are unsure about potential consequences of an action, you should not use a privileged account to test the outcome.

Case 3 can be prevented – provided the IT infrastructure has robust mechanisms in place that match skill and knowledge to privilege. However, do note that there's often a strong *soft* element – teaching, coaching, mentoring, classes, exams, and finally decision-making to allow someone access to privileged resources if they show sufficient level of expertise. We will look at this in more detail as we discuss other commandments. Historically, most concepts of separation of duties and privilege stem from this case (rather than case 1 as one might assume).

If you watched the news in 2013, you no doubt would have seen news stories about customer payment account data being hacked and stolen from several major companies, including the retail giant Target. Hackers used multiple methods to weave their way through various firewalls and systems to place malware on computers to gather private customer data. We can only speculate the twists and turns the hackers used in order to find, gather, and then retrieve the sensitive data; but we do know from Target's "*updates on Target's security and technology enhancements*"[9] what steps Target took to prevent similar breaches in the future. *Enhancing monitoring and logging, installation of application*

---

[9]https://corporate.target.com/article/2014/04/updates-on-target-s-security-and-technology-enhanc

whitelisting point-of-sale systems, implementation of enhanced segmentation, reviewing and limiting vendor access, and enhanced security of accounts were their five main improvement areas. Separating roles through enhanced security of accounts was a major portion of their action plan.

By limiting vendor access, reducing account privileges, disabling vendor accounts, and expanding password vaults, they eliminated many of the exploitable privileged targets within their computer environment. By broadening the use of two-factor authentication and developing additional training on the use of password rotation, they made sure those who used the accounts were the intended users. The enhanced monitoring would have caught many of the exploits, especially if automation and processes were implemented to quickly react to the alerts. I'm sure vendors working at these large companies are now insisting on these safeguards so that they won't become the ones blamed for the next computer exploit.

Case 4 is the hardest. There is no technology that will stop determined malice, especially within the confines of a company. A worker with access to privileged resources will be able, given sufficient time and sufficient opportunity, to circumvent even the most complex solutions.

Unfortunately, too much effort is wasted on protecting companies from this (corner) case rather than focusing on the first three cases. It also creates a compound problem of its own – the more mistrust you "invest" in your technological stack, the more fragile the human equation becomes. It will reflect on risk-taking, innovation, speed of change, cost, and morale.

But let's complicate things a little more, shall we?

The Compass Is Pointing South

The big issue isn't a "lone nutjob" wreaking havoc through the company's IT assets. It is the invisible creep of "good guys" toward the unethical activities, without anyone really noticing.

In the conversation between Alex and Wendell, the new employee was exposed to unethical behavior right from the start. Alex acted from the position of authority (assumed rightness) and – the worst thing – he might not even be aware that he is doing anything wrong!

Over the years, Alex had developed practices that best suited his style and needs. He created the bastion host to make his work easier (on the surface, it's a good thing because Alex can do more for the business). The same approach led him to creating privileged access for Belinda. Alex's moral compass is working fine – as far as Alex is concerned. And he might not be able to externalize his actions and view them with an objective perspective.

This is a case of cognitive bias creep.[10]

The bias creep manifests in multiple ways – we ignore failures, we trust information that confirms our beliefs and preconceptions, we ignore those that contrast or contradict them, and because something we do seems to work, we keep doing it.

It applies to all of us; we often do things with the conviction we are acting in the best (and most ethical) way. And along the way, we make mistakes, because we've never had a golden baseline against which we could measure our actions.

Conclusion

Account management is one of the most important things in system administration, because ultimately, everything comes down to user access and permissions, and what people can do granted the right privileges. This is also a ripe field for ethical violations, both intended and unintended.

---

[10]www.nap.edu/read/19017/chapter/7

We can only protect against a limited number of scenarios where damage is caused in a deliberate manner. Instead, we need to focus on the large and complex gray area where unethical behavior happens as a result of missing procedures, ill-defined steps, conflicting instructions, and personal habits.

The best way for system administrators to protect themselves from themselves – and minimize the risk of damage in the IT environment – is through the separation of roles. Privileged accounts should only be used when absolutely necessary. Each such use should be logged so that any issues can be debugged with ease and clarity. Privileged accounts must not be used for personal needs, even if they seemingly assist with work requirements. A healthy IT environment will have monitors in place that can detect and alert on any technical violations in the account management process so they can be quickly rectified.

Now that we have privileged access, we are now exposed to a whole new range of challenges, the chief among them being privacy. We are going to discuss this in the next chapter.

CHAPTER 2

Respect Privacy

Even though he'd been with the company for only a short time, Wendell liked working with Belinda. She had this calm, quiet manner, and he wasn't afraid of asking her any questions. With Alex or Henry, you never knew if you'd step on thin ice.

"Hey, Belinda."

"Hey, Wendell, how's it going?"

"Oh, great." Wendell rubbed the crown of his head. "I need to ask you for a favor. Can you set up a work area for me? Mike asked me to run this little project so I get to know the customers better, and I need some disk space allocated."

Belinda pulled a chair from an empty desk next to hers. "Sure, no problem. Have a seat."

Wendell sat down and watched Belinda work. The wrapped scripts that the team used did not look so alien anymore, and he was getting comfortable with the syntax and terminology.

"How much do you need?"

"Uh. Say 500 GB?"

"Sure. You know what, I am going to give you the disk space, but I'm also going to give you all the permissions, so you will be the data owner. You'll also be the owner of the group that has access to the space, and that means you will also have the ability to add or remove group members, if you need someone else to work with you on the project, all right? You won't be able to resize the area, but if you need more space, just let me know, okay."

"Sounds excellent."

© Igor Ljubuncic, Tom Litterer 2019
I. Ljubuncic and T. Litterer, *System Administration Ethics*,
https://doi.org/10.1007/978-1-4842-4988-8_2

Belinda typed down a long command. "What's this project about?"

Wendell put his elbows on his knees and leaned forward. "Mike wants me to run a little experiment. He wants me to see if there are any correlations between our customers' home addresses and store locations. Like if they go shopping at a certain time, like coming back from work, they might go into a store that's closer to the workplace than their home. But if they shop over the weekend, it's more likely they'll do it at a location that's in the vicinity of their home address. Something like that. I guess Mike wants to get me familiar with the data models we use. That's all."

"Oh, that's cool. I'm sure you'll learn a lot from that exercise. You know, just the other day, Alex set a high account for me so I could run this application for one of my customers. They were having performance issues, and I needed the privileges to be able to troubleshoot. I also found a lot of useful correlations in there."

"Yeah, he told me about it."

Belinda turned toward him. "Do you know what data you're going to use for your exercise?"

Wendell grimaced. "That's the thing I'm still thinking about. I thought generating random dummy data using this old script that Gopal wrote, but I don't know how useful that's going to be. It's not like we'll be using this information for anything real."

"I'll tell you what." Belinda snapped her fingers. "How about I give you a copy of my customer data? I can transfer the files into your work area, and since you're not going to use your data analysis in the production, it'll be fine. Just make sure the data is secure, okay?"

Wendell brightened up. "Of course. That sounds really cool. Thanks."

Belinda made a wry face. "Can I ask you for a big favor?"

"Yeah, sure."

"I actually have a problem that you might be able to help me with. I have a project where I'm trying to clean up full disks and delete unused home directories. Like if the usage goes up to 95%, I will then archive any folder that's had no file inside it accessed in the last 3 months, or if the user hasn't logged in, I can then just reduce their quota to a few MB. But there are a few directories that keep growing. These are home directories of several users with temporarily locked Linux accounts, but there must be processes out there that are still writing to these files."

Wendell rubbed his chin. "Hm. Well, I guess we can run an environment-wide script that checks if any processes are holding open file handles to these home directories and then see what we can do next."

Belinda wagged her fingers as if she were typing. "Could you?"

Wendell moved over to the edge of the desk so he could work on his laptop. "Give me like 10 minutes to write the script. Then take a look to make sure I'm not going to destroy anything, and then we run it."

Wendell liked the challenge. He enjoyed brushing up on his scripting skills. Moreover, he found it the best way to get to learn the new environment. Even though it was all familiar technology under the hoods, the things were set up ever so slightly differently from his last workplace.

"Okay, I think I've got it," Wendell said. "The script is in our group work area."

She looked at the code. "Let's run it."

A few minutes later, she got a report and started going through the results. "Nothing too obvious here."

Wendell frowned. "So something is writing to these files, but it's not like one continuously running process. So I guess there must be some scheduled task that runs every now and then, does some writing, and then exits. Let's try something different. Let's map the size of all the files under these locked accounts. Then we check again every 5 minutes for say an hour and see if there are any changes."

"Just in time for the lunch then." Belinda smiled.

"Oh yeah, I'm starving. Let me rewrite this script, and then we can go."

After lunch, Belinda had a fresh set of logs to sift through, but this time, she did make progress. One of the accounts had a large mail spool, and it kept growing.

Wendell pointed, and accidentally touched Belinda's monitor. He hated when it happened. He did not like leaving fingerprint smudges on the screen. "I guess there are some automated tasks running in the environment, sending emails to the user. Like when a batch job finishes running. Those are still enabled, I guess."

Belinda looked up from the log data. "Can we check which processes are doing that?"

Wendell tsked. "Tricky. There's no way of knowing how these processes actually send the email. Hard to tell."

Belinda raised an eyebrow. "But...maybe we can take a look at the user inbox and figure out what's sending the emails. BTW, do you have an idea how to open the mail?"

Wendell nodded. "Yeah, we can try that. There's this neat little text-based mail parser we could use." He launched a new terminal window on his computer and showed her how to use it with his own local mailbox.

"Great." Belinda glanced over once or twice, looking at the command structure and the flags. Then, she opened the customer mail. "Okay, so these are actual reports from a customer," Belinda muttered. "Maybe it's some sort of test they set up a while ago and just forgot about it."

"Most likely. Let's sort the emails by size."

Belinda relisted the data. "Oh yeah, definitely. I know this guy's name. We worked with them on creating a disaster recovery plan. So what they're doing is they compile some statistics on user logins every hour, zip it, and then email it. That way, if their main data center goes down, they can be sure the backup web servers are set up correctly and that there's no problem with external connectivity."

Wendell sighed. "Well, they might actually need this data. We should probably talk to the user's manager and see what he wants to do with this."

Belinda smiled. "Thanks, Wendell."

"Sure. This is helping me a lot."

Belinda nodded. "You always learn the most when you work with actual production data. The other week, Caesar asked me for help. He had his customers input some values incorrectly into their database, and he asked me if I could help him with that. We do so much with our customers, but you don't always know what they're actually doing with their data. But once you do a real production environment change, it all kind of clicks."

Wendell was in an upbeat mood, happy that he'd been able to help Belinda with the data growth mystery. "Let's send an email to the manager. Who's going to write it, you or me?"

"Well, they're my customers. I'll do it," Belinda said.

Why Should You Respect Privacy?

Privacy is one of those things that are inherently intuitive and self-explanatory, and yet also requires deeper scrutiny when the topic is raised. The root of the word privacy implies a certain individual seclusion and freedom, which, on the surface, runs contrary to the expectations of a public workplace where we interact with dozens and hundreds of people. Indeed, it is only recently, in the digital age, that the notion of privacy became associated with public scrutiny.

The rise of the machine had transformed how we interact with our environment. In the past, sharing news was a difficult thing, complicated by the challenges of long-distance travel and low literacy in the general population, making news messengers a valuable, respected, and *trusted* element in the community. The invention and application of electricity obsoleted the mechanical propagation of news almost overnight, allowing people distanced by thousands of miles (or kilometers, if you will) to communicate with one another with only a short time delay. The advent of the computer made the distances and time lapses even smaller, culminating in a near-real-time reality that we enjoy today. Things that happen on one end of the globe are instantly recorded, registered, and shared by millions of people worldwide, with almost no barriers or filters.

The proliferation and pervasiveness of modern information has also created a powerful side effect. In the past, people had more freedom in choosing which information to consume. If they did not want to read a newspaper, they just would not. Nowadays, this is almost impossible, as every digital medium is an almost limitless well of new information, whether we want it or not.

Our desire to absorb information is, in a way, inversely proportional to our exposure and the accessibility to the said information. And with the personal space into which we can choose to allow information to trickle in shrinking, the need for privacy rose to the forefront of our priorities.

With any digital device being a vector of data exchange, the boundaries between what we deem private space and public domain are blurred. We need ways and methods to limit the exposure of what we deem private information.

This need, however, does not immediately translate into what we perceive to be public functions, like our workplace. But the concepts of privacy apply there just as rigidly as they would to any individual.

In this regard, privacy should no longer be treated as a vector of self. It is a measure of exposure by which any person, group, or a collective of data could be harmed if shared outside defined limits.

If you work in the IT industry, your life is that much harder. Information has become the backend of pretty much every business out there. Even companies that have nothing to do with information technology will retain some sort of IT staff or lease such services. System administration effectively means almost unlimited access to hardware, software, intellectual property (IP), and vast amounts of data generated by businesses, internally and externally.

Each one is a potential trap, waiting to ensnare the unwary.

And then, privacy becomes more than a measure of exposure. It becomes a critical pillar by which businesses can be destroyed.

Not helping is the mass of data breaches that we have witnessed in the past decade. Almost weekly, there is a news bulletin on this and that company that had its data stolen. From credit card data to emails, addresses, and shopping history, entire archives and databases are being siphoned out of the company's premises and unleashed into the wild.

Concerns around privacy are growing as people share their personal data with companies such as Google, Facebook, and Microsoft in exchange for no- or low-cost information and services. Privacy terms are clearly defined in legal terms that, unfortunately, the average user of these services does not read or cannot fully understand. Once privacy terms are defined, companies must take every precaution to not only follow their own terms but also follow the privacy laws set in each of the unions/ countries/states/regions where they operate.

Even though the United States did not have specific cyber laws around privacy, the CEO of Facebook was called before Congress to explain how personality data from users was shared with a third-party company. This third-party company was then hired to assist in a US presidential campaign, where personality information could have been utilized for advertisement targeting. Most likely, the team collecting the personality data did not plan for it to be available for other uses beyond its initial intent. Most likely, it was passed to the third-party company with the best of intentions. But were the Facebook users who took the test notified of the change in usage? Were the initial researchers notified? Once the mistake was noticed, who was informed? Was there an attempt to immediately rectify the mistake? Ethical behavior not only helps prevent accidental and unlawful sharing of private data, it also promotes action to get the right people involved to quickly correct privacy issues.

Each and every breach of this nature erodes the trust and reputation of the companies involved, may include hefty fines and monetary compensations to those affected, and sometimes carries criminal responsibility for company owners, executives, and even employees.

Privacy breaches and the blurring of boundaries between what we deem personal and public domains have created a backlash across the industry, as countries implement rules and regulations designed to give users more control over their data. The EU General Data Protection Regulation (GDPR),[1] made in 2016 and implemented in early 2018, is a powerful example whereby the extra-governmental European Parliament enacted a regulation designed to protect the private citizens of the European Union and the European Economic Area. Similarly, in the United States, the state of California has just passed the Consumer Privacy Act Bill,[2] which aims to address numerous digital privacy concerns and is slated to come into effect in 2020.

On the other hand, many countries either still do not have laws that define digital privacy or use outdated laws that do not conform to the modern technology landscape, creating inconsistency and confusion in how data is treated. There's nothing simpler than sending a bunch of files halfway across the globe, but the legal implications of such an action can be immense.

As a system administrator, a developer, or just an innocent tech support person, you are the thin line of the wedge.

The intended goal of this chapter is not to heighten your sense of paranoia. Far from it. We're going to provide simple and clear guidance on how to behave ethically in a complex, ambiguous, and perilous world of data. Often, you cannot control the data, but you can control how you behave and react to situations that bring you in contact with the data.

Respect Privacy

Privacy is the measurement unit of trust. If you are given data, you are given trust.

---

[1]https://ec.europa.eu/info/law/law-topic/data-protection_en
[2]https://leginfo.legislature.ca.gov/faces/billTextClient. xhtml?bill_id=201720180AB375

If You Need to Access Private Information, Get Permission

The conversation between Wendell and Belinda is a story told a thousand times over across the entire IT industry. Work is rarely done in isolation, and you may need to rely on help from your colleagues. Quite often, you will be exposed to new vectors of data, whether it's routine system logs or customer analytics. Each such encounter is an opportunity to learn new things, but it is also a test of ethical behavior, even if people do not necessarily treat it as such. Regardless of what specific situation you face, if you do need to handle private data, you should request authorization from the data owner – a person or entity responsible for the data.

If You Accidentally Release Private Information, Tell

Data leaks can happen. Will happen. Even with best intentions, practices, and tools in place, you may accidentally expose private information. Sometimes, the exposure may be small and the damage minimal or nonexistent, but you should still make sure that the data owner is notified. If someone entrusts their data in your hands, it becomes your responsibility to manage that data in a clear, transparent manner.

Protecting Private Data with Clear Owners

There were several things done well in the story. Wendell was allocated private data space, and Belinda made sure to enable Wendell with the right permissions to manage the data.

I am going to give you the disk space, but I'm also going to give you all the permissions, so you will be the data owner.

Wendell requested disk space for his work project, and Belinda also responded by assigning him all the necessary permissions to be the data owner. This is important, because all data needs to be owned in an unequivocal manner. There has to be a designed person who will be responsible – and accountable – for the handling of relevant data. The responsibility will vary based on the type of data used as well as specific activities related to it.

You will also have the ability to add or remove group members.

As the data owner, Wendell also becomes responsible for all work done with the data stored there. Again, this removes ambiguity. Wendell is the single point of contact for data handling, and he can delegate his duties as necessary. This also makes the work procedures more efficient, as there is no more need to contact Belinda and request additional changes to the allocated disk space.

As the owner, Wendell is accountable, and with the ability to add and remove members to the disk area, Wendell is also responsible for any work done here. In turn, if people need access to the data stored in Wendell's area, they will have to request permission from him.

Without Authorization, Private Data Is Vulnerable

Data owners must control all access points to the data. Such points need to be identified and permission explicitly granted when they are accessed and used.

I also found a lot of useful correlations in there.

Belinda's story exposes a number of delicate issues associated with the troubleshooting of her customers' application performance. While her intentions are good, and it is even her work duty to fix problems related to the customer flows, she exposed herself to a potential breach of customers' privacy by running their applications and viewing and processing data and drawing conclusions thereafter without their explicit knowledge and permission.

How about I give you a copy of my customer data?

Belinda may have permission from her customers to store and access some of their data, but it is unlikely she has the same approval to share that data with her colleagues. By accepting the copy, Wendell inadvertently assumes responsibility for Belinda's customer data. Moreover, neither Belinda nor he asked the customer if they are willing to allow such a move.

Furthermore, while earlier Belinda did follow the right procedures in assigning Wendell ownership and control of the disk space for his test project, she herself did the opposite with her own data. She decided to create a copy, and thereby introduce ambiguity into the system. Perhaps the copy of the customer data now becomes Wendell's responsibility, but is he also accountable for Belinda's customers?

I can transfer the files into your work area, and since you're not going to use your data analysis in the production, it'll be fine. Just make sure the data is secure, okay?

Belinda makes several assumptions here. Wendell may actually end up using some of the data analysis for purposes other than his test. Wendell has not fully defined the scope of his experiment, and therefore, he does not know what he may need to do with the data. The results may prove valuable enough to introduce changes into the environment. In such a case, Wendell needs explicit approval from the customer that their data can be used for purposes other than the agreed scope with Belinda. The customer may even be willing to such use, but the framework needs to be clearly defined, and an explicit permission given.

Data security is a whole different dimension. By making sure that the data is secure, Wendell assumes accountability for the data. Moreover, Wendell does not know what security level is required. How sensitive is the data? Are there any guidelines or requirements in place? Are there any nontechnical clauses that he should be aware of?

In fact, by implicitly assuming accountability for data security, Wendell puts himself outside the system administration zone into the legal zone, for which he neither has the authority nor expertise. As a system administrator, Wendell must not be a lawyer. His interpretation of what constitutes as secure may not align with the company's policies – or even more importantly the customer's policies.

An unauthorized copy of the customer data, even if it is well secured, is an additional vulnerability for the company. What if a hacker got access to Wendell's credentials? What if he gave group access to another person, who then copied it to their laptop? Before encrypted laptops became the norm, the biggest company fear was that an HR laptop would be stolen.

However, even if Wendell is faced with a potentially complex situation that mandates data security, there are things that he can do to ensure maximum ethical behavior, on his and everyone's behalf. We will discuss the best approach to data privacy and security later on.

Wendell and Belinda did not blatantly set out to look at private data. Is there ever a time when it is fine to look at private data?

Consider this real-world example:

> *A system administrator's manager's manager asked her to use her privileged access to get information from a file that neither of them owned. The high-level manager then told the system administrator to not say anything about accessing the file to anyone, especially to the direct manager. Even though the system administrator was very uncomfortable about accessing these files, she felt that this high-level manager was authorized to make the call.*

Was the high-level manager the right person to get permission from before accessing the private data? Should the system administrator have told someone else about viewing the private file? What is the ethical thing to do in this situation?

The manager was not the data owner since he clearly did not have explicit rights/permission to gain access to the data. What if this was part of his job, such as the chief information security officer (CISO)? There still should have been a third party approving the override of permissions. If the CISO needs to override, then permission needs to be given by a manager above the data owner. If the manager needs access, then they need to get approval from HR or the CISO. Having the desire to see data and then giving yourself approval to override permissions is a great conflict of interest.

As a system administrator, even if your manager is demanding you do it, you *must* get authorization from the data owner before accessing the private data. Moreover, it is also useful checking company policies, to ascertain data access procedure rules are clearly spelled out. Since unauthorized data access can have serious ramifications, a system administrator should make sure they have written policy protection to avoid being fired for refusing data access to a manager. If the data owner is unavailable, then the person overriding that owner's authority cannot be the person requesting access to the private data.

Protecting Yourself by Quickly Informing Owners

No system is hermetic. Every time you manipulate data, you run the risk of mistakes. Eliminating errors is impossible. They can be minimized through efficient processes and automation. But when mistakes do happen, and if they involve exposing private data, it is imperative to inform anyone involved – from the data owner to persons, groups, or businesses whose data is impacted.

Avoid Accessing Private Data

Belinda invested effort to protect the privacy of her customers. This is an important principle that should drive the technical considerations and the logic used in tools and scripts needed for work.

> *I will then archive any folder that's had no file inside it accessed in the last 3 months, or if the user hasn't logged in.*

Belinda's screening logic for disk cleanup is methodical, and it also respects the privacy of the data owners. Her script only checks whether the top-level folder has been accessed and does not examine the file contents inside.

> *Environment-wide script that checks if any processes are holding open file handles.*

Wendell knows this is a practical, thorough method for analyzing data usage. The script runs across the entire environment, which ensures a single, common set of results. It eliminates the chance for mistakes and allows good visibility of the overall status in the data center. The script logic also respects data privacy; file handles are non-identifiable and merely indicate that certain processes are actively using certain disk areas, but they do not disclose the contents of these areas and the relevant files in any way.

Tell Data Owners if Private Data Is Exposed

In general, you should avoid accessing private data without the data owner's authorization. On the other hand, if you do require access for legitimate business purposes, you should get that permission before you attempt to access the data. Lastly, if the private data has been exposed, you need to tell the data owners. If it wasn't you who exposed the data, then encourage the person who was responsible for exposing it to tell. In the most extreme cases, especially when the private data was exposed maliciously, you must take the responsibility to tell the data owner if no one else is available or willing to do so. When big companies get reprimanded for not protecting private data, it is usually delays in reporting that cause the most people to be upset, not the actual breach.

Take a look at the user inbox and figure out what's sending the emails.

In her attempt to be diligent and efficient, once again Belinda decided to take her troubleshooting one step further and access customer data. This is a similar pattern to what she did with the application performance analysis. Her data script was anonymous and it avoided accessing file contents, which is exactly what she chose to do now.

Wendell probably didn't realize he was complicit in this transgression by providing Belinda with the tools to parse the mailbox data. Caught up in the moment with passion and curiosity for the problem at hand, Wendell forgot to step back and examine whether his actions lead to improper, unsanctioned use of the customer data.

It may not be a natural thing to do, but it is important to segment the work around any data manipulation. With each step, Wendell needs to ask himself whether the work has been approved by the data owner and whether the customer has given permission for such access.

These are actual reports from a customer.

Belinda and Wendell did eventually get to the bottom of the problem with the disk space growth. Along the way, they also exposed customer data. They opened a mailbox and examined data reports that may include sensitive, privileged information not meant to be shared, and definitely not meant to be seen by system administrators. By fixing one problem, they created another.

Wendell did realize that Belinda and he did not have the sufficient authority to resolve this on their own and that they should talk to the user's manager. What he should have done is suggest they obtain such permission from the manager before opening the mailbox, and not provide any tools to allow his colleague to access customer data without permission. More importantly, since they have already accessed customer data, they should notify the customer and explain what has been done.

There is another important element here. Wendell and Belinda did decide to contact the manager, which seems like the right (ethical) thing to do. However, we do not know whether they wish to contact the manager to inform them about the fact they have accidentally accessed private data or just to ask what to do with it (get additional information and/or permissions to handle email). If Wendell and Belinda are only asking for clarifications, they might not even be aware that they have done something wrong. If they are "telling" that they have accessed private data, they are doing the right thing, but the ethical question around initial access still remains.

In either case, most likely, the manager will then make it clear that what they did was not right. Furthermore, they should have requested permission to access the email in the first place – and subsequently gone through another round of approval to handle the contents.

A chain of approvals for data access may be necessary here, starting with the user's manager all the way up to the customer. Sometimes, this course of action may not be clear. It might not be possible to identify the data owner, the customer may not be reachable, and there are dozens of other reasons where complications may arise. The next section should help simplify things.

Privacy from Scratch

How does one go about designing the "perfect" work environment that respects the privacy of all entities involved, across all data vectors? This sounds like a very amorphous and thus difficult concept.

The answer lies in the data.

The technical considerations for the IT environment infrastructure and data management built around privacy will depend directly on the data. In other words, you should start by mapping out the data.

Data requires two primary attributes: ownership and classification.

- Ownership – Every piece of data, regardless of its form or content, must have an owner. The data owner will be a business entity that is ultimately responsible for the data. The **data owner** may also be a **data custodian**, whereby they manage the data (or a portion thereof) and ensure that it is usable by those who need it and secure from those who don't have a need to know. Both these functions understand the **data content** and how it is and can be used. Many times, they will be the primary user of the data (such as email).

- Classification – This attribute will impact how the data is managed, including data transfer, storage, retention, backups, archiving, access, and any other type of possible use. Data classification will be set by the data owner in conjunction with the **information security officer**. In some cases, the data owner will only define the data sensitivity and leave the technical implementation to the information security officer. In other cases, the data owner may mandate specific policies around the data use or storage. Across the industry, typically, data will have classification levels like **public**, **confidential**, **secret**, or **top secret** (not the movie). Each level comes with its own protection methods. For instance, confidential data may be accessible by anyone in the company, but its use outside the company could still require approval from the press office. Secret information will most likely require encryption. The full extent of data classification and security is beyond the scope of this book.

Once these two attributes have been defined, it is possible to architect the work setup that will meet the requirements. For instance, in most jurisdictions worldwide, medical data of patients may only be stored in facilities that are local to the jurisdiction, preventing any transfer to other countries. In such a scenario, for instance, you will architect backup, availability, disaster recovery, and other solutions around this stringent requirement.

Other types of data, based on their classification, may require encryption, infinite backup retention, vetting of work personnel by government departments, and more.

Once the data has been defined, it needs to be managed. **Data management** encompasses the entire set of operations around data. This journey includes every step from data creation to its storage – and sometimes subsequent removal. You need to map the trail (follow the breadcrumbs) and understand how the data moves and morphs from one point to another.

While it is impossible to state every possible data management type, it is possible to scope the management broadly as storage, transfer, and use.

- Storage – Nonvolatile data will be kept as a permanent record. The manner of storage will be dictated by the classification. The technology used for storage will also be determined based on the data type, volume, and content. Privacy-oriented data storage requires that any copy of data be recorded and access monitored and regulated. To that end, much like data needs its owner, the underlying storage medium requires one. The data owner will then nominate one or more data custodians, who will have the ability to nominate and grant approval for **data members** to access the disk space and data. In some companies, the data owner will be the same person as the data custodian. With companies that have customers, the customers will often be data custodians or data members, too.

- Transfer – Data will rarely remain stored without any access, and it will be moved from one medium to another. Every data move needs to be accounted for. If you do not control the data flow (such as was the case when Belinda copied customer data to Wendell's disk), you cannot guarantee privacy. If you cannot control the flow, you then must ensure that the **data integrity** is maintained. For instance, email traffic sent from one person to another will often go through multiple mail server nodes, some of which you may not have access to or own. Mail encryption and the use of digital signatures can ensure that the data has not been tampered with. Such policies and practices will be defined based on data classification by the owner and the information security officer.

- Use – Data use will be any access and processing of stored information. It could be done by the owner themselves, or it could be done as part of work project, where application logs or collected analytics are processed to gain insights and drive business logic. It is important to **map the data usage** and account for any such occurrence. If you do not have the full understanding of how the data is utilized, you cannot guarantee that the privacy is being respected or data classification (confidentiality) maintained. The mapping needs to be done by the data owner, data custodian, and customer. Finally, data can be processed from one classification into another, or it could stay within the same classification. For example, confidential customer data could be analyzed and processed and presented as something like the number of customers per region, which can then be presented as public data.

This is illustrated in Figure 2-1.

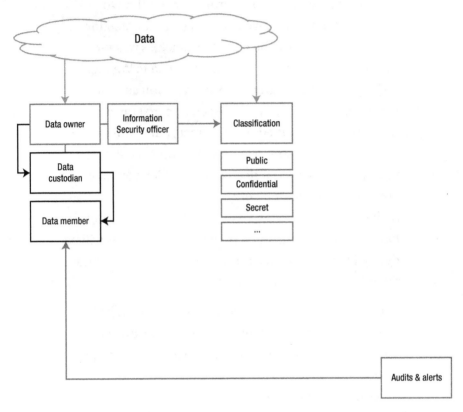

Figure 2-1. *Data classification flow with audits and alerts*

What's Your Role in All This?

System administrators will find themselves at every step of the data flow
and use. They will be responsible for the health and utilization of the disk
space. They will create and assign initial data ownership based on policies
(such as the new data owner paying for the allocated quota). They will
be capable of making changes to the disk and ownership based on the
direction of the data custodian.

If you need to handle data and make sure you do not break this commandment, then you have to make sure of the following:

- Data has an owner and is classified – you follow the policies.

- If you require data access where you have not been explicitly nominated, then you should not view the data without the data owner being present or providing specific instructions.

- If you need to change the data – store it, transfer it, or use it in some way – you will be creating a new breadcrumb on the data trail. This needs to be mapped, and therefore, you require the explicit approval of the data owner.

In some situations, though, the decision-making will not be so simple. There will be scenarios where you are handling a crisis, and you will need to make changes that do not adhere to written policies.

When that happens, you can seek permission from people who have the authority to override existing policies or processes. Sometimes, it may be the **manager** who, under certain conditions, will be able to act on behalf of some of the earlier stated roles. It may also be a division or department director, who will be able to set new policies or override existing ones in an emergency. Likewise, the chief information security officer (**CISO**) for the company would likely be able to do the same thing. If the situation involves personal data, the **HR manager** might be able to step in and, along with the manager, provide necessary authorization to override existing processes and access private files of employees. Ideally, this would become an override process rather than an exception.

In my experience, the most common reason for needing to override the process is when the data owner is not available, such as being on a long sabbatical. When access to project data was required, then an override from a manager from that project as well as the employee's manager was required in order for the system administrator to allow another project member to access the private data. Another less common occurrence was a manager needing to access files within one of their employees' personal drive as work. In those cases, human resources needed to provide approval. As a system administrator, you never need to be the one making the decision about if the private file can be exposed.

We can see this flow illustrated in Figure 2-2.

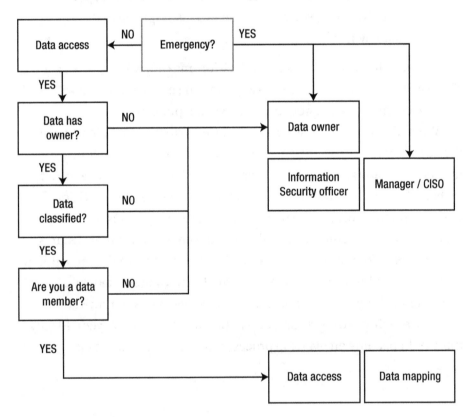

Figure 2-2. *Flow chart for emergency data access*

If one of the functions does not exist, you can override the process by going to other functions in the organization; for example, in the second step of the process, if there is no data owner available, data ownership assignment would then be given to the IS officer, manager, or CISO.

Lastly, we can use software to help with all stages of the data management process. In Chapter 1 (Separate Roles), we mentioned auditing, alerts, logging, as well as version control and configuration management tools. All these can be used to provide insight into how the data is handled, and make management easier, more transparent, and more efficient.

For instance, if data transfers are repetitive, they can be fully scripted. Completed operations can be audited for success, including parameters like data integrity, data manifest, and other attributes. Failures can be flagged, so that they can be examined for any possible issues.

Data storage can be monitored, including disk area usage and quotas, inactive disk space, disk area ownership, and permissions. If possible, a history will be kept of data changes and use, with version control providing a full mapping of access. In general, all data access should be fully logged. The exact processes will depend on how the environment is set, specific data types, and data usage. This is shown in Figure 2-3.

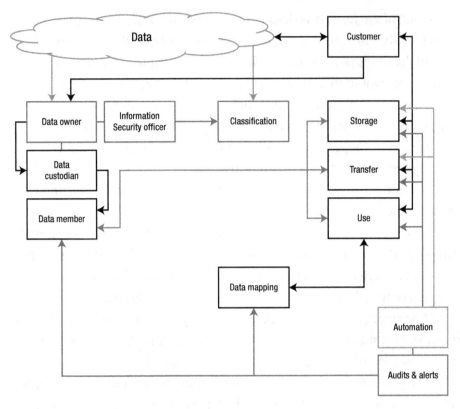

Figure 2-3. *Data access automation and logging*

Conclusion

Privacy sounds like an amorphous concept, and its implementation can be daunting in living, breathing IT environments. Security administrators and developers face daily dilemma every time they have to interact with private data as part of their duties. It is impossible to envisage or predict every scenario where data may be misused or leaked.

The solution is not to. The ethical approach to privacy is that you should not make assumptions or decide for yourself how to handle private data. Instead, if you do have to handle such data, you can abide by a few simple, generic rules that are applicable to all use cases. Data needs to be owned and classified. Data use needs to be mapped and documented, sometimes with the aid of automated tools. In line with the classification, you need explicit permission to access and change data from its relevant owners. If you do accidentally access private data, you need to notify the data owner. In emergency situations, you may have to use a different chain of approval to get the work done. Such conduct will ensure that you behave and work in an ethical manner that respects privacy.

> *Data needs to be owned and classified. Data use needs to be mapped and documented, sometimes with the aid of automated tools.*

And now that we know how we can access data in a manner that respects the privacy of its owner, in the next chapter, we will talk about when and why we should or should not change data.

CHAPTER 3

Do Not Change Data

"Tell me," Wendell started. "Do you ever dream about work?"

Caesar chuckled. "Dream? Well, not recently, no."

"It's just I'm seeing all sorts of anomalies in this data set that I've got from Belinda, and I just can't get my head around it. It's been bugging me lately, and last night, I even dreamt about this project."

Caesar moved his mouse cursor so his screen would not go blank. "That means you're working too hard."

Wendell sighed. "Can you maybe help me? You might be able to figure out something."

Caesar stretched. "They don't call me Rain Man for no reason."

Wendell had to smile. "They do?"

"No. All right, so what have you got?"

Wendell opened a document, showing several graphs. "Mike asked me to get more familiar with our data models, so I've been correlating information left and right, but some things just don't make sense for me. I'm not 100% sure if my methods are wrong or if something's off with the numbers."

Caesar was looking at the graphs, thumb pressed against his chin. "For instance?"

Wendell pointed at his laptop screen. "Mike wants to know if there are any correlations between our customers' home addresses and store locations, right. But then I get something like this example here. I've got a person living in Victoria, Texas, but the data shows that they shopped at a store in the city of Victoria in the country of Grenada."

© Igor Ljubuncic, Tom Litterer 2019
I. Ljubuncic and T. Litterer, *System Administration Ethics*,
https://doi.org/10.1007/978-1-4842-4988-8_3

Caesar snapped his fingers and leaned back. "Oh, we get that all the time. Actually, to be honest, it was Belinda who set me on the right track here. I was having similar problems, and I wasn't sure what the source of the anomaly was. Belinda then helped me with the customer data, and we ran some additional correlations, and I finally figured it out. You just need to do a different type of queries."

Wendell wrote a few notes down. "Okay, that makes sense."

"Don't feel bad, bro. These inconsistencies happen quite often, and you couldn't have known. I've helped our data analytics team write new reports that ignore these obvious typos when they generate their weeklies. Simply exclude any match where the customer's country does not match the shop country."

Wendell nodded.

"And this is not a new thing either. Mike complained that his reports to his management look bad because of these odd glitches. I got pulled in to figure out how to fix it."

Wendell rubbed his knuckles. "No problem. This is actually good, as it gives me better understanding of how we analyze data and how we interpret the results we get. But going through all that stuff feels tedious. Is there an automated way to screen the data for anomalies?"

Caesar smiled. "Of course. I actually maintain a shell script that goes through the database and sanitizes these anomalies. I run it any time I need to produce any kind of report. I'll send you a link. Use it as you like, and if you encounter any new anomalies, do let me know, and I'll update the tool."

"Thanks." Wendell wrote down another note. "I also wanted to talk to you about monitoring and logging, since that's kind of your baby."

Caesar chuckled. "A proud father."

"So can you briefly run me through it?"

Caesar leaned forward. "Yes. So first, I've got a bunch of stuff configured to make my life easier. You know how it is with logs. You easily get swamped with noise, so you miss things. I've got a script that sends me an email only when there's a critical alert of any kind. Then, I use the dashboards when a system throws an error and I need a quick view of its basic performance metrics. Finally, I have *another* script that sends me an email with a daily digest, so I can look for correlations to environment-wide problems."

"Sounds like a pretty robust setup," Wendell commented.

"Well, it has to be. Otherwise, I'd be constantly overloaded. I need to be efficient and remove noise, so I don't feed you and Mike with useless data."

Wendell looked at his notes from the past few weeks. "We use central logging for all our infrastructure?"

"Yes and no. We do send all server logs to a central collection node over the network and then rotate the logs daily. Then, we generate analytics from the logs, so we have system performance and usage statistics graphs. We don't do any remote logging for test and dev environments. Let me show you a report."

They spent a few minutes poring over the data and looking at the graphs. Wendell noticed something strange in one of the plots. There was a massive spike in usage that lasted for only about a minute. It looked like the web site activity had gone up by a good 800%.

"What did we do there? Was there some product launch or something interesting at that time?"

Caesar waved his hand. "Oh, no. Sorry. That's a logging issue. Sometimes, log entries get written multiple times, and then you see these odd spikes. But that's fine. I just filter out the duplicates and retain the one original entry for that time stamp, and that's it. We get normal data, and we can have a clean report. Saves a lot of headache when the dev and marketing start panicking for no reason how our traffic is suddenly going up and they have no idea why."

Wendell nodded, but he wasn't sure this was the best approach to the problem. "Do we know why the log entries get written multiple times?"

Caesar made a rueful face. "No time to troubleshoot that, buddy. We'll get there. Daniel has promised to help me with that, actually. He has a load of experience working with data collecting and reporting tools, and he is going to help me get access to the log generator. Normally, you don't get that in the tool version we use, but Daniel knows his way around, and he thinks he knows how to access the software logs and figure out if there's a problem there."

Wendell nodded again. Well, it would be worth hearing from Daniel, to see what he had to share on the logging duplicates problem.

If You Control the Data, You Control the Narrative

As we have mentioned in Chapter 1 (Separate Roles), there are several possible permutations in the decision-making process. You can make good decisions based on good data, bad decisions based on bad data, as well as bad decisions that stem from one's misunderstanding of the available information. There is of course luck, but that's usually a scarce commodity in the business world, especially when you are serving customers.

It is difficult to control all the factors that influence your work. You will rarely have the luxury of dictating every step of the process. Whether it's people, external parties involved in the work, the timing of different elements coming together, or even the underlying rules of physics, there will be a whole bunch of probabilities stacked against you.

However, there is one thing that you can control – and that's data.

In Chapter 2 (Respect Privacy), we talked about the explosion of information. Indeed, the IT world is one giant database, containing billions upon billions of data records of every kind, the sum of our computing experience mostly from the past 30 odd years. This data forms the backbone of the decision-making process in companies and drives strategy, investment, and product development.

The use of all this data can render wonders. Over the past few decades, we have made great strides in technological and scientific progress. We have successfully mapped the human DNA, discovered the Higgs boson, and enabled millions of people to talk to their friends on the far end of the planet, in real time. We use data to predict demographic and economic trends, and the stock markets run on clever algorithms that make our hearts skip a beat now and then. Every facet of our lives is dictated by the massive use of data, and this usage is doubling every two years.[1]

This same data can also wreak havoc when misused.

System administrators, software developers, and IT technicians find themselves in a rather precarious situation. They are often not data custodians themselves, but their access to privileged systems and resources gives them the ability to access sensitive information with significant business impact. Their duties often require that they interact with this information.

And this brings us to the aspect of control.

System administrators often sit at data traffic junctions, and they have the ability to change raw streams of information coming into data centers into higher forms of logic and order. In fact, sometimes they will be required to do so, especially when collecting things like system performance metrics, security logs, and sometimes even customer data.

Indeed, the system administrators won't necessarily always have the ability to dictate which data gets collected or why or how it ends up being stored in long-term archives across the globe. But they do have full control of how they access and use that data.

But this does not only apply to system administrators. This is relevant to anyone working with data (and it does not have to be strictly technical data). This is applicable in the academy, among researchers, and applies to managers and software developers handling application and customer logs, too.

---

[1]`www.emc.com/leadership/digital-universe/2014iview/executive-summary.htm`

On its own, data does not have inherent value until processed and analyzed. It is this step that transforms raw numbers and letters into meaningful, powerful logic, which we can then use to make our lives better, safer, smarter. It is this step that governs decision-making. Bad data will make even those highly skilled in the subject matter derive wrong decisions.

Data manipulation has been an inseparable part of data usage since the dawn of humanity. However, the word manipulation is no longer used to just indicate a high skill or level or usage. Nowadays, it bears mostly negative connotations and has become associated with data changes designed to deliberately skew results toward a preferred conclusion. And the reason is companies, businesses, organizations, as well as individuals have been using – and changing – data to achieve their goals; change the data, change the narrative.

But it is almost too easy to dismiss deliberate data tampering. The real problem is that people will often inadvertently, even innocently, make changes to data, because they do not fully understand or appreciate the risks of such actions, because they feel pressured to present a "rosy" or "inflated" picture of expected results, and because they believe that data changes are legitimate if there's a good reason to make them.

As someone with access to data, whether you're a system administrator, researcher, or manager, you will most likely find yourself in the second scenario: you will be asked to collect and analyze some data. You may discover that you have too much information and that your database cannot handle the input volumes, so you might feel tempted to discard parts of the data. Or you may choose to filter out certain records because you believe they are not useful. Or you may have results from a test that do not unequivocally provide the conclusion you've expected, and you need to make redo the whole thing over.

And by doing any one of these, you may put yourself in an unethical situation.

Do Not Change Data

If you change the data, you effectively change the snapshot of the reality at the time the data points were collected. This creates a skewed picture of the situation and will lead to incorrect results, even if your analysis methods are perfect.

Changing data has numerous long-term repercussions. It may be downright illegal. It may erode the trust that others have given you, which could lead them to disregard or discredit your results in the future. It will cause you or those affected by the results to make costly, maybe even dangerous, decisions based on results derived from manipulated, skewed, or partial information. In some situations, this could be embarrassing. In others, this could cost people their lives.

> *One example of a business changing data that resulted in significant damage was the Takata airbag recall. Having inaccurate test result data contributed to deaths, injuries, and tens of millions of vehicles recalled.*[2]

Results Are Results, Good or Bad

It is impossible to overstress this point. No matter how bad of a picture the data portrays, the data should not be changed. Businesses often create an unfair expectation of their employees by demanding positive results from work projects or asking for bombastic figures. Over time, this makes people try to force their work and results toward expectations. In turn, this leads to bad results being ignored or glossed over, which can cause significant damage in the long run.

Ideally, every work project with quantitative results will have defined success criteria up front. It should also be based on a hypothesis that can

---

[2]www.nytimes.com/2015/11/25/business/takata-said-to-have-manipulated-testing-data-for-troubled-airbag-inflaters.html

be tested in a repetitive manner. If the results of the test show data that do not align to the success criteria, they indicate that either the original hypothesis was wrong or that the success criteria were set incorrectly. The data should not be changed to match either one.

Bad results have merits; they can help you decide what not to do, which is as important as getting good results. You may not have a successful model for your product on the first go. Iterating over several failed models usually leads to a more successful final version of your product. This is not dissimilar to the evolutionary process in nature. Of course, there are scientific methods that can help both make the proposed work model more *workable* and analyze the available data in a more accurate manner.

Use Automation and Filtering to Understand the Data

The conversation between Wendell and Caesar touches on a number of delicate points, mostly because there's no simple, clear-cut separation between ethical and unethical areas. Somewhat like Wendell's data.

I'm not 100% sure if my methods are wrong or if something's off with the numbers.

Wendell is not certain if his data analysis is correct, so he has decided to seek advice from a colleague who has more experience in the subject matter. This is always a sound approach. Working with team members can help uncover problems and inconsistencies in work methods and procedures, as well as highlight additional angles that can make the data analysis more robust.

Moreover, Wendell is also trying to understand whether and where there might be a fault in his work. A systematic approach is always a good thing, as it allows you to isolate problems. Sometimes, issues may be caused by multiple, interacting causes, and troubleshooting them is quite difficult and time-consuming. It is always advisable to try to reduce the problem to the minimal set of significant factors. This saves time and effort and makes data analysis simpler.

Is there an automated way to screen the data for anomalies?

Wendell is trying to adopt some of the lessons he had learned from Alex and Belinda. He is looking for ways to automate the data filtering (regardless of whether such an activity itself is the right choice). In general, automation can help streamline processes, reduce errors, and make work easier, as we have seen in previous chapters.

I've helped our data analytics team write new reports that ignore these obvious typos when they generate their weeklies.

Caesar's work methods are also quite commendable. He is also very keen on automation, and he is involved in helping other teams improve their work. Cooperation across teams is vital, especially in data-rich domains inside the IT industry, as compartmentalization leads to unnecessary duplication of effort and solutions. By being involved, Caesar also has the opportunity to provide an impartial, outsider's view of the problem other teams may be facing, without the ability to solve it effectively as they could be too emotionally invested to have a more philosophic understanding of the issue at hand.

Caesar does try to be methodical and keep track of his actions. The transparency in his work aligns with the lessons we learned in Chapter 2 (Respect Privacy), and it can help resolve problems should they occur with data analysis. Moreover, Caesar suggested that Wendell come back to him for any tool updates. A centralized data reporting facility is helpful in avoiding duplication, inconsistencies, and unethical access of data.

I've got a script that sends me an email only when there's a critical alert of any kind.

In addition to automation, there are other benefits to Caesar's insistence of using scripts to sort and filter data. Namely, by filtering information into buckets based on their severity, priority, and importance, he can focus on analyzing important data first. This way, Caesar can avoid data overload, which is common with many monitoring and alerting systems.

We do send all server logs to a central collection node over the network and then rotate the logs daily.

This is another example of healthy data retention and log rotation practices. We have already discussed these in association with user accounts in Chapter 1 (Separate Roles), and they are fully applicable to all aspects of information technology and system administration. A well-documented process of data collection, processing, and storage minimizes the risks of unethical access, even by accident.

Moreover, sending logs to a central collection node is done without filtering. This means all log entries are copied over, including potentially bad data, which can be useful for a range of different analyses, including security, forensics, customer activity patterns, resource usage and load, and more.

Removing Bad Data Removes Good Information

While Caesar did establish several useful, ethical practices, he also did commit a number of unethical violations. Wendell's role in this situation is delicate. He did not make any of the changes himself, but he is privy to a situation where data has been accessed (possibly without the right authorization) and changed, creating a skewed picture of the operational business environment.

It is sometimes difficult to find balance between snitching on your colleagues and trying to correct them, as such actions may be interpreted the wrong way by those involved. However, there are some clear ethical guidelines applicable to Wendell and Caesar's story.

Simply exclude any match where the customer's country does not match the shop country.

*I just filter out the duplicates and retain the one original entry
for that time stamp, and that's it.*

We can see a common theme here. Caesar is not happy with the bad
data points, and he has taken steps to remove such data from his reports.
While Caesar is semantically correct, removing "bad" data points only
masks the underlying problem.

We do not know why the database records include these bogus data
entries. By removing them, Caesar also eliminates the opportunity to
troubleshoot and understand the issue at hand.

The longer-term effect of his changes could mask additional
problems – by removing the data entries, Caesar also removes the visibility
of the anomaly, therefore removing the opportunity for *someone else* to see
the problem and possibly fix the source of the problem, provide resources
to fix the problem, or prioritize efforts properly to understand the anomaly.

For example, if there is a large volume of "bad" data entries, removing
them may result in underreporting, which could be interpreted in many
ways. The company's leads may have a false sense of complacence, not
suspecting that a certain portion of customer data is wrongly classified
in the database or that these could actually be issues with the customers'
experiences, which could directly impact the bottom line.

You will lose key indicators if you change data.

Underreporting may also hurt future capacity planning. It is possible
that the IT teams plan upgrades to their hardware infrastructure based
on the current and forecast utilization demand of the resources, like web
servers and the database. Using skewed metrics (after being sanitized by
the team) can mislead into wrong projections; utilization beyond optimal
parameters, as the actual usage will be higher than the reported usage; and

degraded experience for the end user, which again can impact the business revenue.

> *Story from the IT trenches: There seem to be more real-life examples of overreporting utilization rather than under-reporting. In the system administration world, this usually results in the over-purchasing of compute resources. In one example, management and finance no longer trusted the data, which resulted in a lack of resources in later years. In another example, the utilization data was scrutinized after servers sat idle for months; the person responsible for the data was moved to a new "opportunity."*

Caesar's work violates both the second (Respect Privacy) and the third commandments (Do Not Change Data) discussed here. He would need permission to access and analyze the data and then specifically request that he be allowed to make changes from the data custodian or the owner.

Wendell should point these to Caesar. He should suggest an alternative approach that allows both the original data to be preserved without any changes and additional analytics performed separately.

> *I actually maintain a shell script that goes through the data and sanitizes these anomalies. I run it any time I need to produce any kind of report. I'll send you a link. Use it as you like, and if you encounter any new anomalies, do let me know, and I'll update the tool.*

We've seen this quote just in the preceding text, and the reason why it's written here again is that it also has several unethical connotations. Caesar's script is not part of the documented data access process. If there are issues in the script, they impact the reports, and people reading them are not aware that the data has been changed (i.e., data integrity compromised in transfer). Caesar also implicates Wendell by suggesting that he do the same thing, making it more difficult to understand problems in data logic and any subsequent resolution.

If You Suspect an Input Error, Go to the Source

Sometimes, you will be convinced that the results are wrong – not merely bad (or exceptionally good for that matter). If you believe your hypothesis is correct, and there are no errors in your models or the analysis, then you can suspect the data.

Data should be inviolate – but that does not mean you should access it or its interpretations at face value. Indeed, if you believe that the original, raw data is incorrect for some reason, you should go all the way back to the source.

In some situations, this could be sensor readings from an IoT device, performance values from a graphics rendering server, web site statistics, or any other metric. If you believe the readings are incorrect, you will need to understand the process of data sampling and collection and eliminate any errors there. For example, a sensor could be miscalibrated, or the web site statistics might be based on a data vector that creates false values.

If you identify an error (and not because you want to make results better), you can make changes to *how* the data is collected, but once it's collected, it should not be changed.

Ask for Help Finding the Source

Wendell and Caesar did try to be diligent in their work. They did not work blindly with their data sets, they performed analyses and tried to correlate information before taking the next steps.

> *I've got a person living in Victoria, Texas, but the data shows that they shopped at a store in the city of Victoria in the country of Grenada.*

Wendell had a sound approach in his work. He had decided not to make any changes and instead consult with a colleague. He was also looking at the shopping data and the customer's address to understand the discrepancy in his analysis. Moreover, Wendell should persist with this approach when it comes to Caesar's data, too.

69

Belinda then helped me with the customer data, and we ran some additional correlations, and I finally figured it out.

Much like Wendell, Caesar also did thorough work in trying to understand why the results he was getting seemed incorrect. He asked for help from a colleague, and they worked with additional data sets to understand and correlate results.

It is always useful to compare (and examine) multiple sets of results, to understand if there are any anomalies, especially if a specific set is known to be valid and can be used a standard or a baseline. Indeed, if there are anomalies, it might be possible to understand the root cause of the problem, or at the very least isolate the step of the data analysis process of the component in the data access chain where the issue occurs.

Easy Leads to Issues

Throughout the story, we saw several cases where there seems to be anomalies in the data collection and analysis. The most sensible approach is to troubleshoot the issue at the source – the step where the data is generated and saved in the first instance. This could reveal issues with the application business logic or an incorrect system configuration. There could also be other reasons for the invalid data points, none of which can be identified and resolved at later stages in the process.

No time to troubleshoot that, buddy.

This is the perennial excuse in the IT industry. Quite often, people have significant workloads and shifting priorities, and there are certain things that will be difficult to accommodate in the tight, busy work schedules.

Wendell has the right approach of trying to analyze the issue at the source, and he should insist that this be done in a structured, planned way. Much like the physical laws of conservation, be they energy, spin, or the electric charge, there's also the universal IT equivalent – the conservation of problems. Unless solved, the issues will not go away.

Overall, this is definitely a difficult scenario. Quite often, there is a tradeoff between solving problems and opening a Pandora's box. Sometimes, people may just seek the "easy" way out. But it is paramount not to hide anything. Data spikes can cause panic in the marketing department, which will get the attention of management to purchase the software that will help debug the issue and determine the root cause of the duplicates. In the end, not changing the data is the right thing. Also, those spikes might be someone hacking in to steal data.

> *Normally, you don't get that in the tool version we use, but Daniel knows his way around, and he thinks he knows how to access the software logs and figure out if there's a problem there.*

There are multiple issues here. Daniel's approach circumvents the known, established processes, similar to what we've seen with Alex. This is a violation of the sixth commandment (You Shall Not Go Where You Are Not Wanted). Daniel and Caesar need authorization to access the files on the log generator. They need permission from the data owner, who in this case might be the vendor of the log generator appliance or software. There might also be privacy issues involved, as there could be sensitive data involved, and they require separate attention.

The Scientific Method

Data analysis is a highly complex and often time-consuming activity. Moreover, it requires a relatively deep understanding of statistical methods and tools, something that is neither trivial nor common in the wider IT industry. While most system administrators have good knowledge of systems, they are usually not well versed in the mathematical analysis. Moreover, it is often assumed that statistics are the domain of the academy and research and that there is no place for such an approach in a down-to-earth world of IT operations. Sometimes, data analysis is handled by dedicated teams of business intelligence.

And yet, we're seeing an explosion of data across all tiers of the IT world. While seemingly mundane entries in system logs do not look exciting or revealing when examined in a sporadic fashion, they can often reveal important patterns when analyzed on scale. But even for smaller, isolated projects, having the right methodology and strict analysis rigor is quite important.

Data Integrity

If you need to analyze data, regardless of the size or perceived importance of the data, there are ten things that you need to do before, during, and after the analysis.

Data Sources

- Data source needs to be clearly identified – You must be able to pinpoint the definite origin of the unedited, raw data values. In some cases, data output may already be processed by "black box" systems (like sensors), and you will only have access to the subsequent results as your data.

- Data source needs to be protected – Your environment should have mechanisms in place that prevent arbitrary changes to your data. These can be in the form of permissions to logs and databases, encryption, or alerts on raw data access and change. Write Once, Read Many (WORM) devices can be used for sensitive, important data. In such devices or systems, the data cannot be changed once written.

- Derivative information and conjectures need to be stored separately from the source data – If you need to process and analyze data, you need to do this without altering the original data set in any way, possibly working with a temporary copy of the original data values. This way, other people can work with unedited data, too. Furthermore, they will not be exposed to your analysis, which could skew or bias their interpretation and understanding of the results.

Automation and Auditing

- Data needs to be audited for integrity, not for accuracy – Your systems should reveal if there are problems with data collection or the structure of your data sets, not whether the values make sense or align to your expectations. The analysis of results will reveal if there are *other* problems with your data. If the data is determined to be inaccurate, change the data collection process for the next cycle. Make sure you record and document the change. Moreover, automation helps with repetitive tasks and reduces human error.

Hypothesis, Methodology, and Errors

- There must be a well-formulated, testable proposal before any data analysis is done – Do not just blindly search for patterns in the data, as there will always be some. Correlation does not imply causation. Moreover, some data interpretation will most likely have zero business value.

- There are no good or bad results – If your hypothesis proves to be incorrect, that is a valid conclusion, and you should not change data or methods to adjust the results to your liking.

- Data analysis requires the awareness of what data looks like – Blindly applying statistical methods can lead to gross mistakes. A great example that illustrates this phenomenon is Anscombe's Quartet,[3] four data sets that have nearly identical simple statistics, but look completely different when graphed, as shown in Figure 3-1.

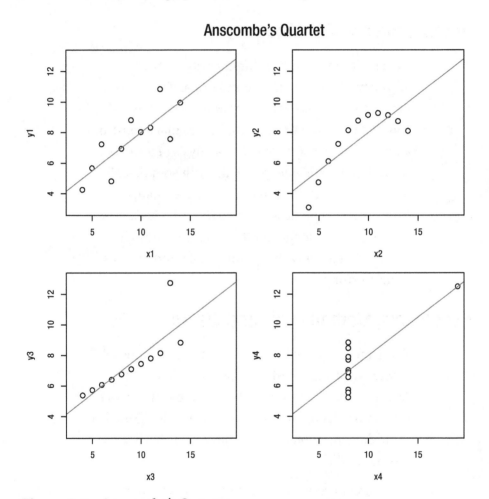

Figure 3-1. *Anscombe's Quartet*

---

[3]https://en.wikipedia.org/wiki/Anscombe%27s_quartet

- Methods must be reproducible – If you give your work to someone else, they should be able to do the same work and obtain the same results as yours.

- Logical errors and problems must be fixed before any additional analysis – There can always be problems and complications when working with the data. It is possible that your methods are incomplete, your systems might not be processing or analyzing all the available information, or you could be collecting incomplete or incorrect data sets. You must make sure that your entire chain, from raw data to results, is complete.

Documentation

- The analysis must be fully documented – There are many benefits to maintaining a solid paper trail of your data analysis techniques. Transparent, accurate communication is always useful. Written documentation of your past work can be useful to other people in the business. It will also allow you or anyone else to revisit a previous problem or experiment without having to rediscover all the findings.

This way, data analysis becomes a tightly controlled loop, from a clearly identified source that is protected from and audited for changes via formulated, quantitative hypotheses to a methodical analysis with defined goals and open, transparent procedures.

Additionally, deriving from the lessons we learned from previous chapters, you can use the building blocks of ownership and privacy to make the data handling even more robust. Data should have owners, its use should be mapped, and any access logged. This way, you can make sure not only to respect the privacy of your customers you will also maintain the integrity of stored information and provide clear, unbiased results based on data only. The workflow is illustrated in Figure 3-2.

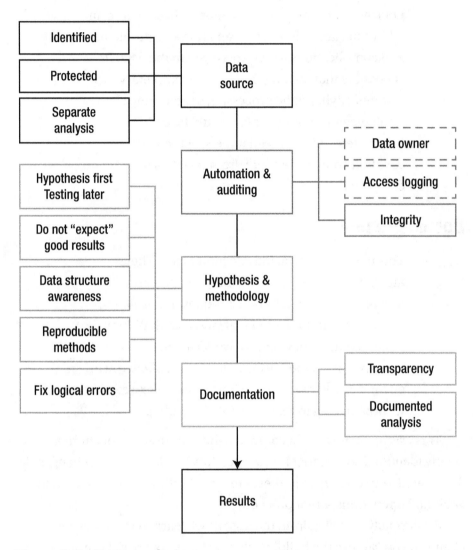

Figure 3-2. *Data analysis process*

Help Others Be Ethical

As a system administrator straddling the highways of data, you are in a unique position where you might possess a much higher level of situational awareness than people working with the data. You might be able to spot anomalies and issues in systems, data collection methods, data transfer, or even the analysis. If you do, you should inform the data owners or data custodians and help them fix any inconsistencies and gaps in their workflows.

Sometimes, your "customers" may be people with limited understanding or access to the underlying IT systems, like researchers or marketing teams. They might not have the ability to look under the hood and figure out why their data sets or results look wrong. You will be able to assist them, both by pointing out the ethical ways of processing and analyzing data and performing technical investigation and troubleshooting of the affected systems.

> *Story from the IT trenches: In a previous workplace, we had a database administrator who also had a good working knowledge of the data stored in the system. When he noticed data points that looked to be typos or inaccurate measurements, he would update the source data values in the database, not observing the formal data cleansing process in place. He did not notify anyone that he had made these changes, I only knew he did this because I watched him do it as he was cross-training me!*

On top of that, you may have a better overall understanding of the bigger picture, given your wider access to systems and data, as your customers may only be exposed to a small subset of the total pool of information. They won't necessarily be able to see all the patterns, but you can assist them by helping them understand the interdependencies and interaction among different components and systems in the environment.

Conclusion

Working with data is an inevitable, integral part of system administration. Sometimes, you will be asked to assist in processes that include data analysis. It is vital that you adhere to strict ethical principles in your work. We learned that data needs to be owned and classified, and data use needs to be mapped and documented, sometimes with the aid of automated tools. Now we can take this one step further.

Data sources need to be identified, protected, and audited for integrity. Data analysis needs to be based on a reproducible theory with well-documented, repeatable process. You should not seek good or bad results, as these could and will skew the perception of your business environment and negatively impact your work in the long run. You can use automation to aid you in the storage and handling of data and results to minimize human errors.

However, data handling is only one of the many temptations of the Garden of IT. The exposure to data will also lead you to information that can potentially carry serious ramifications for you and your company if misused. Indeed, in the following chapter, we will also learn how to behave in the gray area that is intellectual property.

CHAPTER 4

Do not Steal Intellectual Property

"There will be an investigation ..."

Wendell looked around the meeting room. Facial expressions ranging from bemused to concentrated and to worried. He wondered what his own expression showed.

Wendell leaned back, thinking back about his first weeks with the company, up through the day of the big data breach. He felt as if things had gone really well during his onboarding. He had met people and learned many new things. He received server access early on, and all the data he needed for doing his job. Everyone on the team was very helpful.

Things had really gone well, and now this data breach ... But he had nothing to worry about. He hadn't really done anything wrong.

Had he?

Wendell thought of a few minor things that happened that weren't 100% ethical, such as getting the root password on a piece of paper or getting a copy of actual customer data to experiment with. Then he was given scripts to change customer data that might possibly be used to cover up evidence of unethical behavior! But he knew he handled each situation appropriately and ethically in every way.

Thinking about all of this began to make Wendell feel concerned that even though he knew he'd done everything ethically, Mike and others on the team might decide to blame him for the breach simply because he had access.

© Igor Ljubuncic, Tom Litterer 2019
I. Ljubuncic and T. Litterer, *System Administration Ethics*,
https://doi.org/10.1007/978-1-4842-4988-8_4

It is always easier being wise in retrospect, he thought.

Wendell pondered on the encounters with his other team members over the past few weeks, trying to recall any possible unethical situations. He remembered his interaction with Daniel was quite odd.

"I need to see a man about a thing," Wendell joked as he walked to Daniel's desk. He wanted to talk with him about getting access to a data analysis software for his project.

"What do you need?" Daniel asked, holding a large mug in his hands. He looked distant, but Wendell knew him to be quite astute and sharp.

"Statistical data analysis software. The software I have is really basic; I need something more powerful."

Daniel tapped a random beat on the rim of the mug; it had a flaking Yoda print on it. "Hm. The thing is, there's this really cool program that I'm using, and I think it would be perfect for you; but I'm testing it with the customer, and it's actually covered by NDA, so I can't talk about it."

Wendell raised his eyebrows. "Oh, well."

Daniel shrugged. "Let's see what else we have." He turned to his computer and started searching through known catalogs and repositories of open-source software. He looked at this and that product, humming and then shaking his head before scrolling on.

"There are a few tools with evaluation licenses, but I don't think this is what you need. Some of them are restricted to academia only. Nothing here. Let me check on a crackware site to see what they have there."

Wendell didn't like where this was going. "Wait!"

Daniel was focused on his search. "I think I found what you need. Here."

Wendell read the list of features. It *did* look exactly like what he needed. "Well, we can buy it then. How much does it cost? Can you go to the vendor's official site and check?"

Daniel pursed his lips. "Unfortunately, it makes no difference what the cost is. Since it's not in our planned budget for the year, there's no way we can get funding to purchase it. Mike's never going to approve it."

Wendell sighed. "So what then?"

"Well, I suggest you try the software, get the hang of it. If it's really valuable and useful, and you want it used in production, then we can ask Mike to add it to the budget for the next year. Unfortunately, it could easily be a year, a year and a half, until the money is available."

Wendell made a pained face. "That sounds…bureaucratic."

Daniel chuckled. "Tell me about it."

Wendell thought about his project, and felt frustrated by the notion of having to put everything on hold just because he couldn't buy a piece of software for his work.

Daniel noticed his expression. "I know how you feel. Let me show you something." He opened a console window and punched in a few commands.

"What's that?"

"My torrent machine. I keep it in my home office. It's isolated from work and other systems I have. I use it to download software. So we can search for your statistical analysis tool and get an unlocked version."

Wendell watched as Daniel placed – what was supposedly – a valid copy of the software into the download queue. "Do you do a lot of torrenting?"

Daniel shrugged. "Some. Mostly movies. I don't often do that, unless I really can't find them elsewhere. I don't seed much, and I delete the files after watching them. The thing is, I don't like spending money on movies I'm not really sure I'm going to like, you know. Here, let me show you my recent downloads."

Wendell smiled. "Nice! I like your taste in movies."

Daniel smiled back. "Great minds think alike." He raised a finger. "But fools seldom differ. People often forget the second part."

Wendell scanned Daniel's collection. It was rather big, years' worth of cinema and rentals. Wendell started to wonder if he *ever* deleted any movies. "I used to download movies as a kid, but now I'm using several streaming services. You pay a monthly subscription. They are not too expensive, and you get unlimited access to a pretty rich catalog. I think that's a fair alternative to torrents. Maybe you can try that."

Daniel nodded.

While waiting, Wendell started thinking about the different statistical models he wanted to try. In theory, he could do them the *hard* way, with lots of mathematical calculations, but it would really be nice if he had a seamless tool he could integrate into his workflow. A few minutes later, the torrent download was complete.

Daniel snapped his fingers. "There we go. I'm just going to transfer the file over to the work laptop. It will take a few seconds. Now, let's scan the file with the anti-virus, just to be on the safe. All right, I'm giving you access to my shared folder so you can grab the software."

Wendell nodded. "Thanks."

Daniel leaned over. "Look, sometimes the procedures are really slow and complex, and they just get in the way. Especially when you're testing things out, it's better to find a backdoor solution than no solution. I was in a similar situation last month when I set up the torrent machine. Elwood was able to get me some old server disks to put into my home office system. Mike approves home systems but wouldn't approve extra disks. Elwood made it happen for me!" Sitting up straight again, Daniel continued, "I suggest you talk to him if you need a home system."

"Makes sense. I'll try out the software this afternoon," Wendell nodded. "Thanks again."

Daniel waved his hand. "Don't mention it."

A License to Skill

Chapter 3 (Do Not Change Data) taught us about data. But we didn't really care about the data contents and what they represent. Quite often, data translates into higher forms of logic, often with a unique value. The human glue that puts everything together is what we call intellectual property.

Throughout the ages, there has been a philosophical battle between the tangible, physical world of tools, machines, and goods and the spiritual, ethereal world of ideas and concepts. While products are essentially the end manifestation of ideas, it is the tangible that gets all the fame and recognition. People often find it easier to attribute value to things they can interact with in a physical way than things that only exist in a dimensionless world of thoughts.

As humanity progressed into the industrial age, the notion of intellectual property became more prevalent. As the old concepts of trade and barter were replaced with modern economy (which in itself created a significant mind shift in that paper notes could bear value), businesses, guilds, and trade organizations began to assemble frameworks that would give recognition and compensation to people's ideas and products. Trademarks and patents were born.

At this point, technology became a massive life-changer, leading to significant development and improvement in commerce, healthcare, and communication. Even today, we can point out people and their solutions that revolutionized our lives – steam engine, light bulb, telegraph, radio. Behind every one of these inventions is a person, and quite often a series of legal documents and agreements that codify the ownership of products and their intrinsic ideas.

For many decades, this system was a well-oiled machine. But then the Internet came.

Almost overnight, the average person transformed from someone dependent on their local newspaper for news and their TV set for knowledge into a wild, uncontrolled explorer, roaming the World Wide Web, with free access to pretty much any information. Anything that exists in the digital form is now available – documents, books, games, software programs.

None of these is truly tangible.

The technology landscape has changed at an unprecedented pace, but our perception of value still remains rather old-fashioned. Nowadays, people still struggle with (or choose to ignore) the complexity behind digital products. When you run a piece of code on your machine, you can easily forget that there might be hundreds of people who made that code run and perform its intended tasks. We don't consciously think about the immense logistical infrastructure that supports our digital lives, built from thousands of products, assembled from thousands of ideas.

Even this book spawned from an idea. Many hours of work and research translated into a few kilobytes of text and images that do not reflect the collective input of thought that went into it. So, if you downloaded this book from the Web in an "unofficial" way, perhaps you should consider buying it online. After all, you're on Chapter 4 (Do Not Steal Intellectual Property)!

System administrators happen to sit in the midst of this intellectual pool.

As "traffic" wardens, system administrators are exposed to a whole spectrum of data, ranging from seemingly trivial logs to confidential information that might expose the company's IT security or trade secrets. Quite often, system administrators are not aware – nor do they fully understand – the importance of the intellectual property they manage. Internal classification may help stratify the value of data and knowledge embedded in the digital form, but there are many other vectors of intellectual property that may not have any formal definition in the business.

For example, software may be free for home use but not for corporate use. Or it may be available only under certain conditions (like jurisdictions or product types). What happens if you search online for a concept or a phrase that is closely associated with technology being developed in your company? Can you talk about patents?

There's also the *temporal* dimension. A product release could be a secret until the official launch, when it becomes public domain knowledge. There are time restrictions on certain types of intellectual property, and they are not always obvious. These tie into a wider legal framework, the details of which are beyond the scope of this book.

Moreover, developers, system administrators, and technicians will not always be privy to the finer details of permitted use, and they end up violating rules or regulations, finding themselves accused of theft or misconduct, without even being fully cognizant of the extent of their actions.

We already discussed permissions and privacy as well as how to manage data in an ethical way. This is a good primer for handling the finer aspects of the intangible world of digital property, which we will now discuss in detail.

Do Not Steal (Intellectual Property)

The word theft has a very specific connotation. It implies a **deliberate action.** Indeed, the loss of intellectual property is in the forefront of many businesses nowadays. It has even sparked a trade war between world superpowers,[1] with the US administration estimating the damage from IP theft into hundreds of billions of dollars annually.

The loss can stem from **accidental leaks**, caused by inadequate security or data classification measures, but such accidents do not exonerate those involved and sometimes even carry a legal responsibility. And then, of course, your actions can be interpreted as malicious regardless of your intentions!

You may think the first part is obvious. After all, if you ask anyone whether they intend to commit theft, they will (most likely) deny any such intentions. However, the problems creep in when you take deliberate actions you do not construe as theft that can nevertheless be defined as such, for example, if you grab a piece of software you "thought" was okay, but didn't thoroughly examine the terms and conditions of its usage in your work environment.

The second part is even murkier. Not only will system administrators sometimes be exposed to situations where ownership, copyright, and branding are ambiguous, they may find themselves taking actions based on limited or partial knowledge, using their own interpretation of the

---

[1]https://money.cnn.com/2018/03/23/technology/china-us-trump-tariffs-ip-theft/index.html

permitted frameworks. Or they may act not thinking about the intellectual property loss implications. This can result in complicated situations where neither the cause nor the effect is immediately apparent, and they only become noticeable after significant damage has already been done.

If You Need to Use Licensed Software or Documentation, Get a License

In Chapter 1 (Separate Roles) and Chapter 2 (Respect Privacy), we learned not to tamper with data and to make sure we protect the privacy of our customers. The next step is to ensure that the intellectual rights of companies whose products are used in the IT environment are respected, preserved, and protected.

Software may not be tangible, which makes it more difficult to fully understand and frame its purpose and easier to dismiss its value. If you require new software in your environment, you need to make sure that you have a legitimate business reason to use the software and satisfy the usage requirements. We will discuss how to do this in detail later in the chapter. First, let's examine what Wendell and Daniel did.

Finding the Right Software

He turned to his computer and started searching through known catalogs and repositories of open-source software.

One might say that software is only as good as the search term used to find it. On the Internet, this can be somewhat daunting, and it can be difficult to differentiate between so-called good and bad software. Daniel's approach is sound and methodical, whereby he starts with a known list of programs that are considered reputable, and there is a good chance that he will be able to find suitable candidates for Wendell's work.

Moreover, as we will discuss in greater detail later in the chapter, quite often open-source software is distributed with permissive distribution and usage licenses (although this is not a guarantee), which can be helpful when engineers and system administrators need to evaluate new software products without having to go through a long approval process to buy and install applications.

> *There are a few tools with evaluation licenses, but I don't think this is what you need. And then, some of them are restricted to academia only.*

Daniel shows some understanding of the different strata of software licenses and their terms of use. It is useful to have some familiarity with software licensing, as it can help developers and system administrators make the right choice when they require new software. Ideally this should be the domain of a dedicated business entity, but typically, only the largest companies will have the required resources to support this function.

Products with evaluation can often be used without any restrictions during a short period of time. Daniel also understands that some products are restricted by usage. Quite often, online software stores will state the price of the product, the type of license, and whether any evaluation is available. It is possible to discern whether such software can be used without additional approvals or cost.

Avoid Temptation

> *Let me check on a crackware site.*

Daniel has no legitimate business purpose going to web sites that offer "cracked" software for download. While it may sound like a cliché, web sites that offer unauthorized copies of software are often associated with other types of illegal business activities. Sometimes, such web sites will bundle malware with tools that supposedly help users "unlock" software copies, including Trojans, keyloggers, and adware. You may also be unwantedly exposed to adult content or illicit drug dealings, which are illegal in certain jurisdictions but also a gross misuse of work assets. This is a rather blatant example of intellectual property theft, and by going there, Daniel is violating the commandment of this chapter.

Can you go to the vendor's official site and check?

Wendell's approach was far more ethical than that of his colleague. He was opposed to visiting the crackware site, and he raised a number of valid points that should steer Daniel and himself in the right direction – how to buy and use the software in a safe (and legal) way.

There's no way we can get funding to purchase it.

Daniel's comment exposes further ethical problems in his reasoning. He uses an administrative problem as an excuse to search and obtain the software by other means, some of which can be considered illegal. His claim that the manager would not be able to secure the necessary approval to purchase the software is also a conjecture. The correct way to address this issue is to request Mike's approval and then seek an ethical alternative if the funding is not available. Future chapters will have more details about not accessing illegal sites, following procedures, and communication changes.

As system administrators, Wendell and Daniel should focus on staying ethical, which includes abiding by existing processes and rules, like the software management and purchase chain. This also means promoting ethical work, refraining from violations, and making sure that they maintain a safe and secure business environment.

If You Have Unlicensed Access, Fix the Hole and Get a License

IT setups are complex, living, breathing things, with thousands of components interacting in a giant orchestra of electricity (and an occasional beep). Sometimes, there will be unintended violations of rules and regulations. For instance, you could end up using an expired version of a program, for which the company no longer pays nor has the license. While the software had been obtained following due processes some time ago, it may no longer be available, and any further use can constitute a breach of licensing terms.

Being ethical is a continuous process of improvements, which also includes audits that can identify and flag deviations from the established norms. If you discover an unlicensed use of software in your work environment, this could be an artifact of inadequate license management and auditing rather than deliberate malpractice. In such situations, you should alert the relevant business entities, stop the software license violations, and help them improve their auditing process, so that future instances of similar scenarios are correctly spotted and actioned.

On the other hand, if you do require the use of expired or unlicensed software, you should obtain the correct licenses for any future use. You should still make sure the gap in the process is correctly identified and fixed. In this chapter, we came across several issues, which Wendell should have helped close.

Staying Compliant Is Easy

I'm testing it with the customer, and it's actually covered by NDA, so I can't talk about it.

Nondisclosure agreements (NDA) are a common practice used by companies to allow some amount of data sharing and cooperation when working on confidential projects. Daniel is mindful of his obligation, and Wendell understands and respects the restrictions. NDA should not be misconstrued as a lack of trust. In some situations, one employee may have access to certain technology or products while their colleagues do not and vice versa.

NDA are a specific subset of the privacy commandment, and it is very important to be aware of them and strictly follow their framework. If you believe that someone else should be allowed access to restricted information covered under NDA, you should consult the data owner and request explicit permissions to disseminate the information.

> *I'm using several streaming services. You pay a monthly sub-scription. They are not too expensive, and you get unlimited access to a pretty rich catalog. I think that's a fair alternative to torrents.*

Wendell tries to steer his colleague toward a more ethical option when it comes to digital content. Wendell shows understanding of the intellectual property associated to digital content. He ss mindful that Daniel's downloads were not obtained in an ethical (or even legal) way. Rather than being confrontational, Wendell presents an alternative solution to the problem, which is more likely to result in a positive outcome.

The Slippery Slope

> *My torrent machine. I keep it in my home office. It's isolated from work and other systems I have. I use it to download software.*

Daniel uses his computer resources to download programs, which most definitely goesagainst the distribution and usage terms of said software. While his system is isolated from the work environment, he broke the isolation when he copied a piece of software to his laptop, so he could share it with Wendell. He also implicated his company in his "home" activity, because he used the company's assets (his work machine) to distribute software that he had obtained in a rather illegal manner.

We've encountered something similar in Chapter 1 (Separate Roles). Alex's use of a personal bastion was a violation of the eighth commandment (Communicate Change) and the ninth commandment (Do No Harm). The existence of a privileged backdoor access into the network potentially allowed Alex to cause damage in an unprecedented and unexpected way. Daniel has an unauthorized system connected to the work environment, which is also used for out-of-work purposes, including illegal downloads.

Daniel's work is neither documented nor part of any established process. There's also an additional risk that he may introduce malware into the work environment. The perfunctory scan with an anti-virus program does not guarantee the software is safe for use.

Wendell was not happy with Daniel's use of the crackware site, and he should have objected to the use of (personal) torrents to obtain software for his work needs.

Do you do a lot of torrenting?

Some. Mostly movies. I don't often do that, unless I really can't find them elsewhere.

The discussion about the illegal use of software extends beyond the software needed for the statistical analysis of Wendell's data. Ever since the proliferation of high-speed Internet, unauthorized downloads of movies and music have posed a big problem for the entertainment industry. For many years, there has been a gap for providing access to the full catalog of films and music, including geographical restrictions, where people in some countries had no legal way to enjoy some of the content. The music industry has largely caught up, but there are still films that are not available for rent or purchase.

The lack of pay-per-view content may make one feel justified in downloading movies, but we should not forget that there is significant cost to producing films and that we should pay for the work done to make them. Wendell's suggestion to use streaming services with a monthly subscription is a reasonable compromise to this phenomenon.

Look, sometimes the procedures are really slow and complex, and they just get in the way … It's better to find a backdoor solution than no solution.

Again, similar to the budget approval point, it is not the place and role of system administrators to define workarounds for inefficient procedures or the ones they do not like. Backdoors violate known processes and reduce the security and integrity of IT systems. If Wendell and Daniel believe that certain procedures hamper work, they should work with the relevant owners to change or improve them.

Managing Licenses and Intellectual Property

Today, it is virtually impossible to run a business without an IT component. Even companies whose core trade rests far outside the domain of IT are relying on a strong, complex – and often growing – backend of hardware and software infrastructure to support and sustain their essential functions. This creates a delicate situation where system administrators often have to act as authoritative sources on matters closely associated with their subject matter, but not quite their area of expertise.

If you find yourself in a well-established IT setup, there will most likely be a foundation of software license management in place, and you will be able to refer to it in the course of your work. If you're starting from scratch, you have an opportunity to make sure you follow a robust process that minimizes the risk of software theft and accidental IP losses. You can start small; even a simple spreadsheet can be used to track the installed software and available licenses. As your organization grows, you should think about dedicated assets – both human and software – to manage the license catalog.

> *Remember, if there is an IP leak, people will not necessarily assume good intent on behalf of those involved. You may call it an "accident," but you could be blamed for a deliberate act of negligence or even theft.*

Definition of Intellectual Property

Intellectual property theft extends beyond just buying or leasing licenses for software used in your IT environment. You may also commit IP breaches by misusing logos or brand names.

Software does not have to be a product you see and interact with, like a word processor, a game, or an office suite. Software[2] is **anything digital** that you could obtain on a computer. This can include online documentation, image files (like logos), or software libraries that are used by other programs or applications.

The most basic example of a violation is releasing a software project to the public, using an online code repository like GitHub or GitLab. You could be bundling code from other projects and using their logos and brands, without being aware that this might require a special permission.

Even if you do not use other people's code in your project, the presence of third-party images and names might create an impression that your project is endorsed by the other entities or make people wrongly associate unrelated projects to your work. While this will typically affect software developers, system administrators could also find themselves in a similar situation, if they publicly release administration tools, utilities, or scripts.

Software Licenses

Software often comes with a usage license that explains what you can do with the software and under what terms. The most permissive license places the intellectual property in **public domain**, meaning it has no exclusive intellectual property rights (they may have expired or been revoked, or the original owner decided to share their work without restrictions). More restrictive licenses allow for only a limited number of users, prevent redistribution, and disallow reverse engineering of the software code.

---

[2]https://en.wikipedia.org/wiki/Software

You need to understand the license and agree to its terms before you can use the software. If you do not have the authority or knowledge, you will need to refer the decision to the business entity that can. This is very similar to the data ownership concept we discussed in Chapter 3 (Do Not Change Data). Software needs to be classified and its usage correctly and precisely determined.

License Classifications and Misconceptions

The classification will usually include:

- Home vs. work use.

- Free vs. payware.

- Open-source vs. closed source (whether the software code is available to the general public or kept private by the software owner).

- Libre vs. proprietary (whether the software has any distribution and/or usage restrictions).

Side by side with the classifications, there is also a range of misconceptions:

- A common misconception is that **open-source** software can be used without any restrictions. While open-source software is often distributed with permissive licenses, such as GPL[3] or MIT,[4] unrestricted use is not guaranteed just because the software source code is public and accessible.

---

[3]www.gnu.org/licenses/gpl-3.0.en.html
[4]https://opensource.org/licenses/MIT

- This brings about the important distinction between open-source and **libre** software.[5] The former exposes its code, but the usage is still restricted based on the license under which it is distributed. The latter allows for unrestricted use, although technically it might even be closed source in nature. Most often, libre software will also be open-source.

- Another common misconception is that **free** software can be used without any restrictions. The confusion stems from the implied meaning of the word free. Software can be distributed without cost, but its usage may still be restricted. The cost may also depend on the setup. For example, some programs are free (zero cost) for home use, but you will need to pay for commercial use. In other cases, you will be able to use an application for up to a certain number of users or computers without any charge, after which you will have to pay for additional licenses. The cost does not imply any type of redistribution rights. Proprietary software may be offered for free (e.g., Skype, Google Chrome), but you are not allowed to resell or redistribute these products, and you have no access to the source code. Libre software is often free of charge, as well as open-source.

- Academic, nonprofit organizations and charities may also have special clauses that do not apply to the general public or corporations.

Story from the IT trenches: Our server admin created some impressive graphs each month, which his manager used in

---

[5]https://en.wikipedia.org/wiki/Free_software

his presentation at the directors meeting. One month, the admin was out for a couple of weeks when the scripts ran to create the graphs; unfortunately, the script output reported a licensing error. His manager was rather upset since he was planning to use the graphs to highlight some recent server throughput improvements. It turned out that the graphing software was never purchased; the server admin had been reinstalling the software every 90 days in order to restart the clock on the evaluation license.

An evaluation license should never be used in production. Once it is clear that the product meets the needs of the business, then the ethical thing to do is to purchase a license before moving it into production. The server admin in this example could have easily asked his manager for the funding before automating the monthly graphical report.

Software Restrictions and Expiration

Licenses also define how many people are allowed to use the software, and they may have expiration dates. There could also be other restrictions, like geographical location (or jurisdiction), industry type and purpose, and more.

- Licenses can be attributed to **individual users** (accounts or organizations).

- Licenses can be closely **tied to hardware**. For example, you may be allowed to deploy a piece of software on ten servers, regardless of the number of users. Or you may only use it on specific types of hardware (like physical vs. virtual systems) or a limited subset of hardware (systems with less than four CPU cores, for instance).

- Licenses may only be valid for a **certain period of time**. Some software may only be used for several months, after which it must be renewed. Other programs may have annual subscription. You may also be granted perpetual licenses that do not expire.

Table 4-1 shows the different permutations of licenses and their restrictions. In most cases, it is impossible to decide whether certain restrictions apply just by looking at any one aspect of the license type, and a more detailed analysis is required to determine the terms of use and any possible limitations.

Table 4-1. *Permutations of licenses and their restrictions (Yes/No/Both)*

Licensing restrictions	Cost	Source	Account	Hardware	Time
Home	B	B	B	B	B
Work	B	B	B	B	B
Open-source	B	Y	B	B	B
Closed source	B	N	B	B	B
Libre	N	Y	N	N	N
Proprietary	B	B	B	B	B

Software License Management

Given the large number of available options, it becomes very difficult to manage software by hand. Even a small number of applications can be quite challenging, and manual methods do not scale beyond very small businesses.

Software management, much like data, requires a business owner. The **license owner** should be a technical expert, with a good understanding of different types of licenses, classifications, and exceptions.

The license owner will manage software using some form of **centralized database** that will list every type of software used in the

company and all the systems and users associated with the software. There
should be an **automated process** to register new software and map its
usage to accounts and systems. Regular **audits** should be run to analyze
any gaps and noncompliance in the usage of software in the organization.

There should be a well-defined and documented process on how to
introduce new software into the company, including initial evaluation,
purchase, registration, distribution, usage monitoring and auditing, and
renewals. System administrators and developers who need access to new
software will consult the license owner, as shown in Figure 4-1.

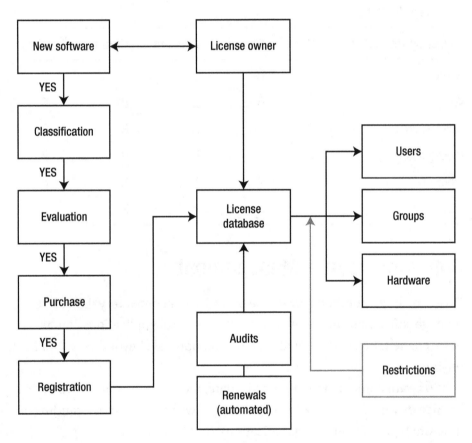

Figure 4-1. *Software license management workflow*

To minimize disruptions in the work and streamline the process, the automated framework could also include lists of permitted (whitelisted) and restricted (blacklisted) software so that system administrators and developers can speed up testing and deployment. For example, if a piece of software is known to be libre, without restrictions, then its use can be allowed without any additional work. Likewise, if a piece of software is distributed as part of an ecosystem, then no special requests are necessary. For instance, most Linux distributions come with licenses that also cover software included in the software channels (repositories). These allow system administrators to install any new application or library from these channels without having to go through a special process.

> *Story from the IT trenches: Our department purchased a CAD software tool, which IT then packaged and published on the application distribution site. This made it easy for our team to install on our desktops. This also made it easy for people in every other department to install the software as well unbeknownst to us. When a software audit was done several years later, the company (thankfully not just our department) had to purchase more licenses than were originally purchased in order to not be fined by the software vendor.*

In this story, the IT department had a great software packager but did not have methodology for restricting installs or doing internal software licensing audits.

Software Development and Copyright Infringement

The other side of the IP coin is the software that your company develops and ships. When you distribute software, you are responsible for setting the terms and conditions for its usage. This will often be reflected in the software license attached to the product. In most cases, the license will apply to your users, but it may also affect you.

The choice of the license will dictate how you ship and distribute your software and what restrictions you are allowed to use (if any). Likewise, if you use components from other software projects, you will have to abide by their licensing and distributing terms.

For example, the GPL is a highly popular license in the software world. The Linux kernel, used in hundreds of millions of servers powering the Internet, giant cloud data centers, and supercomputers, is licensed under GPL. Part of the success of Linux is attributed to the permissive nature of the license, as well as the fact the kernel source code is available. Indeed, GPL guarantees end users the freedom to run, study, share, and modify the software.

Since software products are rarely developed in complete isolation, there's a good chance you will be reusing existing libraries or parts of code that someone else has already developed. This is a common practice; it saves times, promotes collaboration, and allows you to use well-tested, high-quality software components without developing everything from scratch. This also means that your code contains intellectual property created and designed by someone else, and this needs to be reflected in the software license.

Do not interpret the law; refer the matter to an expert in this domain.

If you are using software components other than your own, then you need to make sure you are not violating any existing terms. This is very difficult to ascertain manually. Applications like Black Duck[6] allow you to research open-source projects and mitigate license compliance risks.

---

[6]www.blackducksoftware.com/

Patents, Trademarks, and NDAs

It is equally important to **protect** your company's IP as much as it is to respect the property of others. While you can deliberately misuse the software products, you can also accidentally damage your own company by using wrong information at the wrong time, despite best technical safeguards in place.

Companies often protect their own work by registering patents with patent offices around the world, which guarantees certain rights under complex, layered legal frameworks. Patents precede modern computer systems, with documented use of the concept going as far back as the medieval Republic of Venice.

However, until patents are registered and granted the protection, the ideas and concepts embodied in their descriptions are vulnerable to exposure that could invalidate them. As a most blatant example, if you post a patent proposal on a blog somewhere, someone else could try to register this other than yourself or your company, which could then lead to the intellectual property being granted to another party. Or it may result in a long, costly legal battle whereby multiple sides claim first rights to the patent's embodiment.

In your course of work, you may come across technical documents that explain products, concepts, and algorithms – or you may actually be writing a patent proposal yourself. If you're doing the latter, a common temptation is to actually search online for similar ideas, to see whether someone else has already solved the problem, so you can save yourself time going forward with an idea that was already patented elsewhere. But once you "submit" the idea online, you relinquish it to the Internet.

- **Do not search online** for technological concepts, ideas, algorithms, or similar phrases that are used in product descriptions or drafts, whether composed by yourself or someone else. If you do need clarifications or additional information, consult with the **legal entity** in your company how to proceed.

- **Do not discuss** these concepts and ideas with other people, unless they are part of a group working on the patent. You cannot control what other people do and how they share information, and they may accidentally leak them, possibly invalidating your first-right ownership.

- **Stay silent.** Even if your legal department has successfully submitted a patent proposal to a patent office, you still need to refrain from any public discussions about the idea. Quite often, there's a period of "silence" related to patents, which can extend for many months or even years until the official paperwork has been completed. **Consult** with the legal entity whether you can talk about patents and associated technology.

The same approach applies to nondisclosure agreements (NDA). While they may not necessarily cover new technology or patents, the same rules apply. You should not discuss or share the information, and you should not make any actions that could compromise the terms of the agreement.

Conclusion

Intellectual property is all too easy to ignore. It's not tangible, but we must not forget the hard work, time, and cost invested in creating digital products. System administrators have an obligation to protect intellectual property just as they would protect hardware assets or data.

The protection of IP comes in several layers – the correct classification of software and use of licenses; how to protect (and respect) the creation of others, be they patents, trademarks, logos, or software; and the use of a centralized software management framework that allows for easy selection and detection of necessary software products and their licenses.

As we've seen in this chapter, intellectual property does not reside in an ethereal vacuum. It has roots in products and hardware components, things that are very much tangible. The next obvious step is to talk about physical property, which is going to be our next topic.

CHAPTER 5

Do Not Steal Computers

"Now listen y'all," Elwood continued, probably more loudly than necessary. "Trigger discipline. That's the most important thing here. You never put your forefinger on the trigger unless you gonna shoot."

Wendell saw a bunch of heads nod. Gopal was smiling. Mike looked somewhat impatient. Wendell could imagine the manager's discomfort for letting Elwood run this one. He had probably thought it was one less headache, and maybe even something everyone – well, half of the team that showed up anyway – would enjoy, but now he must be having second thoughts.

It was an odd team activity, that's for sure. Shooting old hard disks.

Elwood sure was a proud Texan. On the way to the wilderness area, Elwood shared bits and snippets about his life, one hand on the steering wheel of his truck, one moving slowly about the cabin as he talked. Quite amusing, Wendell thought. There was something instantly likeable about Elwood, which was probably why Mike had agreed to let him run this *somewhat* unconventional team building activity.

"Keep your gun pointed toward the target. Never turn around with a loaded weapon. Got it? Let's make sure we all do this nice and safe now, y'hear?" Elwood turned toward the back of his truck, where he had an impressive rack of weapons on display. "So what do y'all wanna shoot? How about you, Wendell? You're the new guy, you get to choose first."

© Igor Ljubuncic, Tom Litterer 2019
I. Ljubuncic and T. Litterer, *System Administration Ethics*,
https://doi.org/10.1007/978-1-4842-4988-8_5

Wendell felt a spark of excitement go through him. He had never been that much into weapons, and he had never fired anything bigger than a BB gun. But now he could choose anything he liked. "Uh, I don't know. What would you recommend?"

Elwood grunted. "You got beefy arms, you can handle a kick. Let's say you go for this nice oh-five. Gotta hold the grip with both hands, all right."

From what Wendell remembered from the movies, he thought oh-five was for shooting aircraft, but apparently, there was a handgun of that caliber. He picked the heavy, massive thing and took his place at the firing lane. Imam was next, holding what looked to Wendell to be an assault rifle.

Elwood came over. "Don't worry, big guy. It's gonna be fine." He grinned. "You nervous?"

"Excited," Wendell answered.

"It's simple. You see that old hard disk over there at the 25 yard line? Aim like I showed you, breathe out, shoot. I'll set you up with a clip of APs first, then we'll switch you to holler points. You'll see the difference when you hit the target." He chuckled. "If you hit the target."

"I'll do my best," Wendell said, and no matter how much Elwood tried to scare him, he was still amazed by the recoil when he fired.

The two hours breezed by in a cloud of loud bangs, smoke, and laughter as they slowly relaxed and started enjoying themselves. To his credit, Elwood made sure they never got reckless, so no one tried any John Wayne tricks.

"It's time to put the chairs in the wagon," Elwood said.

"So who won?" Imam asked.

A box full of old hard disks later, most of them sporting big holes, the group was driving back to the office.

"I hear you want a freakin' home media system?" Elwood asked Wendell, chewing on some gum.

Wendell noticed he had grease spots on his shirt. On the other hand, Elwood's was spotless. "Yes. You must have heard that I was talking to Daniel and Caesar about it. So. How does it work to get a system from the office to take home?"

Elwood smacked his lips. "It's pretty simple. Just fill out the home system form and then get approval from Mike. Bring the form to me and then I'll set you up with an old system."

"Old system?" Wendell wrinkled his nose. "Those systems that were just replaced are pretty crusty. Any way to get something a little newer?"

"Well, hold on there, partner. You've only been here a couple of months." Elwood grinned. "Don't expect me to give you the prize heifer!"

"Well, there at least must be a way to add a couple of old disks."

"Sure, I have a whole box of them in the back of the truck with holes in them!" Elwood chuckled and then nodded. "Actually, I have another box in the office that are still really good, it would be a shame to shoot holes in all of them. Sure! I reckon I can add a couple to your system, but you still gotta be meticulous about keeping track of all the assets, even the stuff we took out shootin' today. If a disk has any sort of IP on it, then it doesn't leave the building unless I dispose it in the shredder. You don't want these disks to show up on eBay or something."

Wendell had read enough stories about people getting in trouble thinking they could earn a spare buck by selling company scrap online. "Of course not."

"When we get back, I'll show you the piles of disk pallets waiting to be destroyed."

Elwood turned the radio on. The twang of country music filled the cabin. "Don't tell the boss, but I took home an almost brand-new disk array just a few days ago." Elwood leaned over as if he were about to tell a secret, but he couldn't contain his excitement and spoke even louder, "Let me tell ya, I've been waiting for it to become available since replacement hardware arrived last quarter. It was used on the production database server for the BI team, but the department replaced it because it didn't have the right capacity. They went to Belinda and had their storage profiled, but she couldn't allocate them any high-performance disks from the other projects, so they bought a new one. I labeled the one they got rid of as surplus equipment in the inventory system."

Wendell nodded, drawn in.

"So I had it plugged in this last week, so it gets acclimatized to the temperature and humidity of my media room, and then I'm going to make it my home DVR and my movie library. I'll show you when we get back, and maybe you wanna help me with the setup."

"Sure thing. How big is the array?" Wendell asked.

"It's an external array with 16 disks."

"You'll be able to store quite a few shows on that thing," Wendell joked.

"Heck yeah."

"What are you using for your media server?"

Elwood looked over and winked. "I've got a server that was purchased as a spare a couple of years ago. No one ever uses the spare servers, so I took it home as my *home system*." Speaking louder now, "And I sure need more space now. Gopal and I found a whole bunch of movies in the marketing department file share. I wanna get a copy of those into my movie library before Belinda comes asking questions or deletes them." He chuckled.

Wendell pursed his lips. "I heard there's a guy in marketing who's mining Bitcoin."

"Heck. Really?" Elwood shook his head. "They sure are a wild bunch."

"So you had fun today?"

Wendell grinned. "Yes, it was a blast. We should make this our regular team building activity."

Elwood gave him a light punch on the shoulder. "Well, we're gonna have that other box coming for scrap next month, so you can have another go then. What do you say?"

Wendell rubbed his arm. "Sounds great."

Elwood chuckled and turned the radio volume up.

In the Palm of Your Hand

In Chapter 4 (Do Not Steal Intellectual Property), we dealt with the difficult concept of ascribing value to software. It is only in recent human history that we reached the ability (and need) to create products that have no physical size or weight, and most of us still instinctively struggle with associating the same level of ownership to digital property as we do with tangible goods, which should make the topic of this chapter dead easy.

Don't steal computers – it should be obvious.

Alas, the reality tells a different picture.

Humans have a much better understanding of physical property, but this ability goes against other primal instincts we have brought with us from the prehistoric savannahs and into the data center – the need to hoard in the face of scarcity.

The digital revolution isn't dissimilar to the massive socioeconomic change of the late 18th and early 19th centuries, when machines took over manual labor and created a powerful ripple effect of migration, change, and opportunity. Over a relatively short period of time, a relatively stable market was transformed into something that would look completely alien to people from just a generation before.

The late 20th century saw a similar shift in the division of labor across the globe. The computer made the world smaller and faster, connected billions of people in a virtual soiree, and created immense opportunity for innovation and growth. At an unprecedented pace, electrical engineers, physicists, and the odd rebel studying the arcane art of computer science suddenly became the pioneers of change. And among them, system administrators became the gatekeepers to endless wealth of data – and physical resources.

Few people working in the IT industry would consider themselves the quartermasters of giant warehouses, full of whirring, noisy machines, rack upon rack of expensive equipment, delightfully elegant laptops, tons of forgotten cables, mice and monitors, all theirs to control. But whether it's solid-state drives or bales of silk they look after, the instincts are the same.

Theft is blatantly obvious, which is why few people would ever resort to outright stealing hardware resources from their company. But we have come up with many innovative ways of creating a milder perception of the reality that lets us get away with what is essentially the very thing no one would think of doing.

Among the many professionals in the IT world, data center technicians, system administrators, and support personnel are the ones with the greatest access – and thus the greatest temptation – to hardware resources. Every day, countless assets are added, removed, or written off inventory lists. No matter how organized these databases are, there is always a percentage of misplaced items. It is almost too easy to decide that this "lost" hardware doesn't really belong to anyone.

Then, companies also have aggressive hardware management policies, which often revolve around support contracts rather than the actual usability state of hardware resources. There isn't a system administrator on planet Earth who hasn't bemoaned the wasteful (premature) decommissioning of servers or laptops, just because of arbitrary dates in Enterprise Resource Planning (ERP). Instinctively, we feel a need to "save" these hardware assets, because thousands of years ago, our ancestors didn't really have any spares.

An easy way to justify the odd Robin Hood act of goodness is to reuse _end-of-life (EOL) resources in a way that would still keep the assets loosely tied to the company's databases. Some business do encourage their employees to reuse older systems, but quite often, there is an underground practice of utilizing resources beyond their intended purposes. We justify such decisions through benevolence of actions and the fact such actions are only temporary, that is, employees "loan" old hardware rather than "take it for good." There is also safety in numbers. "Everyone's doing it" has been a popular excuse since the dawn of humanity.

Lastly, over time, people become desensitized to minor acts of misconduct. This is not unique to the IT industry, but is quite prevalent in any organization with a high volume of asset movement and change.

For instance, you wouldn't necessarily consider yourself a criminal for taking home a cheap mouse or an old, dusty network cable. Most likely, no one will notice or mind your appropriation, for the same reasons, and you may associate the lack of punitive scrutiny as justification for your action. In turn, feeling safe and righteous, you might do this again, acting on a hoarding instinct that predates silicon-based products by a good few millennia. As time goes by, you could lose such judgment altogether.

Until someone notices, and then you lose your job over a seemingly trivial matter.

Employee theft is a costly business, with about USD 50 billion stolen annually just in the United States.[1] Such high numbers illustrate that a large number of people will succumb to petty crime, as well as the inability of businesses to accurately monitor and account for all their assets.

With so many elegantly designed computers lying about and a seemingly endless come and go of devices, controlling the hardware landscape seems difficult and complex. Indeed, IT people find themselves in a precarious position. They are expected to come up with innovative solutions that will help keep the work environment safe – they might even be held accountable for when things go wrong. And as gatekeepers, they also have the easiest access to the vast spoils and riches that is their IT environment.

Do Not Steal (Computers)

On paper, theft is simple to define – it's taking possession of property without the authorization from the owner. You should have a clear stance on this matter – if you haven't purchased it yourself (which will be the case in a majority of work scenarios), it does not belong to you.

---

[1] www.cnbc.com/2017/09/12/workplace-crime-costs-us-businesses-50-billion-a-year.html

In reality, though, theft is more difficult to define, because people bend rules and the definition of what constitutes property, ownership, and consent. As humans, we tend to fill in the blanks when we find them, in process, behavior, and rules; and we often do to our detriment. To that end, you should remember the basic premise of this commandment and always use that as your starting point for any considerations related to hardware.

If You Need Hardware, Buy It

Navigating asset management systems can be quite difficult and time-intensive. Quite often, system administrators and engineers won't have exposure or permission to access most of the company's databases. Therefore, employees should not try to crack the complex inventory equations themselves. They should instead stick to a simple formula: if they need an asset, they should purchase the required asset.

Whether it's a superexpensive server or a cheap development board, you should always approach the situation in a consistent, transparent manner. You should request the needed resources from your manager or the relevant authority. They can then forward such requests up the chain until it is satisfied. While it can be rather frustrating to wait for the administrative giant to flex its shoulders (think of Vogons in *The Hitchhiker's Guide to the Galaxy*), it is far more frustrating to have your employment record besmirched over something as trivial as a piece of hardware.

Purchase What You Need When You Need It

> *"It was used on the production database server for the BI team, but the department replaced it because it didn't have the right capacity. They went to Belinda ..."*

This example shows a good practice of hardware management. When the BI group realized that their existing server may not be suited to the purpose anymore, they didn't just blindly rush into upgrading the device.

They conducted an investigation first, to understand whether they had a capacity or a performance issue. This allowed them to find the optimal workaround to their problem. Perhaps they could have made a better choice in the hardware selection to begin with, but even so, they followed the right methodology in solving the issue at hand.

Brute-force solutions to various database bottlenecks aren't uncommon. Due to time, knowledge, or priority constraints, IT teams will often choose the simplest answer – hardware upgrades – even without the complete picture of the problem or its symptoms. Quite often, such incidents will recur, especially if they are caused by logical flaws in the software or the workloads.

Unused Hardware Is Not Yours

"Don't tell the boss, but I took home an almost brand-new disk array just a few days ago."

Elwood's violation of the commandment is quite blatant. He acted without authorization and used equipment for an unintended purpose. On top of that, the new disk array still has book value.

There are many implications to this action. Taking home hardware that has recently been purchased cannot even be misinterpreted as casually tolerated bad practice.

"I labeled it surplus equipment in the inventory system."

Elwood further compounded the problem by mislabeling the equipment. Companies often have strict policies on how hardware is managed, and sometimes, governments and municipalities grant tax reliefs for certain types of business activity. It is possible that Elwood has implicated his company in what could be a tax fraud by classifying assets the wrong way. Additionally, the inventory lists now include items that wrongly picture the state of the IT environment. For instance, this could lead to inaccurate purchase forecasts based on incorrect data, or a business division that expects to find sufficient inventory of a certain kind of hardware may suddenly realize it is not available.

"So I had it plugged in this last week."

However, the biggest issue with Elwood's action is that he has taken disks that were previously used in a production database. It is quite possible that those disks contain confidential data. No measure was taken to identify and dispose of the data in an approved, secure manner. By plugging the disks into his media system, Elwood might even have exposed the data online.

"No one ever uses the spare servers, so I took it home as my home system."

This ties back into the inventory mismanagement. It is possible that another team in the company may require the server for their work and only discover that it is missing when they actually need it. Even if Mike did approve the use of the spare, the server needs to be properly categorized.

For instance, if the server is taken home and used for on-call or training purposes, then it should stay on the books. However, if the server is being given to the employee for personal use, then it should be taken off the books. In some jurisdictions, this could also mean the value of the server being transferred to the employee as income on their taxes. In this case, there should be a correct procedure to decommission the server before it can be repurposed for other uses.

"I heard there's a guy in marketing who's mining Bitcoin."

This is another example of theft – using company assets for personal use while still in the building. It does not matter whether the hardware is used to store media files or generate revenue through computation, in either case it reduces the available IT capacity, whereby power, storage, and CPU cycles are used for personal needs rather than intended business goals. In the end, it translates into unsanctioned activities that could cause a lot of damage to the company, including both reputation and hefty fines.

Wendell should have reported the Bitcoin mining issue, so it could be properly investigated and validated. He also missed an opportunity to put safeguards in place that can help detect similar misuse early on.

> *Story from the IT trenches: While working as a UNIX sysadmin at an aerospace company, I was getting complaints from a few engineers about network slowness over the lunch hour. I thought it was strange that no one else was complaining, but I figured everyone else was at lunch. The next lunch hour, I confirmed that the network was heavily utilized and that packets were dropping. I also noticed that a lot of engineers weren't in the cafeteria and were actually at their computers. Apparently, one of the other UNIX sysadmins had installed flight simulation software on the server network, and now, the engineers were "flying together" every day during lunch.*

If You Need Someone Else's Hardware, Ask for Permission

In an ideal world, you would be able to make hardware requests and have your wishes granted in a fast, efficient way. Most of the time, there will be time and budget constraints, and you will be forced to improvise. However, acting in the gray area between hardware purchase and inaccurate inventory lists does not mean you should err on the side of theft. If you need hardware, and there are available resources in the IT environment, you should identify the owner and request permission for use. Such an approach will eliminate any situations where your actions might be misconstrued as petty theft or the abuse of your position as an IT employee. No matter how urgent or pressing the matters are, you shouldn't make **personal** shortcuts to overcome inefficiencies in your company's work policies.

Unused Hardware Is Less Expensive Than Exposed IP

"If a disk has any sort of IP on it, then it doesn't leave the building unless I dispose it in the shredder."

While the unusual team building activity did have some negative outcomes, Elwood did correctly handle the management of old hard disks prior to taking them out. He understands the need to secure IP, and he did follow the correct procedure to dispose of any storage that may contain confidential data – too bad he did not implement the same policy with his own media system! Lastly, we can only assume that Mike did (tacitly) approve the activity. In this case, Elwood did follow procedures.

If You Find It, It's Not Yours

"Sure! I reckon I can add a couple to your system, but you still gotta be meticulous about keeping track of all the assets."

Elwood's suggestion to Wendell is not following policy. It might be entirely possible that Mike would approve the request, but it needs to be done in a clear, transparent manner. Wendell should explicitly ask whether he can add the disks, even if they are old.

> *Story from the IT trenches: During my time as a manager of a Linux sysadmin team, I would allow/authorize full-time employees (who were system administrators) to take home fully depreciated workstations to be used as test machines for learning purposes. A temporary contract worker learned of this and took home an old workstation he found in the lab. Following a system inventory audit, it was discovered that the workstation was missing. As a result of the unauthorized removal of the workstation, the worker's contract was not renewed, and of course, he was asked to return the workstation.*

"Gopal and I found a whole bunch of movies in the marketing department file share."

In essence, this is stealing disk space from the company for personal use. It encompasses the violation of the fourth commandment (Do Not Steal IP), as well as our chapter's topic. Perhaps there is no physical theft of hard disks, but the use of the storage reduces the available capacity for work in the marketing department. Unaware of the problem, the department may have to purchase additional disks, which ties back to cost and waste.

> *Story from the IT trenches: A sysadmin on our team brought an old file server online in the lab room and connected it to the external network. He locked it down so that only he had access. He then began downloading porn JPEGs to the disk. We discovered it while clearing old hardware out of the lab.*

Elwood and Gopal should also have reported the misuse. It is quite likely that the movies were downloaded illegally, and even if they are legitimate property of the persons involved, storing them on company drives is most likely a violation of their licensing terms.

However, it is also possible that the marketing department had those movies for inspiration – or for use in promotional material! In this case, they may have violated the procedures by not asking to use the onsite storage for this purpose. This could also be a simple matter of insufficient communication or incomplete documentation, which needs to be fixed so that it reflects correctly the proper usage of the file share.

Getting on Top of the Hardware Game

The prevention of hardware theft comes in two main guises – **active deterrents** against misappropriation and misuse and **accurate management** of hardware. Combined, these two approaches can minimize damage caused by stolen hardware. If the safeguards do not stop the stealing, effective systems that maintain a clear and up-to-date picture of hardware assets will help detect the incidents early on.

Furthermore, there need to be clear, simple, and readily accessible **policies** that explain hardware usage at all stages of the asset life cycle. This will allow employees to know what they can do with the hardware, and if they have any questions or concerns, they will have a quick way of finding answers. The removal of gray areas will reduce the moral ambiguity and remove the temptation for misuse.

The Perfect Crime

Before we get into details about removing hardware from the premises of the workplace, let's first talk about misusing computer hardware at work. There's one type of stealing that can be quite hard to detect and prevent: it's stealing hardware without removing it from the building.

Sometimes, people may use (or rather misuse) work assets for personal gain. It can be quite difficult to detect such instances, for example, someone using a company license of a software (say Matlab or Photoshop) for personal data, even though the usage terms and work contract may prohibit that. Or they may use an expensive server to compile their personal code. For all practical purposes, an image or an algorithm used for personal needs is virtually indistinguishable from one used in a work assignment; unfortunately, system tools will typically not flag these types of violations.

The best way to mitigate this "soft" theft is through training, documentation, and pragmatic policies that try to balance reasonable work practices with employees' needs. An environment that promotes integrity on all levels will also help people stay ethical. It also works the other way around: if employees adopt an ethical approach, there will be less loss of capital due to stealing, and then management may be more inclined to permit some nonwork use in certain cases. Quite often, simply not using company equipment for personal gain goes a long way toward mitigating this type of violation.

The Life of a Computer

Hardware inventory management is one of the most challenging tasks in the IT industry. The reasons are many. Hardware comes in many sizes and shapes. Apart from some special equipment, one person, without any great preparations, can carry most hardware resources. This means you can displace a laptop, a server, or a router within seconds, making it effectively lost.

Tracking hardware is also quite difficult. Placing a label on a server is easy enough, but what if you need to take that server apart? Most IT gear consists of modular systems with dozens of sub-components, designed to be interchangeable and replaceable. Furthermore, computer hardware needs two primary resources to function – electricity and network connectivity. If those two are provided, the systems can operate anywhere. You could have a workstation in a dedicated lab on the tenth floor of your office building, or under your desk. Changing the physical location complicates things – but if you unplug a hardware asset, it also becomes invisible to any monitoring agent in the environment.

Moreover, the hardware landscape is vibrant and constantly changing. In a typical IT setting, the work setup will probably remain static for years, whereas employees will be using different devices all the time. This has become even more complicated with the introduction of Bring Your Own Device (BYOD) at many workplaces, as well as the introduction of laptops, tablets, and mobile phones into the work environment. It is not unusual for a person to have three or four computers about them at any given moment, creating a subtle logistics nightmare for the IT and security departments. Each one of these devices requires updates and patching, tailored security tools and policies, and specific software; and often, they are manufactured by different vendors, with different life cycles, timelines, and priorities.

Since no two IT setups are quite the same, the best way to handle hardware is to follow its journey from purchase to its eventual decommission, where it is physically removed from the company's premises and deleted from the books.

- Purchase – You need a process for how to buy new hardware. This process will most likely be determined by the finance department rather than an IT function, but the IT folks will help choose and design the purchase system.

- Acquisition & landing – There needs to be a process for how the purchased hardware is received, cataloged, and introduced into the IT environment.

- Inventory – There also needs to be an inventory database (written records, a spreadsheet, an ERP tool) that will list the purchased hardware according to the policy. The notable details in this database will include the following:

  - Every asset should have a **unique identifier** of some sort. This ID will allow anyone to find the asset, and therefore it should be both registered in the relevant database and available for physical inspection on the device itself. In some cases, the device may be too small or inaccessible to use printed labels, so alternative digital methods can be used.

  - Every asset should also have a **location** – and it will most likely change over the course of life of the device. Tracking hardware physically is a challenge, because devices may not be always powered on and therefore not accessible via the network. Active radio transmitters like RFID tag or Zigbee modules can be used to create a real-time view of all the available assets. Alternatively, the location could be manually updated or derived in an algorithmic manner based on the device's usage, but this can often lead to mistakes and out-of-date information.

- Usage – Through the normal life cycle of the device, the associated metadata that describe the device, including things like serial numbers, operating system, installed software, location in the data center, IP address, and other properties, must be maintained in the inventory. Monitoring and auditing allow you to identify these changes – and maybe even make automated corrections in relevant databases.

- End of life (EOL) – Hardware assets need to be removed from the environment in an orderly manner. This is actually harder than it sounds, because there might be people, groups, or entities within the company who expect computers to last forever and they could have hard-coded rules for connectivity or usage. These will break when devices are turned off. Worse yet, some of these could be silent failures of scripts and tools running in the background without any monitoring, and issues will only become apparent long after the fact.

  - Devices should first be **de-registered** from any **customer-facing services**. This will allow system administrators to watch for any errant connection attempts or logins and inform any business group of possible logic gaps in their software. In turn, this can make the overall environment healthier and more robust.

- Devices should next be **turned off**. Sometimes, this is also known as the "scream test" – whereby you expect someone to notice and complain. In parallel, this is a test of your monitoring and alerting software, which should correctly reflect the change in the device state. If the asset has been disconnected from customer-facing services, there should be no visible change to the users. Resilient and highly available systems will behave this way by design, with the replacement of individual components causing no disruption or downtime.

- If the devices contain important or potentially sensitive data, they may be left turned off but not removed from the inventory to allow for any **regulatory processes**. For instance, the legal department may require EOL-ed storage to be kept archived without any modifications before the media is deleted or shredded. Likewise, there might be a need to reaccess the stored data, and the device might have to be turned on again, to retrieve information (e.g., for forensic purposes).

- Devices should then be **physically removed** from their location, be it the office or the data center, and, in parallel, all relevant database entries updated to reflect this change. This should also include all licenses, software, and associated information. It is vital that all these happen synchronously, to avoid errors in the inventory.

- Lastly, the **decommission** can then occur based on the device's classification and company policies. As we've defined in earlier chapters, it's all about data and the protection of IP. If a device contains any type of storage medium, you will need to handle the **data aspects first**. Typically, hard disks will need to be formatted or zeroed and sometimes even physically destroyed. Sometimes, companies give out old hardware to nonprofit organizations and charities, and there could be additional safeguards in this scenario, to avoid any data leaks or violation of trade agreements (e.g., your hardware ends in a jurisdiction that is not covered by export agreements or licenses).

You must have a defined process and documentation for every step of the hardware's "life." Simple checklists are the easiest way to ensure technicians and system administrators know what to do in every situation. There should also be a "default gateway" scenario, which accounts for any corner case that is not covered by existing policies, as well as lists the relevant business entity that has the authority to make calls on these corner cases.

If your company is large enough, you want to assign a **hardware owner**, who will oversee the entire life cycle. This entity may go by different names, like the data center manager, inventory manager, or similar, but essentially the purpose will be the same. The persons in this role will have the ability to define new policies and refer any questions to other functions in the organization, like the finance team or the information security team. The entire cycle is illustrated in Figure 5-1.

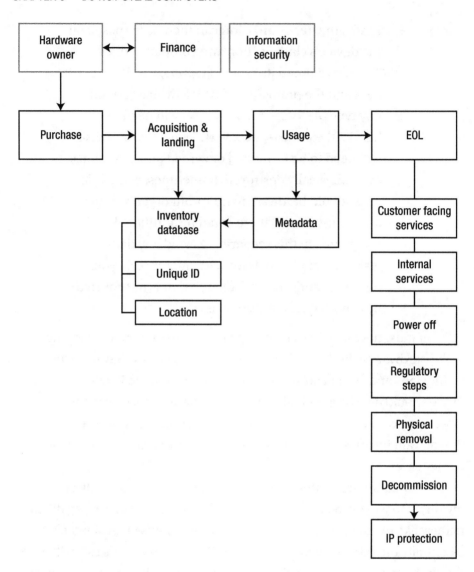

Figure 5-1. *Hardware life cycle*

Behind the Iron Curtain

Clear policies and smart inventory management go a long way toward creating a theft-free IT environment. The more you invest in making sure you can properly track, record, and update your hardware, the cheaper it is in the longer run. However, in some situations, you will need to use additional measures to ensure your hardware stays put.

Physical security of hardware assets may invoke a sense of suspicion with employees – much like any other monitoring systems facing inward. But it is important to remember that securing systems will deter both internal and external players and that physical boundaries reinforce policies even if there's no misuse of hardware within the company.

Industrial espionage is a great example. From companies with entities on an international level, there are attempts to steal premarket samples and hard disks full of sensitive data or, in a rather movie-like fashion, intrude the physical network and plant Man-in-the-Middle (MITM) equipment that allows a rogue party to eavesdrop on network packets. This isn't just the stuff for spy books or blockbusters! Then, there's plain, common theft. Imagine if someone could just walk into your office and swipe a nice shiny laptop left at the desk over lunch.

We will discuss these in much more detail in the next chapter. Here, the purpose of physical security systems is to make hardware more difficult to misplace – and easier to find.

Hardware that is designed to be permanently or semi-permanently fixed (e.g., most data center assets) will be kept in **secure facilities**, both while in use and in storage. The facilities will include various methods to ensure the hardware assets (and any associated IP kept on them) cannot be easily accessed, removed, or tampered with. Typical security will include computer cabinet locks, surveillance cameras, doors with authentication mechanisms, air-gapped data center halls, and others.

- Hardware that is designed to be mobile (e.g., most office equipment) should be secured in a way that **prevents easy theft**. Common methods will include docking stations with a key, cable locks, and keeping the equipment in a secure place when not in use.

- Hardware that is capable of running software should have a **monitoring agent** installed. The purpose of such a module is to provide a network – and possibly location – heartbeat to a central facility. This can be an integrated part of the wider monitoring system, as we have discussed in Chapter 2 (Respect Privacy). If a device "falls off the grid," an IT technician can return to its last known location to initiate repairs or, if the hardware is missing, an investigation.

- If a hardware cannot run additional software, you can use a physical **co-device** to mark the hardware, so it can be tracked. As a (bonus) side effect, this also simplifies inventory management and can lead to a much higher accuracy in the overall (real-time) visibility and state of the IT environment.

- Hardware components which are considered too small or cheap to equip with a tracking tag (like power, network cables, or keyboards) still need to be **properly cataloged and stored**. Ideally, these components will be kept in cabinets or lockers, which require physical intervention to access and use. Any instance of use should be **recorded** (e.g., swiping an employee badge to access the hardware storage facility) and any change in the inventory correctly updated in the hardware database.

- Devices without any associated tracking also need to be **classified**. Broadly, there are two categories: non-individual mostly used for backend hardware (servers, networking equipment, telephony, etc.) and hardware issued to individuals (like a keyboard and mouse). The latter type should be issued to employees **individually**, making each employee an inventory manager for their own hardware.

Story from the IT trenches: At one of my previous work-places, they came up with a rather clever solution to the perpetual loss of headsets, keyboards, mice, and other seemingly low-value devices. They installed hardware vending machines, operated by the employee's badge. Anyone could request items from the available stock, and the hardware would automatically be associated to their name. This made the process faster and more accurate, even though most employees regarded the new method as an expensive gimmick.

Periodic **audits** are crucial for accurate hardware management, especially if you have only partial coverage of all available assets via tracking systems. Audits allow the company to properly and correctly account for any discrepancies or losses in expected quantities and make changes in the operational setup, as current methods and tools may prove inadequate. Gaps discovered in the ability to find all the hardware will allow the data center owner and system administrators to come up with improved solutions. Moreover, they also allow for more precise accounting and purchase forecasts. The hardware security model is shown in Figure 5-2.

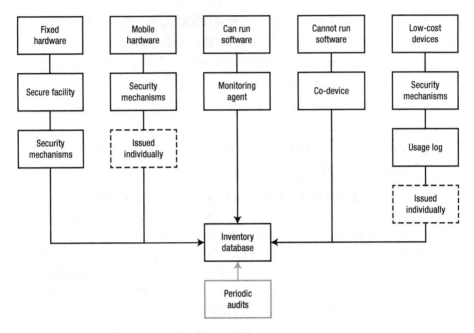

Figure 5-2. *Hardware security model*

Clear and Present Server

Lastly, there must be **no ambiguity in policies**. There should be no situation where an employee could misinterpret the existing framework of procedures and tools so that they end up lugging a spare computer home without being fully cognizant of the violation. The simplest approach is a strict policy that disallows any personal use of work assets. It makes for a much simpler decision-making.

Over the years, the use of work assets for personal needs has become more common and is likely to grow as the lines between what was once typically considered "the office" and "home" have become blurred. This applies to work laptops, phones, as well as cameras, monitors, and similar equipment, especially with globally dispersed businesses that have home-based employees. In such situations, hardware management is more difficult, but it should still be correctly and fully defined. Ideally, it would combine clear documentation with some web-based self-service portal that allows users to track their own hardware, make requests, or check any relevant procedure.

Conclusion

System administrators and data center technicians are not unlike kids let loose in a toy store. Which is why they owe it to themselves to help build a clear, unequivocal, transparent framework of rules for hardware usage. In the long run, it leads to a more robust, better organized, and better maintained hardware environment, with fewer temptations to succumb to the prehistoric urges for hoarding.

Hardware needs to be properly classified, tracked, and managed. The device life cycle must be mapped, every step of the way. You can use both hardware- and software-based systems to create a situational awareness picture of the IT environment, side by side with well-documented policies and procedures and periodic audits. Lastly, there could always be a corner case where there might be no rules or known precedents. In such situations, always make sure to ask, because careers are worth more than a lump of silicon and plastic.

Not stealing IP and hardware, well one might think they are in the clear. But there are other dangers and traps in the uncharted water of the IT. In the next chapter, we will talk about terra incognita, the parts of the IT world where one must not go.

CHAPTER 6

Do Not Go Where You Are Not Wanted

Coming back from a short break, the last person Wendell expected to see standing behind his desk was Frieda from InfoSec. She never looked particularly happy, but today...she seemed in an angry mood.

This can't be good, he thought, trying to keep his expression neutral.

"You left your computer unlocked!" she snapped by way of greeting. Wendell winced. "You're lucky someone didn't delete all of your files! Maybe I should have installed the Bielefeld screensaver on your system, how would you like that? Next time, lock it when you leave."

Wendell stood frozen in place, acutely aware that Frieda's voice carried, and that all his colleagues had stopped working and were watching the scene. He was stunned, and a little scared. The last thing he needed was a reprimand from Frieda before his 3-month assessment with Mike. Then his head cleared, and he wondered: *What's Bielefeld?*

"And you are logged in as root," Frieda continued, taking his silence as an opportunity to hammer her point in. "On more than one terminal. I could have deleted the customer database!"

"Eh, well, actually, I'm just logged into a test server," Wendell stammered.

Frieda narrowed her eyes. "You never know what type of data a test server has access to. Anyone could have copied the customer files."

© Igor Ljubuncic, Tom Litterer 2019
I. Ljubuncic and T. Litterer, *System Administration Ethics*,
https://doi.org/10.1007/978-1-4842-4988-8_6

Uh, I know what type of access it has, Wendell protested, but he made sure to do it very quietly, inside his head. "I was only gone for a minute."

"You're a bad boy, Wendell," Caesar teased.

Frieda didn't seem to notice. "What data do you have on that test system?"

Wendell quickly bent down and locked his computer screen. "I was in the bathroom, and it's only been a couple of minutes. Why do you want to know?" His voice was still shaky.

"I need to know in case you exposed confidential data!" Frieda was on a roll. "Do you know how much it costs security to investigate a mess like this? I'll have to get security footage, check network access, look at USB usage ..."

"There is nothing confidential on my system or the test server," Wendell mumbled, hoping she would back down. He mulled over what he had just said. It wasn't an outright lie, was it? "I'm a new hire. They wouldn't give me access to that kind of information."

Frieda almost jumped. "New hire? Then why did I see you in the data center on the security monitor yesterday? Without signing into the access log!" She was staring right at him and was beginning to lean forward. "What business do you have in the data center?"

Wendell pointed behind him. "I was just visiting Elwood, and he gave me a tour."

"There are no tours of the data center. That is a secure area. Did you think you were at the Neuschwanstein Castle?" She smirked.

"Hey, Frieda, give our 'Dell here a break," Elwood spoke, coming over. He gave Wendell a pat on the back. "I showed him around, so he knows how things work if something breaks. He left his phone behind, and I was with him the whole time."

Frieda didn't seem mollified. "What were you doing by that server at H12?"

Wendell thought he had given her the reason for being in the data center. "I was checking out my test server. The VM, I mean. I didn't know which hypervisor it was running on. How did you see me?"

"You better watch where you go, because I am." Frieda would not back down, staring him, daring him to blink. "Did you see any confidential data while you were in the data center?"

"He didn't see anything," Elwood spoke.

Elwood was looking amused, Wendell saw. But he didn't find anything funny in this whole situation. Then he remembered seeing one of the consoles open, showing some data on the screen. "Uh, no," he said quickly. "I just saw racks of computers. What do you need from me?"

"What's going on?"

Wendell sighed with relief. It was Mike.

Frieda seemed to be just as hostile, Wendell realized. So it wasn't anything personal against him or some trick they played on new employees. "A series of information security violations, that's what's going on—"

"Look," Mike cut in. "Let's keep it down, people are trying to work. Wendell here is a new guy, so you need to give him some slack. He may have made a mistake or two, but that's how we all learn. I asked him to learn as much as he can about the environment, and everyone's been helpful, so if you have any complaints, you can level them at me."

Frieda huffed. She looked displeased – and suspicious.

"Maybe you can talk to Gopal. He can give you some extra pointers," Mike said.

Wendell nodded. At this point, he would agree to almost anything, just to have InfoSec off his back. "Sure thing, Mike."

"I'm still watching you," Frieda said, walking away.

Wendell plopped down in his chair. "What the hell was that?"

Alex raised his head, grinning. "That was, my man, your first encounter with Frieda. Don't worry, she just wants to keep you out of trouble. Maybe."

Elwood chuckled. "All things considered, you handled it pretty well."

Wendell made a wry face. "I did?"

Caesar was there too now, all sly mirth and exaggerated facial expressions. "Oh, yeah. At least you didn't cry."

They all started laughing. Wendell let his nerves settle, and then he joined, feeling silly – and worried.

Here Be Dragons

IT environments, especially data centers and labs, can be wonderful places. They aren't that different from museums showcasing thousands of curious specimens on display. If you look past the dry data, you can see big, complex mazes of amazing technology and tools, interconnected and locked in an intricate dance of digital life. We don't often think about it, but just imagine the amount of effort and precision that makes trains operate on schedule, traffic lights turn green to keep the cities moving, or allow your browser to give you instant answers to all your questions.

All this amazing innovation is a result of the endless pursuit of knowledge that defines human nature. We are inquisitive and curious, and we made it where we are today because we kept on pushing the boundaries of what can be done, in every aspect of our lives, for thousands of years.

Therefore, it should not come as a surprise when you tell a person they cannot go somewhere that they would, on a primal level, resist.

As far as boundaries go, the world of IT feels like it's constructed of paradoxes. On one hand, companies empower their employees to think out of the box, look for solutions beyond known and accepted conventions, and to always try to improve things. On the other, companies create seemingly arbitrary "walls" that are designed to limit access, making the creative work harder.

In the early days of what we classify as modern IT, there were virtually no limits to what system administrators could do. Technology was developed and used on the basis of trust – some of these decisions are still apparent in how the Internet works today and practical limitations in software resulting from generous, permissive designs in architecture. The altruistic approach soon proved inadequate, as businesses and organizations sought to protect their IP and assert higher control over their environments, both internally and externally. In some cases, the safeguards made sense, such as military, government, and healthcare. In others, they were received with less enthusiasm or understanding of the benefits of implemented measures.

As the IT universe (and the Internet) grew, the pendulum began to swing away from the permissive end, leading to more restrictions, both in physical and digital security. While one can debate the benefits and moral implications of the current technology landscape, it is virtually impossible to separate and disassociate security from the core business of any modern company.

This reality frequently creates confusion and frustration among people sustaining the IT backbone. On a philosophical level, most system administrators or developers would agree that there must be some order in the chaos and that some of the security mechanisms are truly beneficial for the sane, efficient functioning of many IT environments. But that sentiment rarely surfaces when people are impeded in their daily work with what can often be described as unnecessary bureaucracy and paranoia.

Driven by our need to excel and improve all the time, people look for – and find – workarounds that allow them to be faster and more productive and deliver results. And by cutting corners, they expose themselves to ethical violations that can cost them their job.

To make things worse, most of the walls partitioning and protecting the IT environments are ephemeral. For instance, a software firewall is merely a set of if-then rules that filters network traffic. Changing them is almost too easy, especially for people with the right credentials and access.

Physical access is easier to understand and grasp – much the same way, people are more comfortable with stealing software and intellectual property than they are with stealing computers. The perception of tangible value helps us frame and respect the boundaries. With software, such limits are hard to grasp and easy to ignore – or work around.

As it happens, system administrators *often* have the powers to make the changes if they feel like doing it. And sometimes, they will do it.

We further complicate things by adding a moral dimension to the picture. When people discuss a security training or a process to get access to a database, they don't just think about the immediate steps needed to complete the task or the potential benefits of these measures for the company or its customers. They often weave in a whole history of news, online stories, past experiences, as well as personal stance and opinion, often tainted with moral and even political connotations. Anti-virus programs, badge readers, and security bulletins aren't just measures designed to keep the company safe – they are a complex emotional saga.

The combination of power, easy access, personal morality, and the need to solve problems is a volatile mix that makes people transgress – physically and digitally – into areas they are not normally allowed. We will find ourselves acting without even realizing that we're doing it. Until something bad happens.

Do Not Go Where You Are Not Wanted

In a situation tainted by ambiguity (your own), the best way is to follow the rules. Ideally, there will be rules that clearly define access, permissions, and the need to know in every business-related case. If these rules do not exist, you should err on the side of caution.

- Rules and restrictions exist for a reason – They could be *wrong* reasons, but there is a process that led to the rules being implemented. If you want to solve the wrongness, you should address the root of the problem. Moreover, rules are like software monitoring logic; you add new entries, but you rarely if ever delete old ones. Over the years, you end up with ancient legacy conditions that no longer apply to modern situations, or the reasons for their implementation have long been forgotten. You need take these into context if you want to fully understand and reason the rules through. Similarly, if possible, old rules should be audited and reviewed for relevance and cleaned up to simplify the work procedures.

- Rules and restrictions protect the company and you – Overall, rules will often limit your access, physical or digital, but their purpose is to protect everyone involved – the company and its assets and you. There are situations that are difficult to fully define by written rules (or the rules would have to be long and complicated as to make their application impractical). In such scenarios, especially if there is high risk of damage – or even life danger – simple rules allow for much easier, faster decision-making.

- Restrictions minimize risks – Some rules are based on the concept of *need to know*. For instance, access to HR files must be restricted for obvious legal reasons. Such a decision has nothing to do with people at hand, and personal trustworthiness of individual employees is irrelevant as a factor when granting access. Similarly, there could be many other systems, databases, folders, shares, labs, data center areas, and even offices to which system administrators should not be granted access. It is important not to associate any moral connotation to these restrictions. Compartmentalization helps companies manage data more securely and reduce cascade damage in cases of breaches, failures, or other complications.

- Common sense still applies – That does not mean you should completely ignore your internal moral compass, disregard common sense and logic, and just blindly follow through with the instructions, regardless of the consequences. If you believe that your actions could cause further damage or complicate matters – even if the dry rules may fully exonerate you as far as liability goes – you should stop to think and reevaluate your work.

If you find legitimate reasons why the existing rules are not suitable, you should drive the relevant owners to make necessary changes. But you should not ignore the rules or work around them just because you decided they are useless or stupid just then and there.

Asking *why* is crucial. But make sure you ask the question at the right time and place. Doing so when you feel inconvenienced is most likely *not* the right time or the place. In such a situation, your question will not result in an impartial, unemotional response. It will be based on wants and feelings and not data and facts.

Challenge the decision-makers, don't challenge your career.

If You Can't Access or if the Door Is Locked, Stay Out

Every IT environment will have some form of physical and digital topology of restricted areas with selective access. These rules will have been created over time, quite often charged with financial, legal, and safety background stories that you may not know – or even be allowed to know.

In order to act ethically, you should learn and respect these rules. You should assume there are good intentions and sane logic behind their implementation. If you believe the rules hamper your work, you should consult with your manager and relevant owners. You should not try to make your own rules.

Restrictions Are There to Protect You

"I'm a new hire. They wouldn't give me access to that kind of information."

This is a recommended policy for people just starting in the company. As a new hire, you should protect yourself by not getting access that you don't understand how to use. Over time, you will be granted (or gain) additional permissions and privileges as you get familiar with the roles and become confident in the work procedures.

"He left his phone behind, and I was with him the whole time."

Most data centers have strict rules, which often prohibit taking any photographs, and quite often, you need to have an authorized escort at all times. Such practice helps deter theft, but it also reduces the risk of injury and damage. Elwood made sure to follow the relevant procedures – but as we will discuss shortly, he also did break other related rules.

You Are Not Above the "Law"

"Maybe I should have installed the Bielefeld screensaver on your system, how would you like that?"

Frieda's jibe comes on top of Wendell leaving his computer unlocked, which we will discuss a bit later, but it is a bad example of ethical behavior. Technically, an unlocked computer does grant her access, but she does not really have any valid reason to be using Wendell's machine, even if it's for the sake of a "funny" lesson. Furthermore, Frieda's role as an information security officer puts her in a precarious position. She has the authority to perform checks and audits on other people and systems, but it is also her duty to help others understand their violations and learn how to resolve them in a correct manner.

"I was in the bathroom, and it's only been a couple of minutes."

From the human perspective, seconds or minutes can be a long time. Computers can execute thousands, maybe even millions, of instructions in that period. Wendell should not use "personal justifications" to bend the rules.

"I need to know in case you exposed confidential data!"

Frieda's demand is within the remit of her role as the information security officer. She needs to understand if there has been any damage and what measures need to be taken to contain it. While this may seem exaggerated, just think of the thousands of data breaches from the past couple of years, many of which had resulted in private information and tons of data from hundreds of millions of users being leaked online.

"Then why did I see you in the data center on the security monitor yesterday? Without signing into the access log!"

This is a fairly serious violation of work procedures, and both Wendell and Elwood are to blame. Elwood should not have allowed anyone in without following the correct procedure. This also serves as a bad example for the new hire like Wendell, who might be more inclined to break rules having seen his "senior" colleagues do the same. Since he does not have access (yet), he should stay out of the data center or follow the correct procedure to gain access. Even if Elwood did not seem to mind, Wendell should have erred on the side of caution – as he eventually (and rightly) was blamed by Frieda for what he did.

Remember, the rules may seem boring or pointless to you, but they exist, and until changed (even through your own intervention and suggestions to the relevant owners), you need to follow them.

"There are no tours of the data center. That is a secure area."

Even if Wendell did get access, that does not mean he can do things that are prohibited by policy. There are many reasons why companies would not allow data center tours. Usually, this is to prevent IP leaks and theft. Sometimes, the workloads running on data center systems could be so sensitive or time-critical that any blunder could result in significant damage (imagine a visitor pressing a button on a server chassis).

"I'm still watching you."

The company should set expectations for employees to be accountable for themselves, not have a nanny. Moreover, intimidation does not work as a reliable security measure in the long run.

If You Find an Unlocked "Back Door," Tell

System administrators and technicians will come across many gates on their proverbial IT journey. As such, they also have the highest chance of coming across misconfigurations in tools and systems.

If you discover a gap in the security coverage of the systems you work with, you should notify the relevant owners. Even if you are not 100% sure you have uncovered a bug or a problem in a configuration, you should still highlight your findings so that experts in the fields can evaluate the potential issue and address it.

Back doors can be anything that allows arbitrary access to privileged systems or exposure of confidential data. This could be lax physical security systems, a software error, wrong permissions, an outdated list of credentials, weak passwords, or a broken corridor camera.

React Quickly When Holes Are Found

"You left your computer unlocked!"

Frieda's comment may sound harsh, but she acted in the best interest of both Wendell and the company. If you leave your screen unlocked, other people can have unfettered access to your system, and they may choose to make changes to your files. This ranges from innocent pranks, where you send an email to the entire company, inviting people over for free pizza (we've all done that, well, *most* of us), to sinister actions like viewing or stealing someone's private information – bank account, annual evaluation, and so on. Then, the other person could also use your workstation to steal intellectual property, customer data, or passwords to sensitive systems. If such a breach is detected, it will be traced back to your account, and you will mostly likely be held liable. Frieda duly informed Wendell of his mishap, and she possibly prevented unwanted access to his computer.

Wendell quickly bent down and locked his computer screen.

At least Wendell reacted quickly and plugged the "hole." This is not the ideal scenario, but his action stopped Frieda from having access to his machine.

Leaving the Door Open

"And you are logged in as root...on more than one terminal."

In Chapter 1 (Separate Roles), we learned about the importance of separation and least privilege. Using the account with the highest administrative privilege can sometimes be necessary, but it is often not the case. Keeping multiple applications (in this case, shells inside terminal windows) open and with the root user logged in can create a security risk, especially since Wendell had left his computer unlocked. This allows unchallenged access to whatever data, tools, and systems Wendell has. Once again, Frieda's criticism is justified, because Wendell did violate the basic principles of secure work with privileged accounts. He should have only done one privileged task at a time and then logged out after completing his work. We will talk about this in detail in Chapter 7 (Follow Procedures and Get Out).

> *"You never know what type of data a test server has access to. Anyone could have copied the customer files."*

This is indeed a likely outcome for a "back door" scenario to the IT environment. Whether opened intentionally (malice or hacking) or by mistake, the back door allows arbitrary access to systems and data. It is possible that Wendell's test server is isolated from the production environment, but there could be problems and misconfigurations that he is not aware of, especially when running as a privileged account.

> *"He also remembered seeing one of the consoles open, showing some data on the screen."*

Wendell should have notified Elwood about this. It is possible that one of the data center technicians had accidentally left the console open. Even though it is a restricted area, the user should have logged out of the server after finishing work.

Protecting the IT Environment and You

In an ideal world, there would be no need for any security, and work would always be done on the basis of trust and utmost personal accountability. Alas, in the real world, this is not possible. Even if there is no malicious intent, people make mistakes. We discussed this in Chapter 1 (Separate Roles), whereby errors and damage can be caused by poor judgment, insufficient information, and a lack of procedures and skills.

A well-designed IT environment reduces the chance for unwanted access on all levels, starting with physical security, continuing with software system access, and ending with privileged access. This includes the following:

- Physical access restrictions – IT environments should be equipped with robust mechanisms that prevent accidental access, infiltration, and brute-force attempt to bypass them. These mechanisms are built to be tolerant and with a low rate of false-positive incidents – if systems trigger more errors than legitimate alerts (like the boy who cried wolf), people tend to ignore them, and they become useless.

- Network access restrictions – In parallel to the physical systems, IT environments should also be protected from software-based attacks and intrusions. There will be separation and isolation of digital enclaves, often based around the sensitivity of data that they contain and the level of privileges they require. Network access restriction tools include firewalls, traffic scanners, heuristic behavior detectors, access control lists, and others.

- Identity access – There need to be systems, both physical and digital, that will challenge identity for any access attempt to places where restrictions apply. If a person cannot satisfy the challenge, they will be denied entry.

- Clear processes – Everyone (employees, on-site contractors, visitors, and guests) should be able to quickly and easily understand where they can go, what restrictions and rules exist in place, and what to do in case the existing setup does not allow them to complete their work.

- Monitoring – The IT environment should include a facility that will poll the access restriction mechanisms. Monitoring tools will have thresholds that allow automated systems and human operators to identify interesting data points, including incidents, anomalous behavior, potential security breaches, and others.

- Logging – You need to log access (both success and failure), as it provides a trail of actions that explains how and when hardware was used. Ideally, you will keep these in a database with constant updates that correctly reflect the current state of permission.

- Audits – The database should be audited periodically for any discrepancies. If designed correctly, it is part of a wider monitoring system and also provides forensic evidence when required.

- Alerts – Systems in the IT environment should have clear rules that always provide a deterministic answer to any access request. Successful entries are logged. Failed entries are logged and, under some conditions, also raised as alerts that can be then further processed and analyzed. Alerts should include meaningful procedures so that people know what to do and how to respond to alerts, especially in emergency situations.

With these in place, there will be fewer cases of casual access violation by employees and fewer opportunities for curious people to decide to wander around, probe, and test the boundaries of their work environment. However, no process is 100% foolproof, and this commandment is necessary so when processes break down, the people will continue to do what is ethically right.

Physical Access

Keeping people out of restricted areas serves many purposes. We briefly mentioned industrial espionage and theft in the previous chapter. Additionally, physical security is designed to provide safe work environments whereby only qualified personnel have access. This is almost self-explanatory if you think about military, hospitals, or perhaps power plants; but most people don't necessarily view the cozy, well-furnished IT offices as anything that requires special measures. There are several main reasons why physical access needs to be restricted:

- Safety – IT environments have their **dangers**. A typical data center is a noisy place, with heavy equipment, high voltage, and possibly open flooring. People working in these areas are trained to work with a certain level of occupational hazard and to recognize potential risks.

- Cost – In general, protecting against internal threats is **costlier and more complex** than external ones. While it is relatively easy to define who belongs inside the company walls and who doesn't, inside the confines of an organization, it is far more difficult to make simple, clear-cut decisions. The sooner you detect a breach or an intrusion, the cheaper it is to remedy the problem.

- Crime – Hardware theft is a product of human nature and opportunity. While it is impossible to change people, you can create an IT environment that deters stealing. In Chapter 5 (Do Not Steal Computers), we talked about hardware life cycle, monitoring, and tagging, all of which can help reduce the material loss. This book is too short to describe all possible tools and ways to implement physical security, and it ranges from ordinary badge readers and locks to biometric scanners, cameras, and other sophisticated sensors.

At one of my previous workplaces, the local data center had a really clever security feature. The entrance to the data center hall was via a rotating double-door gate that had weight pads inside. Upon entry, the person would be weighed and the value associated with their access card. Upon exit, if there was as little as 100 grams (3 ounces) weight difference, the person would be locked inside the cylinder-like gate and the building security and the data center warden instantly alerted. This prevented any unauthorized movement of sensitive or important data center equipment (like hard disks). Whenever there was a need for a complex maintenance, which required frequent entry and movement of servers, the gate was disabled and security guards posted.

The preceding example might seem extreme, but it is much more secure than the similar rotating door at another workplace, which didn't have the weight pads, but only a 1 × 1 foot pressure pad. It became a game to see how many people could fit in the glass cylinder while keeping all of their weight on the pressure pad. Even the visiting hardware maintenance vendor participated in the game.

Physical boundaries help create safer work environments. However, it is equally important to remember that people will always look for – and find – ways to circumvent them. At some point, this becomes a game of diminishing returns. Instead, reinforcing ethics is the last (but most effective) line of defense.

Software Access

There are multiple layers to how software security can and should be implemented. While specific details differ from one IT environment to another, the fundamental principles remain unchanged. We have discussed most of these in previous chapters – as well as in the section "Physical Access" – and combined, they form the **layered stack** that provides the necessary framework for secure work.

- Role separation reduces the risk of damage. We touched on this in Chapter 1 (Separate Roles).

- Account management allows the environment owner to fine-tune access based on identity and need to know. These are the fundamental principles we reviewed in Chapter 2 (Respect Privacy) and Chapter 3 (Do Not Change Data).

- Data management helps prevent privacy incidents.

- License management helps prevent IP violations, as we have seen in Chapter 4 (Do Not Steal Intellectual Property).

- Clear and accurate processes apply to software just as they do to hardware.

- Automation reduces deployment errors and configuration drift.

- Monitoring, logging, audits, and alerts provide an accurate picture of the current state of the environment, including access rights and permissions for all relevant functions.

The full IT environment setup, with both the physical and software access scenarios included, is shown in Figure 6-1.

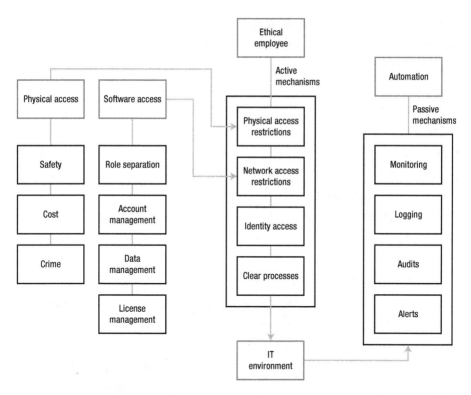

Figure 6-1. *Combined physical and software access stack*

Whitelist vs. Blacklist

The more rulesets and rules a system has, the higher the chance for false positive. Effective security systems assume a *deny all* default approach, whereby all and any type of access is forbidden to everyone, and partial exceptions made (based on identity and function). This is true for both physical and digital (software) tools.

Penetration Testing

As tempted (and clever) as you may be, you should never try to break, harden, or test your IT environment on your own. Penetration testing is a popular method of assessing the quality, resilience, and effectiveness of your security mechanism.

For instance, an IT network is subjected to a series of coordinated, automated attacks and the results analyzed to determine how likely the network is to withstand a real attack from outside. Methods can include specific browser booby traps, enumeration of services, brute-force hacking of routers and firewalls, Denial of Service (DoS), Distributed Denial of Service (DDoS), zero-day exploits, and other payloads. Typically, a third-party company will run these tests, with approval from information security.

You may decide you have similar skills and knowledge and may want to run these tests on your own. Usually, if done without authorization, such attempts result in disciplinary action and even dismissal. Perhaps your technical savvy can be put to good use, but any testing of security systems needs to be approved. Even within your personal space, in the cloud you must request authorization from the cloud provider to do penetration testing. Otherwise, it is indistinguishable from attacks, which are almost always classified as criminal activity.

One well-documented case of a system administrator conducting unauthorized penetration tests happened at our former place of employment. A popular technical author and well-respected consultant, Randal Schwartz aka Merlyn, proactively ran the penetration tool, Crack, on password hashes. When he learned that his personal Internet service provider had been hacked, he wanted to make sure the same thing did not happen at Intel Corporation, where he was working on contract in a lab. Crack revealed 2 of the 30 passwords within the lab where he worked. He then used one of those passwords to gain access to the password hashes on the main server outside of the lab. As his Crack session ran on the main server over several days, one of the server admins noticed the session and reported it to security. The next week, the police came to his home with a search warrant and confiscated all of his computer equipment. Randal was eventually prosecuted for altering a computer without authorization, which is a felony under Oregon state law.

Conclusion

The same kind of curiosity that drives technically minded people to great achievements and inventions also works against them when they are challenged by authority and seemingly arbitrary boundaries. This struggle between achievement at all costs and boundaries set by authorities is common in the workplace; we tend to fight for our "freedom." But the struggle also puts us in a difficult spot, as we could easily conduct ethical violations.

You should respect the restrictions, even if we do not immediately understand the full history or the reasoning behind them. This applies equally to both physical and digital (software) access. When you hit what seems to be an unreasonable restriction, escalate your concern to the policy owner. If you're the one whose job duties involve designing and maintaining systems that restrict access, think of the ideal model as an onion – layer upon layer of security, with cost and risk increasing as you peel them away.

Your systems should be robust, tolerant, accurate, and with an easy trail of evidence. The environment is designed to be transparent, so it does not impede on people's work and routines – which only heightens the chance for violations. Then, if and when things go wrong, your trail of evidence will help you understand and fix problems, as well as any gaps in your defenses. Lastly, it is important to remember that security mechanisms can only do so much. Overall, it is the adherence to the first five commandments that helps keep the stack glued together in an efficient way.

Still, despite best intentions and most having tools in place, sometimes things *will* go wrong. It is only a matter of time – and some complicated probabilities. It is important, even crucial, to have the right tools and systems in place and to behave ethically. Equally, one must know how to conduct themselves when things suddenly go pear-shaped. In the following chapters, we will move away from the *peacetime* scenarios and talk about ethical behavior when faced with uncertainty. We will start with our seventh commandment – Follow Procedures and Get Out.

CHAPTER 7

Follow Procedures and Get Out

When in doubt, run. Wendell remembered seeing that scribbled on a wall in a bathroom somewhere, probably a gas station. Such a strange place for a piece of philosophy. He found it oddly applicable to his situation.

He kept thinking about the past several weeks, all the way up to the breach, and wondered if and how he had contributed to the incident. He recalled his meeting with Alex, all bluster and drama, learning about the separation of roles and the correct use of privileges. He had always done that, hadn't he?

Then, as a stark contrast to Alex, Belinda was nice and helpful, and he felt he had learned a lot from her about data management and privacy. With Caesar, he had honed in the lesson, learning even more about how the company handles customer information. Mike was pleased with his progress and gave him additional tasks to master.

The meeting with Frieda left a sour taste in his mouth, though …

Now, with Daniel. They had done everything by the book, right? Maybe he should not have used that evaluation software, and he should have asked Mike to approve it, but that was a minor thing. And Elwood's approach to hardware was sure unconventional, but the man was a diligent data center manager, and Mike had attended the scrap shootout.

© Igor Ljubuncic, Tom Litterer 2019
I. Ljubuncic and T. Litterer, *System Administration Ethics*,
https://doi.org/10.1007/978-1-4842-4988-8_7

Wendell believed Mike to be a good manager, loyal to his employees. He had supported him and the rest of the team, or, well, at least tolerated the things that had happened, so it couldn't be all that bad. He was pretty sure that Mike would stand behind him, if they pointed a finger at him. Just as Mike had done with Frieda.

After his encounter with Frieda, Mike had encouraged him to spend a day with Gopal learning about how to automate his work tasks in order to avoid using a root shell. Wendell thought more about his interactions with Gopal; was there something they did that could have led to a breach?

Wendell had walked into his initial meeting with Gopal with an upbeat attitude. Gopal, on the other hand, looked like someone had offered him a deal that sounded too good to be true. He looked cautious. Even wary.

"Again, what do you want to do?" Gopal insisted.

Wendell took a deep breath. "I need to get Frieda off my back. Mike thought it would be a good learning opportunity for me to familiarize myself with automation. It should save me time, too. Right now, I am following this long procedure that requires me to run commands from a root shell, and it is taking forever!"

"What are you doing exactly?" Gopal asked.

"Every time I need to make a permission change, I need to authenticate in a shell, make the change, commit my change to a log, and run a test query to see that it's all working correctly. I have to do it every single time, because I'm doing it all by hand."

Gopal flicked his fingers. "That is too much work. Lazy is the way to go. Lazy people always come up with the best inventions."

Wendell grimaced. "I don't want to be lazy. I just want to avoid mistakes, and I guess Frieda was right in getting angry. The thing is, at the moment, I need to make all these group and file permission changes by hand to meet this new campaign goal of the sales and marketing teams. And this is production data, so I have to be extra careful."

Gopal didn't move. "Do you have permission to do this?"

Wendell frowned. "Yeah. Mike is fully aware of the request, and he told me to do what I can to get marketing off his back." He smiled and hoped something in the words he said would resonate with his colleague.

"You got it in email?" Gopal asked.

Wendell nodded.

Gopal looked closer at the request from marketing and then groaned. "I've been avoiding this request in the queue for several weeks, and now it's coming back to haunt me."

Wendell shrugged. "It will help me a lot."

Gopal finally moved, waking his laptop from sleep. "All right. Let me show you some magic tricks." He tapped his screen, making color ripple. "You know this tool?"

Wendell stared at the fingerprint smudge. "Not really. That's a configuration management software, isn't it?"

Gopal grunted. "Yes. The beauty about this tool is that I can make quick changes and have them propagate across the entire environment in less than an hour, and I don't need to do anything manually. You write a recipe, and poof, it's deployed. Magic."

Wendell looked in his notes. "Do we need to get permissions from Mike to use these recipes? Because that's a lot of change all at once. If something goes wrong, I could be in a lot of trouble!"

Gopal squirmed. "This isn't a big change compared to what I usually do. We'll have this done in an hour, and then we can check out the game room."

Wendell wasn't interested in games, he was thinking more about the quality of proposed code changes and whether there would be any impact on production systems as the configuration management changes rolled across the environment, but then, there was the blame angle, too. "Does anyone else check these recipes?"

"No, just me."

Wendell spent a minute or two, trying to read the unfamiliar syntax and understand what the rules in the recipes meant. It didn't look too difficult, but then some of the declarations looked very hard to decipher. "What are these?"

"Groups of systems I defined for when rolling out change. That way, I can control how the recipes get installed."

"Looks complicated," Wendell said.

"No one said automation is simple. But I never do any task twice if I can help it. I put everything into a recipe and deploy it that way. Let me show you something else."

Wendell wrote notes as Gopal talked about the Git repository where the recipes and the monitoring plugins were stored, so that anyone could access them if they needed them.

"Would I also be able to make changes to access permissions in the customer database? That's one of the tasks the sales folks have."

Gopal pressed his hands together. "You can do anything." He paused to think. "We can do it now."

Wendell wasn't expecting that from Gopal, but he liked the idea of being able to go back to Mike with some concrete results.

Gopal waved dismissively. "It's okay. It's a small change anyway."

Wendell sat by and watched patiently. Gopal's logic seemed rather obfuscated, he thought, but he didn't comment. He believed there were valid reasons why Gopal would write these recipes the way he did.

"The change should propagate in about 15 minutes," Gopal said.

Wendell checked some emails while the time ticked by, and then, he ran the sample query the sales team had provided him, the one that would indicate the success of his change. It seemed to work. Then, just to be on the safe side, he ran the query as his own user. To his surprise, he managed to retrieve the results from the database. He felt a knot tighten in his stomach.

"Hmm, I'm not sure the recipe works as it should," he murmured. "I can access the customer data with my own account. I'm going to change the permissions back to what they were."

Gopal almost jumped, checking logs and running commands. "Oh, we made a mistake. Wrong permissions. I'll need to update the recipe, so it will take another 15 minutes."

"But the data is accessible to anyone now," Wendell said.

Silently, they worked on their computers, traversing directories, manually fixing the lax permissions. Fifteen tense minutes later, the right recipe was deployed.

Wendell sighed in relief. It was not how he'd imagined his day with Gopal to go. First Frieda, now this … In the end, he had also done the manual steps he'd tried to avoid all along.

"No harm done," Gopal said and nodded.

Wendell nodded back. He wasn't happy about this at all.

"Look dude, it's not always that bad. Mistakes happen. Not every problem is caught in testing, and moving to the larger production environment always brings up issues. And besides, it's all fixed now." Gopal went quiet for a moment, deep in thought. "You know, with a change like this, it probably would have been good to cover your ass by taking it to the change control board. It just takes too dang long; I try to avoid it at all costs."

Gopal frowned. "Just the previous week, I moved some data to the wrong area, but I was able to quickly move it back before anyone noticed. Thankfully, that time I had approval to make the change, so it was okay."

"Were the procedures wrong?" Wendell asked, genuinely interested. After all, he didn't want to find himself in a situation where he'd be making the same mistake as Gopal.

"Some of the documentation was outdated and some of it unnecessary. You know how it is, someone writes this long guide, like we have all the time in the world to sit and pore through pages and pages of text. You make sure the important details are covered, and you get it signed off."

"By Mike?" Wendell tried to keep up, furiously scribbling notes down.

Gopal smiled. "No. Change board. You know what, after this you should probably see Henry about submitting a change control issue before you make another attempt like this. C. Y. A." He winked and chuckled. "I'm happy you're going to be taking ownership of this area. Makes my life easier."

Wendell was still a bit shaky after frantically correcting the error earlier. Thinking about it, he *really* wanted to do a change control now, but he knew it was too late. Instead, he composed himself and let Gopal teach him some more on configuration management and the convoluted way he did things.

Only Sweat the Hard Stuff

If you ask ten different system administrators how they feel about procedures, there will be at least eleven opinions among them. Some will claim that procedures help them do their work in a more structured way. Others will say that they are a bureaucratic obstacle designed to make their work harder. Others yet will be convinced that procedures were made by clueless managers. To complicate things, different people ascribe different meanings to the word procedure; to some, these are technical how-to steps, to others a long list of legalese, to others yet these might be helpful tips on an online wiki or similar source.

There will be people who will follow the written instructions and rules to the letters, there will be skeptics, and there will be rebels. Some will ignore procedures, while others will try to come up with innovative ways to improve workflows and make procedures simpler and easier to follow. Regardless of the opinion, the inevitable outcome is the existence of a set of principles that define how certain types of work should be done.

Why Procedures Exist

Most people will be inclined to rationalize procedures from a technical perspective. After all, hardware and software products are often complex, and they involve layered mechanisms and interfaces that are not intuitive or self-explanatory to allow uncontrolled access. Indeed, quite often procedures will have a strong technical angle, which explains the technology, the protocols, and usage.

However, procedures exist primarily to ensure consistent results from the one unpredictable element in the equation – the human user.

While software is largely deterministic, and technical steps are often quite repeatable (with a very high level of accuracy), people utilizing software bring in an almost infinite pool of randomness into the system. Different logic and reasoning, skill sets, knowledge, understanding of the situation and the tools, and, finally, different ethical values all contribute to the unpredictability of the outcome. Without procedures, it is impossible to guarantee consistent results when different people operate the system.

The primary purpose of procedures is to create a **common language** that defines how people should perform certain activities. They describe the optimal way to accomplish desired results.

Unfortunately, everyone interprets the word "optimal" their way.

A Clash of Titans

For some people, the risk factor may be the cardinal parameter in their decision-making. For others, it could be the monetary or time considerations. More importantly, for companies, there are often intricate legal restrictions that dictate procedures even if they conflict with what most people would consider optimal. For instance, email archiving is often required for very long periods of time – and sometimes, in some fields of the industry, indefinitely – which can lead to significant usage of storage and cumbersome data retention procedures. There is no immediate benefit to the company in having to allocate budget and headcount to manage old data, except they are required and compelled by law to do so.

The lack of visibility into the reasoning behind procedures can leave people perplexed or frustrated. By nature, techies are inquisitive, and they often like to explore ideas to the fullest, including the context and motivation behind implemented solutions. If they do not have access to those, they may find procedures illogical or baseless.

Furthermore, procedures tend to build up and grow. Adding new ones is very easy, but removing existing ones can be difficult, because it is hard to ascertain whether someone may require them or still be using them. In the end, this leads to more administrative overhead for technicians and engineers, who feel there are too many hurdles standing between them and honest work.

The situation is exacerbated by the passage of time. Sometimes, there are old (legacy) procedures in place, for which the original reasoning has been lost. They may be no longer relevant or outdated – or quite valid still – but there might be insufficient information to allow people the necessary breadth of understanding to agree to these procedures.

However, it's not all gloom and doom.

Over the years, as IT environments became bigger, more complex, and *older*, there was a need for a structured approach to manage procedures. In essence, any task that can be broken down into repeatable steps can be automated. Indeed, the use of **automation** can alleviate some of the burden associated with the continuous buildup of procedures and the human-intensive labor around them.

But automation also requires careful planning – and it is always best to have it introduced early on into the process. Unfortunately, many IT environments have organically expanded, with little forward planning. We will discuss the art of automation later on, but for now, let's focus on human logic.

The combination of all these factors – the work pressure, conflicting mind-sets, and inadequate or insufficient automation – creates a turbulent environment of ideological clashes, an environment in which ethical violations can easily – and do – happen.

The great difficulty in following the "right" moral compass when it comes to procedures is that – unlike more obvious transgressions like theft, improper access, or misuse of resources – procedures rarely have intrinsic ethical value. You are not likely to find an IT document that says you should blatantly disregard the security of your customers' systems. But there might be a procedure that describes the patching sequence incorrectly or has insufficient security standards that leads to compromised systems.

Moreover, because we all have different personalities, knowledge, and motivation, we will almost always act with our own sense of "right." This means that people will find clever ways to do their work and selectively ignore procedures, without really understanding the implications of their actions.

With system administrators, who have privileged access to systems, the implications have a much farther reach. In turn, this is why following procedures is such an obvious and yet such an elusive commandment.

The Growing Entropy

Modern IT environments are hugely complex entities – and they will continue to become ever more complex in the coming decades. As we introduce new technology and systems into the workplace, we expose ourselves to new situations with unknown consequences. Every year, engineers and system administrators are working with data sets that eclipse all past information collected by the entirety of humankind throughout history. We are utilizing technology in ways that were not previously possible.

The chaos needs to be reigned with order – and as cliché as it sounds, procedures serve as a foundation to this balancing act. Procedures and tools, when devised and implemented correctly, can make the work better – more efficient, more secure, often faster, and with fewer errors.

Good procedures, especially when implemented with automation tools, help remove ambiguity from decision-making, help normalize actions by people with disparate skills, and improve the chance for successful and consistent outcome. Good procedures allow easier knowledge transfer and offer visibility into the business logic behind products. When it comes to privileged work, procedures help minimize the risk of incidental and even deliberate damage. Most importantly, good procedures allow system administrators to exercise the highest level of ethical behavior when faced with uncertainty in the environment. Good procedures are also a consequence and a direct result of ethical behavior transposed into written guidelines, which can then be translated into automation.

It all starts and ends with the human.

Follow Procedures and Get Out

In Chapter 1 (Separate Roles), we discussed Alex's use of a personal bastion, which violated multiple commandments, including the topics we discuss in the coming chapters. It also ties into the correct, ethical use of procedures.

Work should be done with the least amount of change, under the lowest privileges needed to perform the desired task, and following known, established methods.

- Least amount of change – The implementation of work in the IT environment should be done with as few moving parts as possible, to avoid interaction between components, simplify deployment, and allow future outcomes to be determined with reasonable accuracy. It is always worth exploring methods to implement change in more efficient, modular ways.

- Lowest privileges – Work should be done in a way that minimizes risk, reduces or even eliminates the chance for error and accidental damage, and reflects a clear separation of roles and responsibilities.

- Known methods – Follow an established path of commands and procedures that have a determined outcome, have been tested and build on the past experience, and have calculated risk factor embedded in them. These procedures are repeatable and can be used by anyone with the right skills in the specific domain.

Any deviation from these norms creates situations that do not necessarily have a predictable outcome or a known resolution and can lead to material and software damage, loss of reputation, or other incidents. It also makes work entirely dependent on personal attributes of whoever is performing the task at that time. The elements of chance and luck should not factor into IT workflows.

We can also draw parallels between what Alex and Gopal both did and provide additional context. Both hold reins to their specific domains, which creates unnecessary dependence on their individual conduct, going beyond the strict needs of the subject matter and work demands. The lack of documentation prevents the rest of the team from participating in these activities effectively. Even if some of the methods used by Gopal may be unorthodox, the use of clear procedures would mitigate some of the uncertainty and reduce the randomness that these changes introduce.

If You Must Use Privileged Access, Use Provided Tools

The world of procedures can be roughly divided into two – scenarios that go according to plan and scenarios that deviate from the expected outcome. A robust set of procedures helps minimize the divergence and reduces the risk of damage when operating outside the known parameters. Sometimes system administrators and technicians will have the right skills (and luck) to take control of an unknown situation and steer it back toward the framework defined in the procedures. But there will also be situations when things escalate.

One of the best ways to ensure the desired outcome is to follow procedures and only use tools (software and hardware) that have been tested and proven to work. This lessens the chance for the aforementioned divergence from the norm and increases the chance for success. Quite often, procedures are a result of a long series of testing and actual work, including difficult situations where damage, outages, and loss of reputation occurred. In a way, procedures should reflect past experiences and serve as an optimal form for getting the job done.

Moreover, the process of implementing these experiences into practice should be as independent as possible. Systems and tools should be able to automatically perform the steps of the defined procedures, study new, unknown scenarios when encountered, and correlate events to past data. This touches on the realm of artificial intelligence (AI), which is a whole domain of its own and beyond the scope of this book, but it is one of the most prominent methods of coping with exponentially growing complexities of modern IT environments.

Automate Where You Can

"Mike thought it would be a good learning opportunity for me to familiarize myself with automation. It should save me time, too."

There are several sound principles in this approach. One, Mike recognizes the importance of having his new employee master the environment in an optimal way, by learning how to use automation and work more efficiently. On Wendell's side, he understands that having the right knowledge will make him faster. This may sound like a selfish reason, but it is a great motivating factor, and for many people (including us authors), time saving can help hone creativity.

"Right now, I am following this long procedure that requires me to run commands from a root shell."

Despite having to invest a lot of effort in his work, Wendell does not cut corners for his own convenience. But he does understand he can make things more streamlined, and he is working on improving his workflow.

"Groups of systems I defined for when rolling out change. That way, I can control how the recipes get installed."

Gopal has a systematic approach to how he manages the environment. He has partitioned the resources, which makes it easier to track and control changes. It also introduces an element of modularity and flexibility and allows him to introduce new recipes (software-based templates for system and application settings) in a staged manner. This is a well-proven practice and is particularly effective when working with configuration management tools and large environments.

Don't Skip Steps

> *"I need to get Frieda off my back … It should save me time, too.
> Right now, I am following this long procedure that requires me
> to run commands from a root shell, and it is taking forever!"*

Wendell ends up only doing some of the steps of the procedure to fix the
problem he faces. Saving time is a great thing, but doing things just to get
people off one's back is often a symptom of a bigger, systemic problem in
the environment or the organization. Wendell does not tell anyone what he
did with his privileged account or log the work.

Conceptually, Wendell should look at Frieda's involvement as the
consequence of his actions – and possibly bad procedures – rather than as
the reason for the "problem" he has. If he had followed the rules correctly,
he would only need to worry about learning new subject matter and
making his work faster. This way, there's an emotional element that can
lead him to hasty decision – and ethical violations.

If a Task Requiring Privileged Access Is Unknown, Log It and Document

While *The Hitchhiker's Guide to the Galaxy* has answers to pretty much
any phenomenon, question, or dilemma faced by one Arthur Dent, there
is unfortunately no such written work for the poor system administrator
lurking in the IT trenches. Sometimes, we end up facing the great unknown.

No matter how exhaustive, procedures cannot cover all eventualities –
nor are they designed to do so. Indeed, it is important to avoid the pitfall of
creating procedures that are so long and detailed they serve little practical
purpose. Instead, they should cover the reasonable bulk of everyday
activities and maybe some of the more high-risk corner cases. There will
always come a moment where existing guidelines will just not be adequate
or applicable.

In such situations, it is important to conduct oneself ethically. We all have tendencies that introduce bias to our work – social and technical – and these are augmented by uncertainty and stress. The natural thing is to "jump to conclusions" or "keep busy" in an attempt to handle and resolve unknown situations, especially if they involve sensitive customer data, monetary loss, or other incidents. This can make people take actions that could violate rules and even laws and put the employee in a difficult position.

Rather than solving the problem at all costs, one should strive to advance the situation into known territory – a **common framework** whereby there is a known method or a procedure to follow through. It is important not to treat this from the problem resolution perspective – it will be unique and will vary from one issue to another – but from the problem management perspective.

In practice, what this means is we cannot control what kind of problems will arise in the environment or always have the right kind of documentation or procedures available. But we can always work systematically by carefully logging all the details of the issue, describing the resolution if applicable, and then updating the system tools (including configuration management recipes) so that future occurrences of the problem can be handled correctly – going from unknown to known.

You Only Live Twice – But Document Once

"You write a recipe, and poof, it's deployed. Magic."

Gopal is following procedures, and he uses a configuration management tool to control the environment in a predictable fashion. In essence, he is transforming an *unknown* state into a *known* state through a series of structured commands that are pushed to the target systems in a staggered manner.

"But I never do any task twice if I can help it. I put everything into a recipe and deploy it that way."

167

Gopal's motivation translates into a repeatable, automated procedure. The recipes are also a form of documentation and allow other members of the team to make changes if required.

"Wendell wrote notes as Gopal talked about the Git repository where the recipes and the monitoring plugins were stored, so that anyone could access them if they needed them."

This is another example of effective documentation that allows the work processes to be captured, stored, and used by the rest of the team. Git is also a version control utility, so it allows changes to be tracked individually.

Procedures, Not Magic

"You write a recipe, and poof, it's deployed. Magic."

The difficult part of this action is that new processes should be documented rather than just *poofed* into deployment. While Gopal's work is structured correctly, at the same time, it is important to be careful and not take things for granted. A wrong recipe can cause widespread damage to systems. It is also important to fully understand how the configuration management tool works, because it is impossible to troubleshoot *magic* in an emergency.

Systems and tools should be transparent – magic as an ingredient is never a good thing. Either it implies that whoever is behind it didn't bother investing time in creating good, clear documentation or that they are holding cards close to their chest, in order to create unnecessary dependency on their involvement.

"Groups of systems I defined for when rolling out change. That way, I can control how the recipes get installed."

Gopal should log the groups of systems so there is a trail of actions that can be traced back and analyzed if there are any problems. Without the procedure in place, other team members will not be able to replicate his work if they need to roll out change, or they may do it in a different way, which could lead to a divergence in the results.

"Silently, they worked on their computers, traversing directories, manually fixing the lax permissions."

Wendell and Gopal should have coordinated their work and documented their actions (as we will discuss some more in the coming chapters). They should have also rolled the fix through recipes, in the same way they introduced the original permission change. The manual method may introduce even more problems into the environment, and there would be no record of that activity. A clear log of the event – the introduction of an untested change, the manifestation of the problem, and the resolution – would provide a good starting point to reflect on the incident and learn how to avoid it from recurring. Instead, the problem will just be swept under the carpet.

Procedures Prevent Ambiguity

If we look at the story we discussed earlier, we can see that procedures revolve around human randomness, ambiguity, and the minimization of risks that diverge from the known into the unknown. Therefore, procedures that are designed to address these issues serve as a platform for a robust, ethical environment.

Lining Up the Dominoes

In a complex environment, getting the job done is a multistep process:

- It has a **well-defined scope** of work that determines the needed outcome.

- It has **written documentation** that explains the work. The documentation may have several components, including general description of tools and principles as well as technical documentation that can be used as reference material for the work at hand.

- There should be a way to **log** all the work.

- There should also be a way to **automate** the tasks.

By looking at this sequence of steps, it becomes apparent that changes cannot be made in isolation, without the wider context of how they affect the IT environment. Any task should have a clear reason and detailed instructions on how to execute it successfully. Therefore, it is also very important to distinguish between policies and procedures:

- Quite often, the scope of work will be reflected in **policies**. These are documents that define **why** certain tasks need (or must be) done. Policies are often made through a committee, and they have political or legal connotations.

- The details on **how** policies should be enforced and implemented will be reflected in technical documentation through **procedures**, which are often created by necessity and experience.

Documentation

Both policies and procedures require periodic updating to remain relevant and accurate. Any change in the environment should also be reflected in these two types of documentation. Typically, a policy change will trigger an environment setup change, which will then be placed into a procedure that enables this change to be safely implemented and repeated if necessary.

```
Policy change ➤ environment change ➤ procedure change
```

Sometimes, incidents, outages, and new discoveries in the operational setup will mandate procedure changes, as the existing set may be found inadequate. In some cases, they will also be reflected in policies.

```
Incident ➤ procedure change ➤ policy change
```

Documentation should not only be relevant for the task at hand, but it should also be meaningful to those who utilize it. There can be several levels of documentation available for a particular task, and they could target different audiences. You should write documentation that can effectively describe the work while taking into account different skill sets, work requirements, and risks.

The documentation you write for your colleagues or peers will often be different from the instructions used by help desk or on-call personnel. There is also the eventuality of the so-called "getting hit by a bus," in which case the documentation should provide a complete and effective volume of knowledge transfer.

Change Control

We mentioned changes (both planned and unplanned) having an effect on policies and procedures. While it is impossible to predict incidents, IT teams should strive to minimize the unpredictability factor in the environment. The formal, structured way to manage change is through the use of **change control** tools.

This toolset includes the use of version control software, configuration management, as well as a "soft" mechanism whereby new ideas are discussed and challenged in technical meetings. Anyone who wants to introduce a change into the environment will have their proposal weighed against known criteria (including scope, size, complexity, risk, and other factors), and if approved, such a change can then be translated into a routine task used in the future. Because it directly impacts both policies and procedures, change control is a form of documentation. We will discuss change control in more detail in the next chapter.

Automation

Well-implemented changes with accurate documentation are repeatable, and can often be automated. Running things by hand can lead to a lack of consistency and errors, often as a result of material blindness. People tend to get insensitive to repetitive tasks and sometimes miss obvious mistakes that would be otherwise quite apparent.

Automation ensures that identical tasks are always repeated in the same way, without the human element of variation. Automation is also cheaper and faster in most cases.

However, automation is more than just a sequence of technical steps cobbled together into a scheduled task or a script. The actual implementation of details is the last step. The main focus is on correctly defining the automation tasks and providing documentation that allows others to implement changes through automation systems.

The most prevalent way to accomplish this is through the use of **version control** and **configuration management** software.

The former keeps a clear, detailed log of every change, so that it can be fully traced and analyzed. This also allows people to collaborate and contribute their own data and code to automation tools without having to worry about conflicts or overwriting other people's work. Popular tools include Subversion (svn) and Git.

Configuration management allows changes to be deployed across IT environments in a staged manner. Work procedures are translated into automatable logic via recipes, playbooks, templates, scripts, and other documents (often written in high-level pseudo-code); and these are deployed via configuration management systems to the IT environment. Software like Chef, Puppet, Ansible, and CFEngine are used to govern large, complex setups with a very high level of precision and minimal overhead.

At our former workplace, our team managed tens of thousands of high-performance compute servers across tens of worldwide data centers utilizing configuration management tools. At that time, CFEngine was the management tool of choice, but additional hierarchy was added to enable global policies to be set while still allowing local data center managers to set site-specific policies. A small team of three to five part-time CFEngine admins was able to manage configurations across this global HPC environment.

At Portland State University, Linux servers are managed using Puppet. Unlike HPC clusters, many servers at PSU have unique configurations. Puppet allows the Linux team to select common configurations in Puppet, as well as define unique settings. These settings are then easily adjusted as customer needs change.

There is a lot of flexibility in how the configuration management works. You have the ability to partition large environments into modular, independent groups to simplify and control testing and deployment of changes. For instance, you can roll a change to only 10% of servers rather than the whole data center.

Configuration management is also designed to constantly redeploy changes into the environment, so any manual deviation from the defined settings will be overwritten in a periodic run. This allows environments to align to a common standard, with improved security and less randomness. To some extent, configuration management tools also function as a low-level compliance and logging mechanism.

The complete stack of correctly defined procedures, documentation, change control, and automation that has elements of version control and configuration management is shown in Figure 7-1.

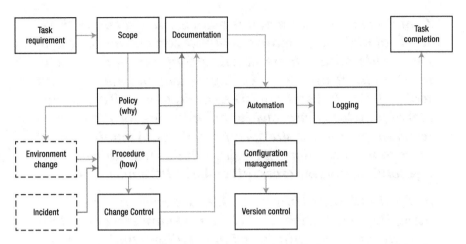

Figure 7-1. *The full flow of getting a work task done in an ethical way*

Only the Privileged Ones

Things do get a little more complicated when system administrators need to run tasks with elevated privileges. In some of the cases, these will be specific activities that cannot always be automated, due to their sensitivity or security requirements. But that does not exempt them from the need for well-defined procedures and the necessity to log the work.

In general, people tend to be opposed (or at least suspicious) of tools that log their work activities, as they believe they are being spied on or that their employer does not trust them and requires constant monitoring. In some situations, this may indeed be the case, but the primary purpose of logging is to maintain visibility and control of privileged work in the environment. There could be legal and compliance requirements, alongside simple necessity to make sure there are as few risks in the IT setup as possible.

Privileged work should always leave a trail. The collected data can be used to find mistakes, but more often, to show that everything was done properly. Over time, it can also be used to improve procedures and make the systems more resilient and secure. Now, if you do require the use of a privileged account, there are some measures you can follow to ensure you are being ethical:

- If privileged work is done, then you need to use a privileged account that is assigned to you **personally**. This will ensure that the work you did is logged specifically as being done by you. Examples include the use of the sudo commands in Linux or special users (like john_privileged), which are allowed to run specific tasks on specific hosts.

- If you have to use a **generic** privileged account, like the administrator account in Windows or the root account in UNIX/Linux systems, then you should also make sure that the environment is configured to log such usage in a way that can be associated with individual user accounts. For instance, a Linux host would log all remote connections via SSH and would have a logging service running. Such a host would also have a process accounting service enabled so that every executed command is also logged. The root shell would have a history, too.

Story from the IT trenches: At one of my previous workplaces, we had an overnight outage of an important customer server, which seemed to reboot without a reason. Checking with the remote support team, they informed us that they had taken no action on the affected system during their shift. However, looking at the process accounting logs (the pacct facility in Linux), we discovered a different version of the story. There was an entry for a reboot command, which indicated someone had logged onto the machine and executed it. We correlated the information to the system log (syslog), which showed a single user (one of the remote support team members) had connected to this server a few minutes prior to the reboot. When presented with this new information, the employee in question did admit to running the command and making a mistake.

Sometimes, you may need to use a privileged account when there are no adequate logging tools in place. This would mean performing work without a trail. If you find yourself in such a situation, you may want to keep a manual record of your activities and search for opportunities where the tasks you are doing could be documented or automated. The more resilient and controlled your IT setup is, the more operational freedom you will have. A clear trail of tasks helps instill confidence and trust and can go a long way toward building an ethical work environment.

Conclusion

Changing the human nature – or even fully mapping it in a predictable, algorithmic way – is an impossible task. But the endless variety of whim and impulse that interfere with our logic and education can be harnessed through accurate, well-defined procedures. Good procedures allow everyone to perform tasks in a uniform, repeatable manner, with lower risks and fewer unknowns.

Good procedures straddle a range of areas: *documentation* that reflects both company's policies and technical, operational experience; *automation* that helps further minimize risks and errors, with the smart use of configuration management and version control; a *clear trail* of information that corroborates the work; and a *process* through which change is introduced and executed in the environment in a structured manner. All of these tools are designed to keep the work known, safe, and predictable.

However, we only briefly touched on the last point. To that end, in the next chapter, we will discuss how to implement changes in an informed, controlled manner – the ethics of change.

CHAPTER 8

Communicate Change

"Remind me again, why do you need to attend the change board meeting?" Henry asked sarcastically, holding a cigarette between his teeth, standing outside in the parking lot, in a quiet spot away from the cars and people.

Wendell had never seen anyone smoke so fast. It was fascinating. One long deep pull and it was over. "Uh, Gopal thinks I should submit my next change to the board to make sure I'm covered, so there are no mistakes."

Henry waved dismissively. He squashed the cigarette against the side of the trash can, and motioned for Wendell to follow him back into the building. That was that. The break was over in less than a minute. "Gopal. He's a master of procrastination. He never goes to the change board when he wants to implement something really quickly, and then always uses it as an excuse to delay things he doesn't like."

Wendell just shrugged. He didn't know what to say. But he did know that Henry liked his theatrics, and once he was done, he would get down to business.

Henry sat down at his desk, and popped half a dozen chewing gums into his mouth. "Let me give you an overview of the change board. Basically, the purpose of the board is to verify that whoever intends to roll out a change has carefully thought their actions through. This means peer review of the technical steps as the first step, the analysis of risks and impact, and having a good rollback plan. You also need to make sure you don't do any big changes before going on vacation or public holidays." He paused and smiled. "Or actually, you do, and let others

© Igor Ljubuncic, Tom Litterer 2019
I. Ljubuncic and T. Litterer, *System Administration Ethics*,
https://doi.org/10.1007/978-1-4842-4988-8_8

handle the mess, so you come back, and it's fixed. Then of course, there are also customer-mandated freeze periods, when we're not allowed to make any changes at all."

"Nothing at all?"

Henry grimaced. "Well, small things are okay, and of course emergencies. Communication is the key. You need to keep people apprised of what you're doing. I hate the word stakeholders, but they need to be comfortable you're in control, and everyone knows what's happening. It helps reduce misunderstandings and silly mistakes."

Wendell wrote down his notes. "This is helpful, thank you."

"See you at next meeting," Henry said. "Make me proud."

The week went by in a blur. Wendell had spent a good few hours agonizing over his work plan, polishing details. At some point, he realized he was overdoing it. But he felt ready.

"... We will migrate one area at a time, verify that all the data hashes match, and then ask the customer to run the test flows. Only if the flows pass successfully will we then migrate the next area."

Wendell was half-listening to Belinda as she walked the board through her proposed change. A customer had run out of space in a project area, and they needed new disks. But they had also decided to use this as an opportunity to clean old data.

"All right, that looks good to me," Henry said after a short pause. "Anything else?"

Imam spread his arms. "Sounds fine to me." Wendell knew Imam was an application developer, and responsible for coding and maintaining a number of tools used for customer data migrations and optimization. Henry said he was always present at the board meetings, acting as a devil's advocate for any change that affected customers.

"Thanks for completing all of the prework, Belinda. The meeting always runs smoothly when you present a change," Henry said. "Okay, Gopal, you're next."

· "So, I've been waiting to bring this to the change board for 5 weeks now," Gopal started. "This actually comes from a customer, and they want to use a different database version—"

"Wait," Henry cut him off. "Hold on. I'm not following. Looking at the form, you mentioned the version upgrade, but I'm not sure how that affects the customer. Is there any change in the actual database schema?"

"The customer will need to check that," Gopal replied.

Henry frowned. "Does the customer know what the version change entails?"

Gopal seemed to be thinking. "Of course. They requested the change."

Henry sighed. "Gopal, we're the experts here, not the customer. Did you explicitly tell them what the version change means for them? I also don't see how you intend to roll back if there's a problem."

"We'll do a staged deployment, one server at a time. I'll push the configuration management changes once an hour—"

"Did you tell the customer about the proposed schedule?"

Silence again. "Not yet."

Henry looked frustrated. "But this is only 2 weeks away. They won't have enough time to prepare for downtime or define the necessary tests to check the database upgrade. Sorry, Gopal, I can't approve this. You need to rework your plan, and we can talk about this next week, all right?"

Wendell wasn't sure if Gopal looked happy or displeased with the rejection. But it was his turn now. He spoke when Henry gave him a gentle nod. "I want to deploy a new model that correlates between customers' home addresses and store locations. This should make our reporting more accurate and also reduce the load on the web servers, as we need to capture fewer data points. Best of all, we won't need admin access for running the old reports."

Henry looked down at the form. "But you will only be doing this with our test server, right, and the data is last year's set from the archive?"

"Yes," Wendell said.

"But there's no actual downtime or noticeable change to the customer." Henry rolled his eyes. "This doesn't really need to go through the change control. You can do this once you've completed the test phase and want to move into the production. Unless of course you win the lottery, then it's no longer your problem."

Imam cleared his throat. "Actually, if we're not doing Wendell's one, since we have some time, I'd like to talk about something that might be urgent. Well, it is urgent. Mike insisted on this getting done right away."

Wendell nodded weakly. He didn't mind. He felt a little flustered that Gopal had convinced him to go through with this plan when it was rather unnecessary. He also noticed Henry didn't like the unannounced interruption.

Imam, seemingly oblivious, continued, "There's a number of corner-case scenarios where our prediction software works really slowly. I thought these were corner case, but they are much more common. When a customer hits one of these, it looks like our engine is frozen, but it's computing the suggestions slowly, about a hundred times slower. So I want to push a fix."

Henry wasn't easily intimidated. "You've been working on the engine for weeks now. How come this is so urgent right now?"

Wendell could understand why Mike had given him the change board hat. He was actually surprised Henry hadn't come up with a lame joke or a quasi-philosophical allegory.

"All the changes are in the repo," Imam explained, "and they have been vetted and approved by the rest of the team. We did code review and testing. So I'd like to deploy this right away. We shouldn't delay this on a technicality."

"Keep the business running," Gopal added.

Imam snapped his fingers. "And I also need Gopal's change approved, because the fix relies on the database upgrade. This is an emergency, and the application change is blocked on this."

So much for the devil's advocate, Wendell thought.

180

Henry leaned back. Several people were milling just outside the meeting room. "We're out of time. I don't like this, Imam, but I understand this is an exception. Please make sure you are monitoring the servers, and if there are any problems, you'll stop and roll back right away."

"Of course," Imam agreed.

Henry sighed. "Any objections?"

Wendell looked around the meeting room, but it was almost empty except the three of them. Belinda and Gopal had already gone out. He wondered what Mike would say, and maybe they should ask him. But then, Imam was quite senior, and he knew what he was doing.

Wendell shook his head.

Changes Through the Ages

In nature, systems tend to exist in a state of minimal energy. Over the course of many millions and billions of years, organisms have adapted and optimized to survive in a way that requires the least resources to sustain their existence. To change that state, additional energy is needed. Whether stripping an electron from its shell or creating a new strain of bacteria, energy is required to effect a change.

IT environments can also be examined through the prism of physics, from the perspective of energy. In a way, data centers and IT labs are somewhat like collective organisms in nature, with a large number of smaller, less complicated entities (primitives) forming a complex, higher form.

The big difference is that we have only had a few short decades to try to optimize our hardware and software, and we are still learning how to do that. Which is why change is an essential part of the data center evolution story. We invest energy, test scenarios, and observe the survival of the fittest (server).

Of course, the analogy may be wasted on someone working the night shift, handling an outage due to a badly configured fix pushed out into the environment without sufficient testing.

The IT world is growing and expanding exponentially, becoming ever more complex. With this unprecedented growth, we are being exposed to the scale and nature of challenges that we never had to face before. There is also a strange duality about it.

We constantly push for changes in order to find the superior technology or solution that will provide the best results, and yet, companies (and customers of said technologies and solutions) are often resistant to any changes, because they don't see a reason to alter an effective, working setup. There is often a struggle between going fast and not breaking things, cost and quality, Skunk Works[1] partisan efforts and being inundated by bureaucracy and data. Sometimes, we are overwhelmed by change, and sometimes we embrace it dearly.

The history is full of examples (one might even say that history is one big, complex example) of changes through the technology world – the good, the bad, and the ugly. One (very) costly example is the loss of a USD 125 million Mars orbiter[2] due to a metric-imperial unit mismatch that was not communicated between two engineering teams.

Another example is that of the Yahoo security team, which did not follow up on their knowledge of a security breach.[3] Back in 2014, they were aware that a *change* (in this case, an intrusion) had taken place in their environment and impacted the users of their mail service, but they did not communicate or follow up on the incident in a clear, transparent manner.

---

[1]Skunk Works is an official pseudonym for Lockheed Martin's Advanced Development Programs (ADP), formerly called Lockheed Advanced Development Projects.

[2]http://edition.cnn.com/TECH/space/9909/30/mars.metric.02/

[3]www.csoonline.com/article/3176181/yahoo-execs-botched-its-response-to-2014-breach-investigation-finds.html

Sometimes, great changes are created, but no one knows about them, and therefore it can take a long time for them to be adopted. Kodak's digital camera[4] was a forward-looking product with amazing new features that took some 18 years to realize because they decided not to communicate the change.

While one may say change is the only constant (be careful when you use this saying in IT offices, some people may decide to ignore you forever), the emphasis isn't on any particular type of change or industry domain. It is all about the **communication** of change.

Winds of Change (and Communication)

Beware the geeks bearing gifts.

—Virgil (system administrator, not the poet)

Quite often, technically minded people, especially in IT circles, tend to be wary of changes, regardless of their origin or nature. They like to view their environment as a steady-state microcosm, existing in precarious balance, and changes are seen as disruptive and often unnecessary factors that threaten the stability and harmony of their proven, working setup.

Their mistrust is not entirely misplaced. Lots of IT changes can be easily labeled with "Not invented here" or "Some project manager thought ..." Lack of communication, insufficient understanding of all the components in the environment both by stakeholders and those executing changes, and inadequate procedures have left a deep scar in the IT world. The resistance to change transcends personal experience (although we all have our share of tragic stories, like the best of Greek theater plays) and has become a background characteristic of IT companies.

---

[4]https://lens.blogs.nytimes.com/2015/08/12/kodaks-first-digital-moment/

This phenomenon highlights two important factors. People are defensive about changes due to an insufficient understanding of their effects. Communication can help alleviate fears around change.

System administrators are afraid of change, because changes are made without communicating what the results will be, what problems can happen, and how the change can be reversed.

In essence, change control is primarily information control, a mechanism that promotes **situational awareness**. When done correctly, it allows every person involved in an ecosystem to easily know the cause and effect of every proposed change. It reduces the margin for error and the margin for uncertainty and minimizes risk of unplanned problems and complications when the change is rolled out. Effective communication also promotes trust, and the change control facility is a very useful, structured way to do that.

Most people envision this facility as a sort of a round table (well, maybe not quite as glamorous) where experts sit and discuss proposed technological solutions in detail. Sometimes, this may be the case, but often, many changes are not sufficiently complex to warrant such an effort. Time is another important factor. It is often impractical to put forward every possible environment change permutation before a council of wise people. In fact, the Knights of the Round Table will usually only make time for changes that are worthy of their attention!

Change control as a means of communication and awareness can also be done using a variety of tools and methods, all of which need to be adjusted to the relevant situation and domain complexity. For example:

- **Version control** tools like Git allow source code change tracking. Any commit can be reviewed in detail and then subsequently accepted or rejected.

- **Ticketing systems** allow customers and support personnel to exchange information in a structured manner, including communication of maintenance tasks, proposed changes to systems and services, review of work plans, and more.

- Teams can run **informal or semi-informal** change control around their projects, or they can have a documented process that allows them to track and review changes. A frequently used process should be put forward to change control; if green-lighted, it can then be used without additional approvals. If the process needs to be changed, then the change control board should review and approve it again. Not every department does this, but it is a good way to save time and rubber-stamping in the change control meetings.

- **Low-risk change** items can use the existing process for tracking and communicating change, but not have the requirement of presenting in the meeting and getting formal approval.

All of these vectors can help shape the narrative around changes, which increase confidence and reduce risk. Conversely, when done badly, change can lead to material and reputational damage – outages, data loss, complications, and plain and simple loss of time and resources.

Poorly communicated change promotes mistrust and wariness, with people less willing to make future changes for the fear of being blamed for any issue that may arise as a result of bad planning, amplifying the general fear of change. This can also stifle creativity, which only reinforces the stereotypical perception around change in the IT circles. Down the road, this may lead to a business or company falling behind in technology and ignoring better solutions as a result.

In many cases, bad changes are a product of ethical violations around **communicating change** – and consequently, they can lead to further ones.

> *Change isn't bad – and even poorly planned changes aren't necessarily bad. If the plan is communicated well, other system administrators can quickly pinpoint resulting problems.*

This puts considerable pressure on people who work in stressful, fast-paced conditions, often with limited exposure to all the governing factors or even the full set of technical data they need. System administrators, engineers, software developers, and technicians will often find themselves spearheading change under suboptimal conditions (with words such as *it's urgent* or *we need it today* echoing in the back of their minds). It is very important to know how to conduct oneself properly, in a way that will satisfy work demands, mitigate risk, and provide effective, useful information.

> **Story from the IT trenches: In the heady days of growth, we were constantly landing new projects and running out of compute and storage capacity. A new storage platform was being introduced to address many of these issues, but the change was going to be disruptive, requiring a major downtime, with massive data migration with new technology. A crucial project deadline was looming, and our (new) management wanted the migration done within a week – half the original estimated time. One of our storage team members decided to sign up for completing the data migration in that time. Could he have done it that quickly? Apparently so. He showed that the data migration had been completed and received a lot of kudos from management.**
>
> **Issues started cropping up soon after the downtime. We began investigating, and it turned out that there were days' worth of inconsistencies in the data – a major problem in product design! It turned out the person had not actually completed the migration in time. However,**

instead of requesting more time, he released the environ-
ment to production while the data sync was still ongoing.
To compound the issue, this was discovered only after
extensive overnight debugging since the person never
admitted to the mistake. Not only was the product design
endangered, we lost far more time trying to recover than
we would have in the planned downtime period. This was
clearly an integrity issue. Needless to say, the person was
let go soon after.

Communicate Change

Ethical communication is all about transparency. Should proposed work
in the environment cause a change that deviates from the established
processes or results, it needs to be told to anyone affected by it. This
could be disruption of service, or this could be a massive improvement in
performance. In both cases, there should be a channel of communication.

Transparency does not mean every piece of information gets "out
there" unfiltered. In some cases, you won't be able to share specific parts of
your work with external customers, or there might be security implications
that prevent full disclosure. However, it is still possible to notify the
relevant parties that their experience or results could change, even if it is
not possible to share specific details.

Transparency also implies proactive communication – you don't
just admit there was a change or a problem because there was an outage
and someone noticed, you also take accountability for your work, accept
mistakes and possible complications in the work plan, and make sure
to reflect those to your colleagues and customers. Consequently, the
communication is also timely and relevant.

If There Is a Change That Potentially Impacts Functionality or Availability, Good or Bad, Inform

It is important not to assume knowledge, awareness, or interpretation of changes in the IT environment. Your customers (or even your peers) won't be privy to all the details you have. You may also accidentally ascribe values to certain aspects of your work that don't reflect the priorities of your customers. Ethical communication can help bring everyone on board and drive toward common understanding of proposed changes.

Two Sets of Eyes Are Better Than One

> *"This means peer review of the technical steps as the first step ..."*

Working with one's colleagues is a very effective way of evaluating the proposed changes. Typically, other members of a team will have a good understanding of both the environment and the tooling, and they will have the right expertise to judge the technical steps. Having another pair of eyes go through the work plan can weed out obvious mistakes and improve cooperation. Peer review is also a great way to communicate the details of the change to the technical staff.

> *"Communication is the key. You need to keep people apprised of what you're doing."*

It is impossible to overemphasize the importance of Henry's statement. Effective communication lies at the heart of every change and allows for smooth running of the IT setup.

> *" ... verify that all the data hashes match, and then ask the customer to run the test flows."*

Belinda's outlined work has many good points. She has a proposed method to verify that the results of her change have been implemented correctly, and there is the communication element, too. The combination of these factors is essential to running changes in complex environments.

"Did you tell the customer about the proposed schedule?"

Similarly, Henry insists on customer communication. The customer needs to be informed, so they can also prepare accordingly. Quite often, changes made on the IT side will require adjusting changes on the customer side. It is vital to coordinate the two sides, to minimize disruption and mistakes, and to schedule the timing of that work. Clients will respond differently (and usually be more accommodating) if they are given sufficient advance notice of important and possibly disruptive changes to their environments. It is all too easy to underestimate how much time a customer may need – it can sometimes be months of preparation!

"All the changes are in the repo, and they have been vetted and approved by the rest of the team."

In this example, Imam makes use of both internal processes and tools to facilitate communication. This creates good visibility of the proposed work across the team, so other people can step in and assist if necessary.

What They Don't Know *Will* Hurt You

"He never goes to the change board when he wants to implement something really quickly."

The *speed* of the change is not a deciding factor in whether the change board should be informed. Instead, Gopal should have assessed the complexity of implementation and potential impact and used those to determine the right communication method and if the change board should be included.

"We shouldn't delay this on a technicality."

Once again, while speed is of essence in most IT environments (everyone wants the job done yesterday), it shouldn't be the defining criterion for change. Making hasty decisions forces people to compromise without sufficient data to make the right ethical choice. The change process must be followed for all changes. If the change board process is merely a technicality, then as was discussed in the previous chapter, Imam should work with Henry to improve the process, not work around it. Change and communication processes should always be treated as a necessary piece of the job.

> *"We're out of time. I don't like this, Imam, but I understand this is an exception."*

In the real world, there are compromises – and there are exceptions. However, exactly for that reason, they need to be clearly communicated. If people don't know about unusual conditions or scenarios, they will flag them as errors – or, worse, ignore them.

If There Is a Change That Has No Potential Impacts, Tell (About Your Great Work!)

Sometimes, it's not all gloom and doom. You may be able to introduce changes without any impact. For instance, if you architect the environment in a redundant way, it might be possible to upgrade services without any downtime for the customers. This is a great opportunity to communicate robust work methods. Likewise, if your changes result in tangible improvements to the experience, results, or perhaps cost, you should communicate these. Your customer may not know about bug fixes, enhancement requests, and new features unless you tell them. You could even communicate security patches, which should help people not worry – and even nurture greater confidence in your relationship.

Moreover, if you run complex changes in an efficient, trouble-free way, they should be discussed in a post-implementation review and used as an example for similar projects in the future. This also includes documenting the environment architecture with the change. In some cases, this could be simply by using Git for communicating. Too often, you hear months later about someone fixing issues in the environment – but they just did it on their own using root and without telling anyone. The technical change offers a great fix, but no one knows about it. Worse, some people may still have it on their backlog list and are planning to spend time on the task.

No Harm in Asking

"But there's no actual downtime or noticeable change to the customer."

Both Henry and Wendell behaved ethically on this matter. Wendell erred on the side of caution (which is preferable over running changes and hoping for the best). Henry made sure that the change did not require approval from the change board. However, there are internal system administration changes that need to be communicated – as we've mentioned, the round table of wise men is not the only entity that needs to be apprised of environment changes.

Show Off a Little

"This should make our reporting more accurate and also reduce the load on the web servers."

In its current form, Wendell's change does not introduce any major risk. But it has a potential to make the environment more efficient. This is a good chance to "show off" his great work. Communication does not have to be just dry updates on task progress. It can also involve highlights on benefits and improvements. In general, people are more receptive and cooperative if they feel there is reward to their work. They may also have useful pointers and suggestions – a better way to do that or an enhancement for it. Wendell may also be implementing a change that has a security issue he may not be aware of.

"So I want to push a fix."

Imam's desire to resolve the problem is commendable, but the way he wants to do it can be improved. At the moment, the implementation of this fix will most likely never be communicated to the customers who are asking for it. They won't know about the effort and the good work, and they will just think that the "sunspots" went away.

Getting the Word Out

In Chapter 7 (Follow Procedures and Get Out), we talked about the use of policies and procedures to reduce the element of human randomness in the IT world. Similarly, communication is a tool (or perhaps the tool) that can reduce the randomness of information exchange and, in consequence, the change that results from it.

When building an IT environment, it is useful to architect systems with a well-defined communication foundation as the *first step*. By design, such environments will also have an effective change control mechanism.

Follow the Breadcrumbs

Communication comes in two major forms: information exchange between machines and information exchange between humans.

In a well-designed environment, changes that affect digital systems should have **clearly defined inputs and outputs** and use **standardized protocols** to communicate. Typically, this will revolve around information storage (databases) and information transit (network). The communication needs to be deterministic and precise, so it is possible to understand the source and destination and troubleshoot any part in between.

Changes that require human interactions should be communicated in a manner that can be effectively interpreted by all involved parties. The effectiveness covers several dimensions, including the volume of information, the **timeliness** of information, and the **accuracy** of information. Most importantly, the communication needs to address the requirements of people involved and affected by the change, both internal and external parties:

- Communicate to other technical personnel (and your future self) in a way that will portray the change as an update to the environment architecture.

- Communicate to customers who might be impacted by the change event and changes to functionality.

The abstract definition may be somewhat difficult to conceptualize. Therefore, as a useful exercise, you can start by following an imaginary trail of information through the environment, in a way that will simulate its intended purpose. For instance, if you have an application server, a very basic information flow will be something like as follows:

1. The service will run on a system inside the data center – this could be a physical machine, a virtual machine, or a container; and it could be hosted in your data center or running in a cloud somewhere.

2. The application will store and retrieve data from a database on a separate machine inside the same environment.

3. The application service will respond to queries from external clients in the form of pages (data, computation, etc.).

The next step is to introduce a change, and then understand how that change will propagate through the environment. A database upgrade is one likely type of change that would affect this setup. It needs to be assessed both from the machine and human perspective.

- If there are any changes in the inputs, outputs, or the protocol, those need to be examined so that data integrity is not affected.

- If there are changes that will affect end users, the changes also need to be communicated to them. The information needs to be timely, correctly reflect the nature of the upgrade, and be provided in a way that will be useful to the intended recipient. For external customers, this could just be a status page notice informing about an upcoming downtime. For internal users, including developers or system administrators, this can include detailed instructions on how to run validation flows and performance tests or how to prepare for the scheduled maintenance.

This way, you can build the puzzle, creating a detailed chart of dependencies in the environment, structured around communication. If you understand how changes propagate and affect different components in the entire system, you can then correctly frame the changes.

Cause and Effect

If you have designed your environment with effective communication in mind, the next step is to introduce tools that will enable changes in a transparent manner.

- Treat it like an experiment – You may want to look at changes with scientific method in mind; formulate a hypothesis and the probable outcome to your change, and design an experiment that will test and validate your theory. For example, if you are introducing a software patch that is meant to improve the performance of a program by 60%, you already have the first part. You now need to devise a work routine on how to patch and measure the performance and also take into consideration actions in case your hypothesis gets rejected (rollback plan). If you realize you don't have the tools or methods to capture and process the results, you probably cannot introduce the change in the first place.

- Changes need to be judged against the communication foundation upon which they rely –
  If you plan to modify a component of the IT environment, then all elements that rely on it should be informed. In some cases, this will require an entire chain of communication to ensure the change is understood by all levels and involved parties. If you don't have the ability to do that, you probably shouldn't go forward with the change.

This scientific approach will ensure that changes aren't just random ripples in the environment. Changes need to be well defined, time-bound, and with outcomes that are measurable.

You Have to Risk IT to Biscuit

On a more granular level, you need to be able to "weigh" change based on its complexity, value (cost of success – and failure), and resources (people and time). It is important to quantify each of these parameters, so that they can be translated into **risk**.

To that end, you could use some form of a **risk calculator** that creates a score for proposed changes based on a number of factors. This could be a simple spreadsheet or a sophisticated piece of software, but the purpose is the same: quantify the risk vs. value factors.

These could be linear or nonlinear, and they will typically reflect the nature of the change. As shown in Table 8-1, you may associate low risk for internal-only changes but high risk for those that affect external customers, any change that affects more than 100 servers could be automatically considered complex, and so forth.

Each score should determine how you address the change – **through well-defined policies and procedures backed up by documentation**, as we saw in the previous chapter. This way, anyone trying to implement a change will know what path to take to get their change approved and implemented.

Table 8-1. *Example risk assessment calculator*

| | | Impacted by service disruption | | |
		Internal < 100	Internal > 100	External customers	Accounts receivable
Probability of disruption	Will	Medium	High	High	High
	Likely	Medium	Medium	High	High
	Unlikely	Low	Medium	Medium	High
	Not possible	Low	Low	Low	Low

As shown in Table 8-2, low-score changes may only require an informal or peer review by team members. Medium-score changes could mandate a preliminary testing on a small set of non-production machines and a rollback plan. High-score changes could mean presence of senior technical personnel during the implementation, extensive testing, and more.

Table 8-2. *Example change action calculator*

Risk	**Low**	**Medium**	**High**
Process and notification	Peer review	Testing and rollback plan	Extensive testing, senior personnel available

196

These tables are only a representative use case, not a template. You will need to determine what values and actions work best for your risk calculator.

Spread the Word

Now that you have a good understanding of the communication framework, the test and implement phases, and the scoping process, the next step is to put this philosophy into practice.

Information is like wave ripples – expanding rings of disturbance. You can treat communication in much the same way. Whenever a ring "intersects" with something in the environment, you will need to make sure the information is correctly received and interpreted. Each interface represents a possible friction point, where things can go wrong due to miscommunication.

Create a Scientifically Framed Change Plan

It needs to outline

- Proposed theory and expected objective

- How you test the theory and measure the results

- How you communicate the progress and results

- Risk – Will determine who approves the plan

Each step of the plan should have three possible outcomes:

- Success – You can proceed to the next stage.

- Failure, go – You continue the work with amendments.

- Failure, stop – You abort the plan and roll back to the original state.

For each of the outcomes, you need to have mechanisms that will register the results and ways of communicating them. The communication needs to be active rather than reactive (e.g., monitoring systems can alert if something deviates from expected thresholds, but they should not be the way your customers learn of possible failures in the change plan).

Quite often, communication of work-in-progress projects and tasks is the **weakest link** in the whole chain. Technical teams tend to assume there is a universal understanding of their domain. They also do not necessarily share their work as they progress (they can see this as distracting or they will want to complete everything before informing others), which can lead to confusion and errors.

> *Did you turn it off and on: We were running a site-wide shutdown maintenance over the weekend, as part of a larger upgrade program that necessitated the migration of large volumes of customer data (several PBs) from old to new appliances. The actual data moves had started a good 2 months ahead of the downtime, with dozens of systems running rsync jobs 24/7 on archived and read-only data paths. To facilitate the migration, the compute team loaned an additional 70 systems to the storage team. The storage team relabeled these machines so they would be correctly classified during the maintenance. Then, on the fateful weekend, the system administrators in the compute team noticed there were 70 systems that had not been powered down – they had been correctly excluded from the shutdown sequence. But this change had not been added to the shutdown master plan, and when the maintenance manager pressed for results (the compute servers gated the next step in the plan), the system administrators powered them off. Again, this was not communicated to the storage team (a meeting room away), and about 2 hours of time were lost powering up the hosts and restarting the data move jobs.*

What's in a Change

In the preparation phase, focus communication on verifying the proposed test plan covers all the necessary parts for a successful implementation:

- Outcomes are measurable – You can quantify the state before and after and objectively determine whether the goals of the plan have been met.

- There is a rollback plan – If the work results in a failure or an unknown condition that has no documentation, there should be a well-defined process to restore the original state of the system.

- There is a communication process for each step, based around possible outcome (as outlined in the previous section).

Furthermore, both the implementation plan and the rollback plan need to cover the entire stack of the environment. In the IT environment, this includes platform-level changes (hardware and software) and configuration changes (code logic and settings). There will also be a risk level assigned for each type of activity.

- Hardware and software changes (new platform, new application, new library, etc.) – Use **asset management tools** to correctly label proposed changes before deployment. They should then be correctly flagged in the monitoring tools in the environment.

- Code and configuration changes – Use **version control tools** like Subversion and Git. These tools provide a clear history of changes, and they can be used as a gatekeeper to progress to the next stage in the change plan. They can also be used to **roll back** changes if needed.

- Risk and change board – Use a **risk calculator** to determine the level of approval needed for the change and follow accordingly – informal or formal peer review, change control, etc.

In the implementation phase, it is important to communicate the actual work being done. The change should be **time-bound** and approvals to progress **explicitly defined**.

- Use **ticketing systems**, **chat**, and **email** to communicate with customers ahead and during the change implementation.

- Use **status pages** for notifications to reduce the need for one-to-one communication on updates that do not require a two-way exchange.

- Complex changes may also necessitate a **project management** function (and tools) as a liaison between interested parties, both internal and external.

Once the change is completed, it is equally important to communicate the results (success or failure). There needs to be a **clearly defined end** to the change. After that point, the change becomes part of the standard environment.

- Verify results (as defined in the change plan) – For instance, performance and regression testing will be done to make sure the new hardware or software works correctly.

- Receive explicit Okay from all involved parties.

- Update monitoring systems and management tools.

- Communicate change end.

- Post-implementation analysis – Discuss both the good and the bad points of the change; drive toward implementation and reuse of processes, methods, and tooling that proved their worth; and make sure the badly implemented elements are not reintroduced in future changes. This analysis should be done within a week after the completed change.

Overall, there are many ways to implement this infrastructure. As environments scale, so will their complexity, necessitating more layered mechanisms of communication mapping and change control. A conceptual diagram of ethical communication and change is shown in Figure 8-1.

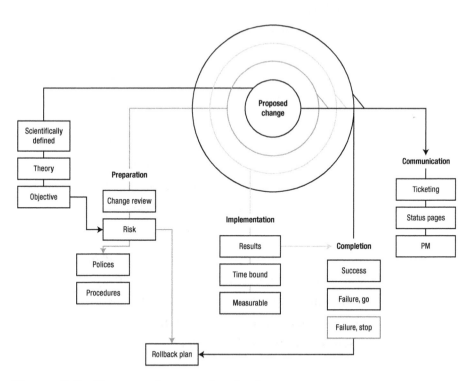

Figure 8-1. *Communicate at the ripples*

Information Vertigo

In large environments, it can be challenging, even daunting, to map the entire network of dependencies among systems. It can also be counterproductive when the volume of information designed to provide clarity about the environment becomes too much to handle in a reasonable manner. To that end, it is important to work from outside in.

- Don't overcomplicate things by flooding people with information – Use the least amount of data to describe and track changes.

- Often, you won't have enough time – Change control board meetings will often be busy, with different groups vying for their spot. Use processes and standards to streamline communication.

- Don't work in darkness – It can be tempting to avoid bureaucracy and trailblaze changes yourself. While such an approach can make for faster work, in the long run, it can lead to undesired changes propagating through the environment unattended. Worse, good changes may be flagged as anomalies or errors, because other people will not have the visibility into your work (as we've seen from the turn-it-on-and-off-again story earlier).

- If something isn't clear, stop and ask – When there are high expectations for you to move quickly, it is easy to move forward even when you are not sure how customers will be impacted by the change. If there's doubt, there's no doubt. Ask for help.

In some way, having a full-blown setup of change control may seem like an administrative overkill that can slow down work. However, years of hard lessons from the IT trenches worldwide show that, in the long run, a structured approach focused on situational awareness (communication and change) is faster and more effective than a haphazard trial-and-error approach.

Conclusion

In fast-paced environments, changes can be stressful and disruptive. The lack of control and visibility over operational work and the fear of blame breed resistance and mistrust that can impair everyone's effectiveness and lead to bad decisions and actions. Communication is critical in keeping unethical behavior in check.

In fact, communication and change are two sides of the same coin. In a well-designed IT environment, the two always go hand in hand. As such, communication forms the foundation of the environment, and it needs to be transparent, proactive, and timely.

Ethical IT setups promote collaboration and trust – communication happens in layers, from informal chats among team members to change control board processes. There's a high level of awareness of causes and effects that propagate through the environment. For any change that is made, both those effecting the change and those affected by it will understand the risks, the expected results, good or bad, and the scope of the work.

However, there is one problem with this premise … It implies that people communicating change are aware of the consequences of their work, be it good or bad. What happens when you cause harm, unknowingly or by mistake?

How do you go about conducting yourself when things suddenly go pear-shaped?

CHAPTER 9

Do No Harm

Wendell grimaced and scratched his temple. He believed learning from mistakes was extremely important, especially for techies like himself. After all, his work was all about making sure other people could enjoy technology in a seamless, transparent way. And that started with introspection, figuring out where things had gone wrong and making sure they didn't happen again.

But whose mistakes?

His? Or others'?

He thought back to the change board meeting, to Henry's questions, to Gopal's rushed answers, to his own budding sense of unease. Maybe he didn't have the experience his team members did, and he was still learning about the environment, but he still could tell when things weren't quite as they should be.

"So, I want to push a fix ..."

It was after hours, and everyone was edgy. Imam sat on the other side of the table, looking impatient. He couldn't really do his work until Gopal was done, and so he spent time chatting and asking questions – maybe too many. Gopal had left the meeting room to work elsewhere, because he seemed annoyed by Imam's attention and couldn't concentrate. Wendell didn't mind Imam's presence, and he actually liked that there was someone who knew customers' applications in and out while the change was being rolled out.

Wendell took a deep breath. "Okay, I think I'm ready."

© Igor Ljubuncic, Tom Litterer 2019
I. Ljubuncic and T. Litterer, *System Administration Ethics*,
https://doi.org/10.1007/978-1-4842-4988-8_9

Imam nodded, fidgeting in his chair. "I'm monitoring the application, go ahead."

Wendell carefully consulted the instructions and typed them in his terminal. He was still a bit shaken from his previous rollout with Gopal. The admin privileges were more of a burden, but no one called them that. Probably because no one would work as a sysadmin that way, he reckoned.

He deployed the new model; it should help correlate customer addresses and store locations correctly this time. He frowned. The model had failed with a permission error. "Damn."

"What is it?" Imam asked, keen to participate.

"Oh, I need additional access to make the model work." He realized he could add the shared account used for application deployments to the customer group to gain access. But then, he wasn't sure if this might cause harm. "What do you think is the best way to do this? Maybe we should ask the database owner?"

Imam pursed his lips. "They have probably gone home. Let me think."

Wendell decided to check where Gopal was at. He opened the IM client and typed, *"How's your work going?"*

"I've upgraded the first database version and schema," Gopal replied after a few moments.

"Did the customer check it?" Wendell typed.

"There's no one around, so tomorrow."

"All right, I think you can push the new model now," Imam said. "I sorted the permissions. A temporary change and I sent an email to the database owner so he knows about it. Once we verify the model works, we won't need it."

Wendell nodded.

A few minutes later, Gopal stepped into the meeting room. "I'm done."

Imam raised his eyebrows. "Already?"

"My change was approved, and you need the new version, so I continued with the upgrades. All the databases are now running the latest release. Well, I guess that's it. I'm going home."

"See you," Wendell said, his attention split between reading the new report results and listening to Gopal.

"Okay, then I can push my fix," Imam said, cracking his knuckles.

Wendell looked up. He was looking forward to this step of their work. Imam's software change was going to fix the prediction software, to stop it from running really slowly. This could be a major improvement in the customer experience.

Imam snapped his fingers. "As I thought. Our firewall is causing all the slowness. In this new version, I changed the port, and now everything is working fast."

"Did you tell the network team?" Wendell asked.

Imam seemed a little distracted. "The new version of the database supports custom scripts, so I want to check that, too."

Wendell knew this feature wasn't being used in the production environment just yet. He didn't think Imam should be testing the extra, and only focus on the slowness fix.

"Well, that's unexpected," Imam said. "The CPU usage is through the roof, and I can see query time going up. Might be the scripting engine. Wendell, can you look up the full functionality in the guide while I debug this? I really want to be done with the change this evening."

Imam's phone rang. "Imam speaking. Hey, Caesar. No, I didn't touch the firewall. Wendell and I are working on a database slowness fix. Yes, Gopal's gone home already. Look, this should be fine. There's no impact." He raised his chin. "Wendell, Caesar is going to send you some firewall logs. Can you look at them please?"

Wendell waited for the email to come through, and then started reading the entries in the log file. It wasn't data that Imam was working with, but it did seem most of it originated from one particular database, and it did contain customer location information. "I think we should stop the cusloc database for now."

Imam grimaced. "If we do that, all our work will be for nothing."

Wendell considered going ahead regardless.

"I'm going to call Jacob," Imam added quickly. "He may know why there's a high level of firewall activity from the customer location database." He picked his phone again.

Wendell pointed at the desk. "Put him on speaker. I want to hear, too."

"I don't know," Jacob said after they had explained the situation to him. "I really don't want to shut a production database down. But I agree, we need to be cautious and continue to explore. The customer may just be running a lot of queries. We give it another half an hour then maybe we can restart the database. Meanwhile, maybe we can ask Caesar to increase the logging level."

"Thanks," Imam said. He dialed Caesar again.

Wendell kept poring through the database manual. There didn't seem to be anything in the custom scripting engine that should suddenly cause a massive spike in the CPU, especially not for some basic scripts that Imam was testing.

"Okay, Caesar says we should look at the monitoring console too. Maybe that will give us a better understanding of why we're seeing all this traffic all of a sudden."

Wendell authenticated his username in the web console and waited for the monitoring dashboard to open up. Imam leaned over.

"Well, it looks like customer data is being read and copied through the firewall."

"Is that normal?" Wendell asked.

"I don't know. The customer may have changed their queries. We should get the on call and see if they can help locate the issue."

"We should notify Mike, too," Wendell added.

"Yup, we should do that," Imam said and picked up the phone. "Hey, Mike. Imam. Sorry to trouble you. Listen, Wendell and I are doing a maintenance ..." He turned the speaker on.

Wendell watched the monitoring dashboard as Imam explained the situation. Mike didn't sound angry or impatient. Wendell had almost expected the manager to be annoyed that things weren't going well.

"... and we want to stop the cusloc database."

Mike hummed. "All right. Give it half an hour, then do it."

Imam nodded enthusiastically. "Okay, cool. Thanks, Mike."

In Harm's Way

While some idioms do not translate well, a non-English phrase that reads *"those who don't work make no mistakes"* is oddly applicable to the world of IT. All of us have, at some point in our professional career, made this or that error in the course of our jobs. Sometimes, there were relatively trivial mishaps, with our individual pangs of guilt as the only witness. Sometimes, these were big mistakes that caused outages. In all cases, we did something we believed was right, which turned out to be wrong.

With computer systems becoming ever more critical in the everyday operation and running of vital infrastructure like power plants, hospitals, traffic grids, and communication networks, the role of IT personnel has transformed from maintainers of tools and platforms into guardians of civilization (one might say the galaxy, but that would be pushing it). Few people have the immediate perception that their work, far from the actual application of technology, can have such dramatic ramifications and impact. It is also an ethical dimension that people haven't necessarily signed up for – and definitely haven't been trained for as part of their IT jobs.

And yet, **mistakes are inevitable**. Over time, the probability of something going wrong in an IT department approaches one. This is a fairly obvious topic – we have already discussed some of its aspects throughout the book. For example, Chapter 2 (Respect Privacy) elaborates on the implications of data loss. We talked about intellectual property in Chapter 4 (Do Not Steal Intellectual Property). But we did not discuss the human dynamic around mistakes.

In general, no one likes to be wrong – in the wrong – or to admit mistakes. Such an approach can be perceived as negative or self-defeating, and it can have direct consequences on one's employment. In turn, people often get defensive when challenged (either by other people or by data they are consuming), which can make them even less likely or willing to introspect, which in turn makes people less likely to identify errors in their work and conduct. That way, system administrators, developers, and technicians end up making ethical violations without even realizing. With people's lives at stake, three or four network hops down the line, the price of ego could be too high to pay.

Badly designed systems or ambiguous outputs can induce further moral confusion. Perhaps the most iconic example of a wrongly architected system is reflected through the Three-Mile Island[1] nuclear accident in 1979. Ambiguous readouts in the station's control center led the operator to believe there was too much water coolant in the reactor, which led to a manual override and steam pressure release.

Few of us can put ourselves in that person's shoes and fully understand the magnitude of the problem they were facing at the time of the accident, but it illustrates the importance of decision-making checks that must be present in our actions at all times.

But the odds are stacked against us. We are **blind to our own mistakes**. It's universal. Just look at any email you've written (or a chapter in a book), and you will notice that you are less likely to spot grammar and spelling errors than a proofreader. This also applies to technical work. If you're writing scripts, coding software, or running commands during maintenance, you may not be able to spot obvious mistakes in your procedures or logic until after the fact.

---

[1]www.nrc.gov/reading-rm/doc-collections/gen-comm/bulletins/1979/
bl79005a.html

The phenomenon is reinforced by **confirmation bias**. As humans, we are more likely to ignore evidence and facts that contradict our beliefs and assumptions and give extra weight and importance to those that confirm them. From an ethical standpoint, you could end up dismissing trains of thoughts, methods, or solutions that don't necessarily align with what you have in mind. For the same reason, you may also ignore or minimize problems.

Don't fight mistakes: (1) they are inevitable, (2) we are blind to our own work, (3) we use confirmation bias to ignore contradictory evidence.

Awareness Is Key

The understanding that mistakes will happen is critical. It is a foundation of a principle called Design for Failure (DFF), which assumes there will be unexpected outcomes. Rather than avoiding or ignoring such eventualities, they should instead be mapped, treated as a certainty; and working back, develop adequate tools to prevent, mitigate, and identify them.

- Prevention – If an error or failure condition is known or can be computed with high probability, the systems should be designed in a way that does not trigger the error or failure conditions. Typically, systems will have safety margins, and there will be thresholds for normal operation.

- Identification – It is possible for systems or people to deviate from expected work conditions, be it a problem in the code or outdated documentation, which could lead to an error. There should be monitoring system in place, designed around safety margins and thresholds, and these should alert when there are errors, ideally before the error conditions are met.

- Mitigation – It may not be possible to prevent mistakes, errors, or failures. In some cases, there will not be a simple, deterministic formula to predict possible error conditions. But if they are correctly identified, the potential harm could be mitigated. For instance, it is hard to know in advance when a hard disk may fail. But the resulting damage can be mitigated through the use of multiple copies of data on several disks, the use of RAID technology, etc.

We will discuss how to implement different elements in a DFF policy later in the chapter. Let's focus some more on the concept of harm.

Not All Harm Is Made Equal

It is also vital to understand that the ethical dimension only extends to situations where there's human interaction in some form, and it is based on the sense of right on behalf of those conducting the work or making a change.

- Deliberate harm – This is probably the least likely case. But it is also the most difficult to prevent and mitigate, especially if it is done from inside the environment. Causing deliberate harm also goes directly against the commandment of this chapter.

- Accidental harm – In most cases, harm is the result of an accident – an inadvertent mistake that results in an output that is different from the expected outcome. It can stem from many reasons, like inadequate or outdated procedures, insufficient operator skill, assumptions made due to time pressure or other constraints, decisions made based on insufficient or incorrect data, and more. Accidental harm stems from good intentions, but it does not absolve individuals from domain responsibility. It is important to note that in some cases, you could be blamed for negligence or deliberate harm if there is a significant gap between expected knowledge and understanding of systems and your work. In other cases, especially where there are privacy or safety implications, certain individuals may be held legally accountable for significant harm. For example, CEOs of software companies, financial or medical institutions, will often be held personally accountable for data breaches or accidents in their businesses.

- Bugs – In some cases, there could be functional flaws in software and hardware that will cause harm. For example, a disk failure may lead to a loss of data, which can be harmful to the users of that data, but it is not an eventuality that can be ascribed to the action of any individual.

The ethical dimension exists primarily in the second category. System changes, like perimeter security and software patches, can address deliberate harm and bugs in code, but they cannot handle logical flaws in our thinking and perception of the environment nor our sense of being right.

Do No Harm

In the IT environment, most people will associate harm with tangible damage caused directly (and indirectly) by someone's work. However, it pertains to almost every aspect of interaction and usage of systems.

Harm could be seconds lost waiting for an application to load to multibillion-dollar losses due to a major incident. Before harm can be rectified, it needs to be identified correctly, and it starts with every action.

IT tasks should be viewed through the prism of consequences, and much like we've seen in Chapter 8 (Communicate Change), they can be treated as scientific experiments. You could ask yourself, what is the expected outcome of the action you're performing? What are you going to do if things go wrong? Have you considered situations and scenarios that deviate from the desired results, and do you know how to handle each one?

It is also important to remember that harm does not have to be directed toward others (and thus necessitate communication). You could harm yourself! For instance, you could lose valuable work if you don't keep adequate backups. You might have to spend more time running system administration tasks if you are using inadequate or outdated tools and scripts.

Because the topic is so broad and generic, it is all too easy to dismiss it or hide it under a veil of everyday processes. However, it is possible to develop an ethical approach to work that is focused on harm and damage and utilize the tools and methods we have learned in the previous chapters, with main focus on communication.

If It Is Likely You Will Do Harm, Stop and Inform

Work-related tasks need to be quantifiable, so that you can understand the level of possible harm that could result from incorrectly executed plans. Typically, risk and harm are closely correlated, and ideally, you will have a 1:1 mapping of the two; if there is high risk in proposed work, then the potential level of harm will be high, too.

Even more importantly, system administrators, technicians, and engineers need to have the awareness that their work could trigger a chain of undesired results. But sometimes, it is simply not feasible or advisable to expect every employee to remember the full range of possible risks and pitfalls in the environment at every given moment. To that end, the likelihood of harm also needs to be precisely outlined, so that engineers will have an understanding of how to act and when to inform others about their work. Indeed, if consequences are well defined, it is easier for people to remember and respect them.

Finally, the most critical element in this equation is the ability to stop and take a step back. Time pressure and exhaustion can fuddle our judgment, and system administrators often find themselves working against the clock while typing half-hearted replies to their managers demanding answers. We have all found ourselves in a situation, past the deadline, grumpy and weary, fighting the environment, and the deluge of questions. It is almost too easy to hit the Enter button and let things happen. In such situations, it is even more imperative to exercise caution. While the phrase "if there's doubt, there's no doubt" sounds idealistic (or cliché), it is a vital part of ethical behavior, especially for people in positions of privilege like system administrators.

But you don't want to be the person who stopped an annual upgrade because you were unsure about a command any more than you don't want to be the person who caused a massive outage. Excessive risk avoidance side by side with the casual attitude to blame the "little guy" when things go wrong tends to skew our judgment and push us into making hasty, unethical choices.

> *One of my first mistakes as a manager was to push my storage admin to continue with the storage server upgrade after he had issues. It was Saturday night, and he said to me, "I'm not sure what is wrong, but I can start over and get this fixed and upgraded within our downtime window, or I can back out and try another day." Of course, I said, "Get it done now." Well...the fix and upgrade did not work as expected, and we went well beyond the downtime window into Sunday. We then spent most of the week restoring lost data. The storage admin did the right thing; he stopped and informed his manager. As the manager, I was just impatient. When you get approval to make a change at a specific time, that does not mean do it or die. If you might "die," then stop doing it! You'll live to try another day. Luckily, for me, I was given a second chance after learning what not to do the next time.*

It is possible to adopt a practical stop-and-inform approach; and it involves timely communication, correct usage of data, and risk factors. Let's examine what Wendell and his colleagues did.

Don't Go in Alone

> *"What do you think is the best way to do this? Maybe we should ask the database owner?"*

In Chapter 7 (Follow Procedures and Get Out), we learned the importance of written documentation and strict work instructions – the idea is to deviate from known outcomes as little as possible and to be able to quickly return to the controlled state. Wendell understands that additional access to the database is not something that has been discussed, and it could have negative impact on the customer. Rather than continuing his work, he exercises caution, and he consults with Imam.

In general, having other people "question" your work is a good way of filtering out obvious issues and fallacies that you as the author may not see. If you can successfully "defend" your chosen tools and methods, mistakes are less likely to happen.

> *"I really don't want to shut a production database down. But I agree, we need to be cautious and continue to explore."*

Jacob exercises caution, and he is sensitive to the potential impact such a move may have on the customers. But he is not being risk averse for the sake of it. In fact, he acknowledges there is a problem and wants to investigate the issue further. Additional information can help system administrators and technicians make safer, more ethical decisions.

> *"We should notify Mike, too."*

Virtually every organization or group of people sharing a cause of some kind forms a hierarchy of power, officially or unofficially. This is a natural thing, which is why the role of a manager has existed since the dawn of civilization. Among other things, managers need to make decisions. Indeed, an integral part of managerial duties is to sometimes take responsibility and ownership of problems and situations that don't necessarily have a well-defined outcome.

The database problem seems to be escalating beyond the ability and authority of the team members involved in the maintenance. At this point, there is a need for someone to step in, analyze the issue on a more generic level, and decide on the next course of action. This will prevent the team members taking unethical steps. Mike will still face the dilemma of not causing harm, but his perspective, training, and authority will be different from the developers and system administrators.

Slow Down and Consult

"My change was approved, and you need the new version, so I continued with the upgrades. All the databases are now running the latest release."

Gopal's unilateral choice to complete all the work without having coordinated it with the rest of the team is a violation of the commandment. The fact his change was approved is not a carte blanche to work heedlessly. He should have stopped after finishing the first system upgrade and waited for Imam and Wendell to test the new algorithm. If there were a problem in the database upgrade, the problem had been replicated many times over to other systems, and rather than having an individual host affected, the entire production base could suffer from upgrade issues now.

Wendell considered going ahead regardless.

Wendell's thoughts resonate with all of us. We have all been in situations where time is of essence and had to act fast, maybe even without having taken all the facts and implications into consideration. In reality, acting rashly or against established principles usually ends up in bigger problems and more harm. As humans, we tend to focus on the miraculous rescues and one-in-a-million shots, but those are isolated instances of sheer luck.

Now, Wendell is most likely correct in his assumption, but he should make sure that his act will not cause an even greater problem. This means being able to fully reason and map the fallout from stopping a customer's production database. Ideally, such scenarios will be part of a DFF policy and included in change and maintenance plans. Since Wendell does not have all the pieces of information, it makes more sense not to do anything.

If You Accidentally Did Harm, Tell

Mistakes are inevitable. In some way, there will come a situation where your actions will result in harm inside the IT environment. This inevitability is part of the work risk in high-paced technology and engineering workplaces, and it should be inseparable from your accountability in your role.

When harm does happen, your conduct after the fact will bear massive impact on the repercussions. If you ignore or sideline the issue or, worse yet, try to cover it up, people may ascribe malice and intent to your actions. An innocent mistake could be interpreted as deliberate harm, and while you may lose your job over less-than-satisfactory work, you will definitely lose it if you're found trying to erase the traces of your mistakes, and you might even be criminally charged.

In general, people are much more tolerant toward those who admit mistakes and take responsibility for their work. This is a very human thing: it gives them a sense of trust, knowing you will conduct yourself fairly – and that you won't try to blame them for your mistakes! Moreover, your peers and colleagues will also understand that they may one day cause harm, so there will be a level of solidarity as part of your common cause. An environment of trust allows for much better collaboration, which can help minimize damage and reduce the risk of future mistakes of similar nature. Last but not the least, the sooner you act after harm is done, the better the chances of stopping any cascading damage, reducing the cost and size of the damage, and collecting data logs that can help analyze the situation and improve the resilience of the IT environment.

Quite often, all of the data breach stories we have heard about were reported months or years after the breach occurred. You can imagine some system administrator ignoring alerts, skipping audits, covering up the mistake, trying to fix the problem, or saying it is not a big deal – before someone else finally escalates the issue. You can then imagine some manager pushing their team to minimize the problem, finding someone to blame, cleaning up the mistakes, and then finally reporting the problem as gently as possible. You can surely imagine the company trying to find a way to spin the issue as minor, to reduce the scope of reporting, to identify one low-level employee to blame, and then coincide the announcement on a major news day. And of course, if the lawyers get a hold of the information, they'll demand that the issue is a major problem, that the scope will include anyone who ever touched the system, that the top-level managers are to blame and should resign, and that everyone should be compensated. How many breaches have happened where the system administrator or the manager covered up the issue? How many were ignored or squashed by corporate execs? How many got past the lawyers without any press hype? The world will never know …

> *I've been in sysadmin situations where the person who caused the problem did not "remember" doing anything, or only provided vague details, or clammed up when they felt like they were being blamed. Because of this attitude, the root cause of the problem could never be identified; processes could not be improved, and automation wasn't put into place. In most cases, it was even worse – we implemented automation and processes that covered every possible scenario that might have caused the problem. This wasted time and money – taking valuable resources to implement and sustain the solutions. Most likely, none of the fishnet solutions would have stopped the problem.*

Your Team Wants to Help

> *"The CPU usage is through the roof, and I can see query time going up. Might be the scripting engine. Wendell, can you look up the full functionality in the guide while I debug this?"*

Imam believes he may have caused harm – or at least, at this stage, there is a complication in the maintenance that might escalate into a full-blown problem. He does not hide it, and he asks Wendell for assistance.

This is helpful on several levels. One, Imam's action raises visibility into the potential issue, and reduces the chance of Wendell continuing work that could trigger further harm. Two, Wendell may be able to provide useful insight and expertise at a stressful moment, which could lead to a faster, more effective resolution.

> *"Imam speaking. Hey Caesar. No, I didn't touch the firewall ... Wendell, Caesar is going to send you some firewall logs. Can you look at them please?"*

Caesar's decision to contact Imam is a sound one. While Caesar has not done any work himself in the after-work maintenance, he feels accountable for his domain of work regardless and chooses to inform his colleagues about the unusual network traffic. He is also sharing additional data that could help troubleshoot the problem and, thus, prevent potential harm.

Don't Ignore Problems

> *"Wendell, can you look up the full functionality in the guide while I debug this? I really want to be done with the change this evening."*

We touched on this example earlier. Imam's action was a step in the right direction, but he hadn't done all he should have in this situation. Imam should have also notified the rest of the team members involved in the after-hours works, like Caesar, so there is no communication disconnect and no work is done in isolation, compounding the issue and making the problem resolution even more difficult to achieve.

> *"Hey Caesar. No, I didn't touch the firewall. Wendell and I are working on a database slowness fix. Yes, Gopal's gone home already. Look, this should be fine. There's no impact."*

Imam's phone conversation with Caesar is definitely an ethical violation. While he did not initiate the call to his colleague, he still had an opportunity to flag the potential problem to Caesar. Instead, he posited that there is no impact, which neither he nor Wendell had ascertained. This is incorrect information that could give Caesar (or other team members) a false impression of the situation. It is evident that Caesar is concerned, as he had noticed an anomaly in the firewall traffic. At this point, Imam should have coordinated the work among all of them and made sure everyone has been told about the maintenance, the issue, and any other aspects of the event.

Prevent, Identify, and Mitigate Harm

One might say that well-managed IT environments are designed and architected by a pessimist. Indeed, the right approach to creating robust, resilient IT setups is through the use of the Design for Failure principle. Mistakes are inevitable, and consequently, there will be harm. Rather than avoiding it, the correct approach is to frame it, quantify it, and then apply corrective measures as an integral part of the solution on every level. As an extreme example, Netflix uses Chaos Monkey,[2] designed to deliberately sabotage parts of the environment in order to test the resilience and redundancy of systems and services. In most cases, such a level of positive destructive rigor will not be necessary, but harm should be part of architecture and operative procedures in the IT environment.

It is possible to structure the Design for Failure architecture as a 3×3 matrix. The columns cover different categories in harm management – prevention, identification, and mitigation. The rows cover different types of harm – deliberate, accidental, and bugs. This is shown in Table 9-1.

---

[2]https://github.com/Netflix/SimianArmy/wiki/Chaos-Monkey

Table 9-1. *Design for Failure architecture*

	Prevention	Identification	Mitigation
Deliberate harm	Physical security measures Network security measures Access control Permissions	Intrusion detection systems Active real-time monitoring of systems with well-defined thresholds and safety margins	Unknown
Accidental harm	Standard and privileged account separation Well-defined policies and procedures Change control Point of no return	Monitoring	Systems redundancy Data backups Backout plan Call for help
Bugs	QA and validation of tools and software	Monitoring	Systems redundancy Vendor support and/ or use of supported software

It is important to note that the mitigation of deliberate harm is very difficult, which is why companies and organizations require adequate measure to prevent and quickly identify any possible instances of deliberate harm. This may not always be feasible, especially if the culprit is an employee with inside knowledge of systems. On the other hand, the prevention of external harm is easier, but it does require significant resources.

Accidental harm covers pretty much any and every action in the IT world, thus specific methods will vary from one scenario to another. However, it is still possible to apply several generic, universal principles that can help minimize the risk of accidental harm.

The use of account separation is a great example of the awareness that you can cause greater damage with a privileged account and that you should minimize its usage. Well-defined, up-to-date procedures reduce ambiguity and minimize the risk of badly executed maintenance tasks. Change control is a great opportunity to discuss work with your peers and discover holes and problems in planned activities.

Point of No Return and Backout Plan

The reduction of accidental harm also has a temporal dimension. The work in the IT space is highly dynamic and often stressful, and people can make mistakes even if everything has been designed correctly.

No plan survives first contact with the enemy.

—Helmuth von Moltke

In this case, the living and breathing IT environment is your enemy. This is especially true if work plans slip beyond schedule, which happens a lot with system maintenance. When that happens, the likelihood for errors and mishaps grows exponentially. You may have your manager or impatient customers breathing down your neck or a hard deadline by which you must complete the work, and working against the clock, you may skip or miss crucial steps that can lead to damage. This occurs because tasks are often unbounded, and they don't have a clearly defined recovery plan.

To avoid these precarious situations, it is best to assume that things will go wrong and slip beyond schedule. This means every change plan should also include a point of no return and a full backout plan, especially for the high and critical changes.

The point of no return is a stage in the work sequence where if things are not going well, it is time to implement the backout plan. Such approach allows for a controlled return to the known environment conditions. While it may be embarrassing or frustrating, there are fewer risks involved than blindly trailblazing forward. This is when disasters occur.

Swallow Your Pride

Another crucial element in the DFF methodology is to communicate problems as early as possible. We all have the tendency to hunker down when handling issues. It is a natural thing and sometimes a direct, personal challenge to our inquisitive nature as engineers and techies. But it can be risky when running important changes in the environment, and it can lead to significant harm.

Informing others of problems gives you opportunity to **pull in resources and ask for help**. If you cover up the issue, then you could just dig yourself deeper into the problem. Sometimes, the best thing is to swallow your pride and do the ethical thing.

In our second story from the IT trenches, we talked about "amnesia" following incidents. Such attitude is highly damaging to the environment and people, way beyond the actual harm caused in specific cases. When there is not sufficient data to properly analyze problems, quite often **it is impossible to identify the root cause**. This means solutions and mitigations are applied without clear understanding of issues. Teams tend to get defensive and use blanket solutions, like automation and processes that cover every possible scenario to the problem, wasting time and money and **taking valuable resources** to implement and sustain these solutions. In the long term, this can be highly demoralizing.

Time Matters

We already know that if you discover harm, you should tell about it. But there's also the somewhat tricky question of **potential harm**. Sometimes, there may be early symptoms of complex problems that cannot yet be fully defined or framed through the lenses of monitoring rules and thresholds.

Hacking attempts represent a good example that covers this angle. For instance, you may encounter phishing attempts, against yourself or your colleagues, or someone may be a victim of ransomware or viruses. While these issues could be isolated or contained and they don't necessarily constitute a wider environment problem per se, time can be critical in such situations.

> *Like many companies, we used Microsoft's Skype for Business as an instant messaging and chat tool in our organization. One day, I received an invite from the CTO to a meeting. I found this unusual, because the CTO and I had never spoken before and I expected any sort of meeting to be coordinated by his PA. The invite message was also rather vague. While nothing harmful had happened yet, I decided to contact the CTO by email and verify whether he'd really initiated the contact with me. Once I learned he had not, we alerted the IS team about a possible phishing attack, and a communique was sent to everyone in the company telling them of these attempts to lure people into conversations where they might expose confidential information.*

Conclusion

Harm is an integral, unavoidable part of IT life. As such, it needs to be calculated and integrated into the work policies and procedures, using the Design for Failure principle. Each type of harm requires its own mechanisms to prevent, identify, and then mitigate if possible.

But appliances and software can only do so much when faced with human tenacity and inventiveness, which is why ethics acts as a glue between actions and consequences. In the course of your everyday work, you should examine every task through the lens of harm and determine whether there is potential for damage or uncontrolled results. If you believe that your work could trigger a negative outcome, you should act ethically and prevent harm. Two crucial elements in this equation include defining the point of no return and the backout plan, which should allow you to restore normal operations should anything go wrong.

Nevertheless, accidental harm will still occasionally happen. When that occurs, it is important to be proactive in managing harm – accountability and timely information can do a lot to mitigate damage. It can sometimes be very difficult to acknowledge one's errors or ask others to help you, but in the broader scope, these can be the difference between honest mistakes and severe ethical violations. Indeed, this will be the topic of our next chapter.

CHAPTER 10

Break Glass in an Emergency

Wendell dialed. The phone rang. No answer. Where the heck was Kiron? "He's not picking up," Wendell said with frustration.

Jacob wrinkled his nose. "I think he's at some networking conference this week. That's probably why."

Wendell huffed. Kiron sure chose a week to be away – right in the middle of a giant breach. "Well, we need the password. I'm gonna get Mike."

Mike came over a minute later, carrying a paper log that he normally kept on his desk. It had several break glass passwords for just this kind of eventuality. "Here you go, Wendell."

Wendell didn't think he was the best person to handle the firewall. Nonetheless, he scanned the page until he located the network admin access password. He typed it into the web interface.

Wrong password, the interface complained.

Alex snapped his fingers. "Oh, the network team has started using a password wallet. Mike, that list is outdated."

Mike's face reddened. "Well, someone should have told me. And what's the password for the wallet?"

Alex blinked. "I don't know. Kiron may have it somewhere."

© Igor Ljubuncic, Tom Litterer 2019
I. Ljubuncic and T. Litterer, *System Administration Ethics*,
https://doi.org/10.1007/978-1-4842-4988-8_10

Muttering to himself, Mike went away. Wendell found himself tapping nervously on the desk. He had worked late into the evening last night, and he was not too happy to have come to work only to find himself neck-deep in a major incident. No one really knew the details just yet, but it looked serious, and that frustrated him even more. He wanted to help fix the problem as quickly as possible and be done with it. The last thing he needed was these little foobars like a misplaced password.

"Got it," Mike shouted from across the hallway, coming back in a hurry. "The password for the wallet was written at the bottom of a printed sheet that Kiron keeps under his keyboard."

"Those network guys are shifty, I'm telling ya," Jacob whispered.

Wendell bristled. Jacob was too cheerful. After all, the production databases were his responsibility.

Meanwhile, Mike had taken over the keyboard, and now that they had access to the wallet, he was feverishly writing down the privileges passwords for the different system types. "Okay, Wendell, I'll need you to make some copies of these and then distribute them to people who need them. Please write down whom you give each password to."

Wendell took the paper, made sure the text was legible, and then went to the printing machine on the north corner of their floor. He came back and started cutting the copies into strips, so there was only one password on each strip. "So, database password, that's for—"

"We don't need that," Jacob interrupted abruptly. "I already know it. Just give it to me; I'll shred it so that I don't have to change it later."

Alex had walked over, looking at the list over Wendell's shoulder. "Since you're busy, I'll take the firewall password. I can do the file servers, too. Belinda?"

She nodded. "Sure. I'll work on restoring last night's backups. I don't need any password for that."

"Just give me the whole list," Henry said calmly. "I'll need several of those for the VMs and the lab systems."

"I'm gonna check the production servers, just to make sure it's all workin'. I reckon I'll use the local console password for that." Elwood smiled at Wendell as he ripped the bottom off of the original list of passwords.

The phone bridge chirped. "I'm here," Gopal said, finally making himself known on the emergency line.

"Hi, Gopal," Mike said and nodded self-consciously as Alex successfully logged into the web console for the firewall.

"Half the firewall rules are broken," Alex muttered. "I'm going to delete them."

Wendell was trying to divide his attention between handing out strips of paper and following up on what everyone was doing. "Shouldn't we use configuration management?"

"No time for that. I'm just going to do it manually," Alex replied.

With no more paper to distribute, Wendell sat down at Jacob's side, watching his colleague work. He felt a bit uncomfortable that he didn't have everyone's level of expertise and familiarity with the system, and he felt he could be doing more to assist.

"What happened here?" Jacob huffed, slapping the keyboard. "My configuration changes are gone!"

"The configuration management tool overwrote your change," Henry spoke up from across the room. "That's going to happen every 15 minutes. What's the name of the server, I'll stop it now. And you too, Alex, unless you want to be making the same changes all over again."

Jacob frowned. "It's *DB01*. But that's not the only issue. The defaults are not what I expected."

Wendell started investigating. "Hm. Looks like Gopal is working on *DB01*, too. He made an upgrade earlier. Maybe he's finishing up the configuration. Gopal, are you still on the bridge? Gopal?"

No response.

"Wait, why are we making upgrades now?" Mike asked.

Alex shrugged. "Ask Gopal."

"Okay, guys, we need to contain this. We will troubleshoot later. For now, we need to stop the network traffic."

"I've turned all the test VMs and lab machines down, so the only access to the database is from the Internet," Henry said.

Daniel had been sitting quietly in the corner of the meeting room. "I removed some of the statistical analysis applications we had on the database, just in case they were causing any problems."

"I think I know how to resolve it …" Gopal murmured on the line.

"Elwood says he can pull out the cables if needed," Mike informed them, looking down at his phone.

"Our admin VLAN is routed through the same switch as the external network," Alex explained, still busy with the firewall rules. "So he'd better make sure he doesn't disconnect us."

Mike typed it back.

"Let's just stop the database, and I'll start the restore," Belinda announced.

"No, no!" Jacob yelled. "No. You can't stop it. We have a major report being generated, and if we stop it now, we may have a corruption."

"What does it matter?" Caesar objected. "We'll be restoring anyway."

Jacob gritted his teeth. "It's more than 50 million records delta since last night. If we restore now, we will never know what those records were. We have to finish the report first."

"Gopal, any progress? You said you might know something …" Wendell asked.

No answer.

Alex made a wry face. "So we had some broken rules, but that doesn't look like it caused the problem. That was just internal traffic to our labs. The data is still going out, and I'm not sure if it's this firewall that controls it."

Time ticked by as people tried to understand what was happening. Wendell had a suspicion it had started last night, during the maintenance, but he couldn't be sure.

"Hey!" Caesar almost shouted. "The traffic has stopped." He smiled. "Someone either fixed or broke something."

Mike looked up. "What did you do?"

A flurry of words exploded across the room.

Belinda grimaced. "Well, I didn't do anything."

Jacob was on his mobile, talking to the customer, his eyebrows raised. "Everything seems to be working well. From their end, it looks normal."

Daniel sighed. "All right, can we go home now?"

Loud music started playing, drowning out the conversation. "Oh, look, Kiron is calling." Wendell answered. "Hey, man. Sup? Thanks for calling back. We had a big issue here, and we needed your help, but I think things are under control here."

"That's good," Kiron said, chuckling over the background chatter of a busy conference. "I only have a few minutes. I'm in a middle of a hackathon. Things are brutal here ..."

"Wendell?"

Wendell shook himself out of his reverie. He glanced around the meeting room, at his colleagues.

Mike inclined his head. "Do you have anything else to add?"

Wendell wasn't sure what the question was. He hadn't been paying much attention since Mike had mentioned the investigation. Wendell's brain was replaying the last few months. This sure had been his most interesting and stressful workplace so far.

"No," he mumbled. Quite stressful.

"I got another meeting," Caesar said. "So I gotta run."

Mike disconnected his laptop from the projector. "Okay, guys; please don't talk about this, not until we understand better what happened. Let's not start the rumor train."

The atmosphere in the room was tense. People were worried, but from Mike's report, it looked like the management wanted someone to blame. Of course. Wendell had a bad feeling it would be him.

"Wendell," Mike called again. "Can you stay in the room please?"

There we go, Wendell thought.

Knowing Emergencies

Emergency situations happen all the time, in every aspect of life. What unifies the different cases is that they elicit the same kind of behavioral response from people: they bring out the best and the worst in us.

The IT world makes for a rather peculiar scenario. On one hand, it is a clean, sterile, orderly, sheltered world where people work in relative comfort, with little to no physical danger. On the other hand, they sometimes make almost whimsical decisions with far-reaching consequences. The nature of IT work does not always reflect the consequences of mistakes and mishaps, which is why emergencies, when they happen, often unfold in an unpredictable way, encompassing a whole range of ethical issues.

For firefighters trying to save people from a burning building or workers on an offshore oilrig, emergencies often have a clear, unequivocal meaning. The true nature of the beast isn't always apparent when it comes to servers, databases, or perhaps network appliances. This is why unethical behavior in emergency situations in IT is common, expected, and disproportionate to the actual incident.

It all comes down to human nature. In general, we tend to **overestimate low-probability risks and downplay high-probability ones**. People are more concerned about nuclear reactor meltdowns than slipping in a shower. Losing 100 GB of data does not feel as real as getting attacked by a shark.

Confirmation bias plays its hand, too. The combination of these two elements tends to make people less likely to spot problems that lead to emergencies and to extend the period of **denial in accepting** the developing conditions of emergency situations.

An emergency is a deviation from an established, controlled state of matters, often defined by a framework of policies and rules. But then, any IT work that deviates from a known set of conditions can be considered as a deviation, and yet, not all such situations end up as an emergency. There are two other factors that must take place for an error to escalate into an emergency:

Time – If you have sufficient time to respond to a developing situation, formulate a plan, and mitigate the issue, it could be an incident, but it will not be an emergency. Typically, emergencies require that conditions deteriorate faster than systems and humans can fix them.

Unknown outcome – Emergencies also mandate that the situation happening has not been observed or documented before and that there are no known solutions or mitigations. If such exist, the incident could be defined as severe or even catastrophic, but it merely requires following known procedures to end or mitigate. Emergencies require a change in the parameters of the problem, from unknown to known, before they can be solved.

Prepare for the Unexpected

Throughout their career, almost every engineer, system administrator, and technician will undoubtedly find themselves in an emergency situation. And almost without exception, such situations will be chaotic, with people trying to resolve issues without a full understanding of both the symptoms and the consequences of their actions. It will make people disregard, ignore, or obviate rules and procedures, in an attempt to quickly resolve emergencies.

This is fertile soil for unethical violations.

It may sound like a paradox, but the ethical approach to handling emergencies is to **expect the unexpected**. This sounds like a cliché, but it ties into the concept of Design for Failure we discussed in the previous chapter. It is impossible to predict, map, or know all the conditions when a system may fail. Therefore, it is impossible to create monitoring rules or mitigations to catch every failure. Indeed, this is a costly and ineffective way of trying to rein in the chaos and prevent emergencies.

Instead, the alternative and ethical approach should be to accept and embrace the possibility that systems will fail and that people will make mistakes. Then, with the understanding that there will be a known outcome (failure), caused by unknown or partially known conditions, you can create scenarios that account for different eventualities and allow for a **controlled response** to the outcome. We will talk about the specific mechanisms later in the chapter.

This concept is known as the **Break Glass** procedure.

Break Glass

Emergencies are delicate situations, often without a precedent. To this end, you need to create a formula that will apply to all emergency situations. This formula needs to encompass the broadest possible range of scenarios, outcomes, and human reactions to quickly developing situations.

Indeed, the existence of a Break Glass procedure not only explains the type of actions that engineers and system administrators should follow during an emergency, it also provides a breathing space, or rather thinking space, allowing people to act in a coordinated, controlled fashion. This nullifies, or at least reduces, the time element that is prevalent in emergencies. Most importantly, Break Glass **minimizes the possibilities of unethical behavior** and further errors as a consequence of the emergency.

It defines what needs to be done in an emergency situation based on the failure condition. The reasons for the condition will not be immediately understood – if they are, it should not be an emergency. The response needs to be clearly outlined – simple, effective, and always up to date.

It defines the communication in emergency situations – a critical and often overlooked element.

However, it is possible, despite best intentions and preparations, that you will still be facing a difficult, unknown situation that may or will require ethical violations. In this case, it will be a choice of lesser evil – you will deliberately choose a smaller violation over a larger one.

Tell Everyone

For many people, the natural response to difficult situations, especially crises and emergencies, is a defensive posture. In IT terms, this translates to hesitation, indecision, and a lack of communication. No one wants to be calling their manager at 2:00 a.m. to tell them there's a problem. Further yet, no one wants to be calling their manager and admit that *they* have caused the problem.

But communication, as difficult as it may be, is vital in resolving emergencies and reducing ethical violations. It allows other people to understand the situation and respond adequately. Customers can take steps to minimize or prevent the loss of data and finances. Other IT teams can assist in the analysis and resolution of the underlying problem that had led to the emergency. A well-coordinated response ensures that the issue is handled in the best possible manner. It signals a level of accountability and personal responsibility on behalf of those involved, including people who may have been responsible for causing the emergency in the first place. Covering up or playing down emergencies is often far worse than the original problem in the first place.

Communication Starts from Within

"Well, we need the password. I'm gonna get Mike."

As a first level of response, escalating to management is a good way to establish a communication channel. While technical personnel are busy troubleshooting the issue, the manager can try to establish a bigger picture understanding of the problem, coordinate work among teams, and provide necessary decision-making, especially if rules need to be broken.

> *"Sure. I'll work on restoring last night's backups. I don't need any password for that."*

Belinda is using standard procedures without the need to Break Glass. She also informs her colleagues of what she intends to do. Moreover, the backup procedure is most likely well documented and logged, as it's part of the standard operational work, so it also provides the necessary trail for any post-event investigation or analysis.

> *"Half the firewall rules are broken," Alex muttered. "I'm going to delete them."*

Alex is telling the room what he is doing. It would be even better if someone was taking timeline notes of the activities, using a shared document, a chat application, or similar.

> *"Shouldn't we use configuration management?"*

Wendell's question highlights several good points. First, he is willing to challenge emergency work (it's not a free-for-all invitation to do just about anything). Moreover, he is doing this in a way that complies with the commandment. Assuming configuration management is set up in revision control, which it should be, then changes will be tracked and can be reviewed as needed.

> *"Okay, guys, we need to contain this. We will troubleshoot later. For now, we need to stop the network traffic."*

Mike is trying to assert some level of control over the situation. He is trying to frame the problem and define the desired outcome and the sequence of actions. Moreover, he is also keeping the scope of the Break Glass procedure small. This allows for quicker return to normal operations after the incident.

"So he'd better make sure he doesn't disconnect us ... Let's just stop the database, and I'll start the restore."

There needs to be effective communication among team members. Telling everyone about the intended work and consequences minimizes the risk of further damage or complications. For example, if Alex's network is disconnected by mistake, it would make it impossible for him to assist in the emergency, or even could make things worse.

Not Telling Causes More Work

"Oh, the network team has started using a password wallet. Mike, that list is outdated."

While the existence of a password wallet is a good security practice, Mike was not aware that a new tool was being used. Moreover, the existing list is outdated, in violation of how Break Glass procedures should be maintained. This means that the Break Glass procedures offer conflicting information to those who need it, and will have two different outcomes, based on which list is consulted.

"Hm. Looks like Gopal is working on DB01, too. He made an upgrade earlier. Maybe he's finishing up the configuration. Gopal, are you still on the bridge? Gopal?"

It would appear that changes were made and have not been documented or shared with the rest of the team. Moreover, Gopal did not communicate his work, compounding the situation. Further actions may actually complicate things, as Gopal's team members may act under wrong assumptions.

Leave a Trail

Both in everyday routine and emergency situations, communication remains a vital, indispensable link that connects the different pieces in the puzzles: humans, machines, and the problems in between. In emergencies, this bears even more importance, because emergencies are typically undocumented first-time cases of unknown scenarios and problems.

It is crucial to provide evidence so that the full sequence of events can be analyzed, especially after the emergency is resolved, when people have sufficient time and leeway to troubleshoot problems in detail. Furthermore, a forensic trail of data provides transparency and clarity into the actions and symptoms and allows the restoration of normal operations once the emergency is over.

In Break Glass scenarios, standard procedures will be violated, and there may be destructive actions that alter the expected state of tools and systems. If there is no trail to how these were changed, it may not be possible to distinguish between the original problem and the emergency work (which also makes the analysis of the emergency more difficult), and it can take far more time to get systems back into the desired state.

It can be difficult collecting information while working on time-pressing issues, but it needs to be done. Perhaps full-blown logs and monitoring will not be available, but it is still possible to keep a trail in the form of emails, chat messages, whiteboard lists, or even pen and paper.

Use Logging Tools

"Oh, the network team has started using a password wallet."

The password wallet is a tool that logs access, so it provides a trail to the Break Glass password.

"Please write down whom you give each password to."

This may not be ideal, but it is better than having no information on password usage whatsoever. A paper log is a reasonable alternative for when electronic trail is not available.

He came back and started cutting the copies into strips, so there was only one password on each strip ... "Just give it to me, I'll shred it so that I don't have to change it later."

Once again, Wendell's conduct is not perfect, but at least he is trying to restrict who has access to each password. Similarly, Jacob's suggestion will reduce the size of the trail. This allows Break Glass to be done without violating the other commandments. Moreover, as a general rule, passwords should be changed following an emergency or a breach, and Jacob should plan for this activity when the incident is over.

"The configuration management tool overwrote your change."

Despite the fact that there is an emergency, Break Glass does not allow for manual changes to system configurations. In general, while handling emergency situations, some changes to normal procedures may be required, but those should be kept to a minimum, and system administrators and engineers should adhere to standard work guidelines as much as possible.

Don't Lose Control

"Here you go, Wendell."

While Mike's assistance is appreciated, the way he handled the passwords is ethically wrong. Mike exposed passwords without a clear need to know and without logging the transaction. Mike could have decided who among the team members ought to handle privileged password access to different management tools, and only shared the credentials with them.

"The password for the wallet was written at the bottom of a printed sheet that Kiron keeps under his keyboard."

Stereotypes and clichés exist for a reason. They are deeply embedded in bad practice. Keeping passwords on a sheet under a keyboard sounds like a sketch from a sitcom, but it is also a bad practice in general. It leaves no trail for who used the password, apart from the obvious, blatant security risk.

" ... he was feverishly writing down the privileges passwords for the different system types."

Mike's conduct provides no digital log of who is getting the password. After the emergency is resolved, there will be no evidence of the use (or misuse) and no ability to revoke credentials. This means the teams will have to rotate their passwords if they want to maintain the right level of access control.

"Just give me the whole list," Henry said calmly. "I'll need several of those for the VMs and the lab systems."

There is no way to track which password Henry will be using. In turn, this means there's no way to review the steps he took since he is doing multiple things at once. If there are complications resulting from the emergency, it will be almost impossible to understand who had access to different systems and if somehow these actions compounded the original problem. This can be particularly tricky with data leaks and breaches, where it is crucial to be able to separate between malicious, external access and routine work on the systems.

"I reckon I'll use the local console password for that."

The use of the local console bypasses any tools that track file access or privileged user activities. Similar to Henry's suggestion, it will make the analysis of legitimate and potentially malicious activity during the emergency almost impossible to distinguish. Break Glass procedures should cover direct access to servers in the data centers in a way that will leave a trail and allow for any forensics afterward.

"No time for that. I'm just going to do it manually."

Bypassing configuration management means there will be no log of Alex's changes. It will make it impossible to distinguish between mistakes, errors, outdated rules, and his manual work during the emergency.

"What does it matter?" Caesar objected. "We'll be restoring anyway."

Caesar's approach is not conducive to helping resolve the situation. Without a log of actions and full understanding of what is happening, the same kind of problem is bound to recur in the future. The less evidence of the issue there is after the incident, the harder it will be for the system administration teams to troubleshoot and understand the conditions that led to the emergency, and this prevents them from devising an effective solution.

"What did you do?"

Actions need to be obvious and transparent. Team members should not need to question one another to understand what was done. A detailed, precise technical log should provide the necessary answers.

"All right, can we go home now?"

This attitude is expected at the end of a long, frustrating day. It is hard to blame people who just want to get away. However, the team should make sure everything is well documented and cleaned up before leaving. This will save them headaches – and exhausting emergency situations in the future.

Ideal Scenario for Break Glass

If one thinks of an ideal scenario, the simple answer is, there cannot be one. It is impossible to create a foolproof IT environment, in which nothing ever goes wrong. In the best case, it will be a setup that effectively and continuously minimizes risk through smart practices, high level of execution, accurate monitoring systems, and robust backup and recovery tools.

Failure Will Happen

The most important thing is to acknowledge the existence of failures, account for them in the architecture and design of the IT environment, and then map them into the ongoing operational procedures.

Failures need to be classified based on two primary criteria: the **probability** that they will occur (low/high) and the level of **damage** that they will cause (low/high). The combination of these two values will determine the risk and the cost that emergencies can incur – and therefore the cost of mitigations and recovery for when the emergencies do happen (see Table 10-1).

Table 10-1. *Determining risk and cost*

Probability/damage	Low	High
Low	Few mitigations Little redundancy	Few mitigations Much redundancy
High	Many mitigations Little redundancy	Many mitigations Much redundancy

Mapping risk (similar to change management) allows the right mechanisms to be put in place. As extreme examples, we can look at other sectors of the industry, like atomic power and train traffic.

The probability of a nuclear plant breaking down is extremely low, but because of the tremendous potential for lasting damage and impact on human lives, nuclear reactors have numerous redundancy systems designed to prevent failures. On the other hand, train failures are quite frequent, but the risk is typically low – people end up coming late to work, and there are traffic disruptions, but the damage is often minimal. This is why trains can be allowed to fail. However, the traffic management of trains is a separate matter altogether, and due to life risk involved, it includes numerous mitigations (automatic braking, train crossing barriers, etc.).

Be Prepared

A Break Glass procedure fills in the gap when the system breaks down. The reason for this is simple: you cannot map every conceivable scenario, and you must sometimes rely on Break Glass procedures. If there is an eventuality that has not been foreseen, planned, and accounted for in the procedure, it is incomplete, and this means that one day, there might be an emergency developing to a Break Glass situation, to which there will not be an immediate remedy.

As such, break glass procedures can be considered the "last resort" solution. They will not necessarily have specific answers, but they will lay down a sequence of actions that should help resolve the unknown state and restore the situation back to business as usual.

Let's go back to the breach that Wendell and his colleagues handled. They did not know (and still do not) how the breach occurred and what sequences of mistakes, errors, or software bugs led to it. But that's perfectly fine, because the idea of Break Glass procedures is not to troubleshoot systems in depth and understand everything. Far from it. The idea is to restore the normal, controlled state as quickly as possible. Specifically, the scenario only requires

- Understanding that there is an uncontrolled usage of data (details are not important)

- Existence of a well-defined procedure that explains what needs to be done in such a situation, for example:

    - Allow 30 minutes for analysis.

    - Terminate network connectivity by removing physical cable access.

    - Perform system restore.

245

This means that Mike's team need not be experts on hacking, because there could be endless vulnerabilities in the firewall or network switch software, in the database, in the customer application, in misconfigured rules, and so forth. What they should have is a documented procedure that includes

- Detection of data egress

- A basic analysis set to allow a nondisruptive fix if possible

- A well-mapped outline of the data center connectivity so that technicians can access and disconnect the affected server (a software-based solution may also be an option)

- A well-designed and tested procedure that allows the system to be repaired or restored to a pristine state with minimal loss of data or functionality

In the end, Break Glass procedures are a combination of steps that can be performed quickly, to mitigate further damage, even when the full state of the problem is not well understood. Rather than being bogged down by inaction, hesitation, and confusion, system administrators will have a clear framework of **what to do**, even if they may only have a partial visibility and control of the root cause for the emergency.

Keep It Together

Indeed, emergencies are not only defined by a loss of control over systems and time urgency, they often involve miscommunication and a lack of coordination. It can be difficult to organize effective work in emergency situations because people rarely train for them and many do not respond well under stress. Here are some things to keep in mind if you find yourself in a computer emergency situation:

- The first order of things is to actually scope the situation so that a problem statement can be formulated. If there is no clear definition of *what is wrong*, there cannot be an effective solution. This does not mean the root cause is clear just yet, but the symptoms are well understood.

- There should be someone in charge – Some companies may have a dedicated **incident manager** function that may also assume such responsibility in emergency situations. However, this can be any person, as long as they understand the requirements of their (temporary) role.

- Communication is essential in building the necessary situational awareness, making sure that people do not work at cross purposes, and facilitating a faster resolution.

Emergency work needs to be predetermined. Now, this sounds like a catch-22 scenario. If the problem statement is known in advance, then it should be mitigated, and there should never be an emergency as a result. On the other hand, if the problem is unknown, how can work be predetermined?

Indeed, it is impossible to predict some failures or the chain of events that follows thereafter, but it is entirely feasible to have a **fallback plan of action** even for unknown situations. While specific tasks will vary from one scenario to another, the general idea remains the same. This is almost like a recipe for what do you do if you get lost in a big city. The street layout will be different in Medellin and Montreal, but the basic idea of asking for directions, using a map, or contacting the police is universal. The fallback plan should be invoked after it becomes clear that there is no known fix to the emergency within the given scope or time or that the risk and damage are too great to allow the emergency to continue – it's Break Glass within Break Glass.

Show a man how to solve IT problems, and he will rest for a day; teach a man how to solve IT problems, and he will be busy for the rest of his life.

The general guidelines for emergency situations should be as follows:

- Instructions need to be **accurate** and **up to date**.

- Instructions need to be **simple** – Time will be of essence, and people should not have to discover how to handle emergencies on the fly.

- Emergency situations need to be **practiced** – Again, it is impossible to plan for everything, but high-risk scenarios can be tested. A regular, periodic emergency simulation drill can instill a level of familiarity with the systems and procedures. Typically, this will be part of a wider, strategic policy called **disaster recovery** (DR). It will revolve around catastrophic failures of significant portions of the IT infrastructure, and the conduct around it, with a focus on restoring functionality and productivity as quickly as possible. DR activities can include data restores, standing up an offsite data center, activating infrastructure services, reinstalling critical applications, and similar steps that might be needed to keep the business running.

Story from the IT trenches: We would have a DR test every 3 months, with the specific details only known to a small number of people, like the customer key point of contact, the data center manager, and several engineering team heads. Without telling the 24/7 NOC, we would bring down between 10 and 25% of the compute environment. They would then alert the on-duty incident manager (who was privy to the finer details of the simulation), who would then gather different teams to troubleshoot the issue, bring

up the remote site online, and then restore normal productivity. Every single time, we learned tons of valuable lessons. There would always be a dozen little things going wrong, from outdated phone lists to missing monitoring rules to asset management problems. Each time, we would get slightly better, but it showed us that we wouldn't fare too well in a real emergency and that constant testing was vital. This was an extremely valuable exercise.

Information Trail

- Emergencies are a ripe opportunity for things to slip through the cracks. People may assume that since things are already going haywire, they can throw caution to the wind. Unfortunately, this creates further problems down the road.

- It is vital to leave a trail of the conducted work and **keep communication channels open**. In a way, emergencies stem from unexpected changes in the environment, with a pressing timetable and unknown results. Communication should be done using the best tool for the task – a real-time messaging tool for immediate communication and email for periodic updates. Phones are useful because people can usually talk faster and convey messages more effectively than in writing, but phone calls rarely have a trail, and it is easy to misunderstand technical information.

- If you are going to conduct a **deliberate ethical violation** of established procedures, thoroughly document it.

- **Review every step** – Working fast may create the sense of urgency, but changes you make in haste may be just as dangerous and risky as the original emergency.

- **Post-incident review** – Once the emergency is concluded, with a full understanding of the root cause, the symptoms, the outcome, and the mitigations taken to resolve it, there needs to be a review that details the lessons learned from the incident. This allows for the analysis of what caused the emergency as well as any unintended consequences that happened due to the Break Glass scenario. This step is necessary to prevent the need to Break Glass the next time.

An effective postmortem of an emergency situation will transform into a future set of policies and procedures.

The overall flow in an emergency situation is shown in Figure 10-1.

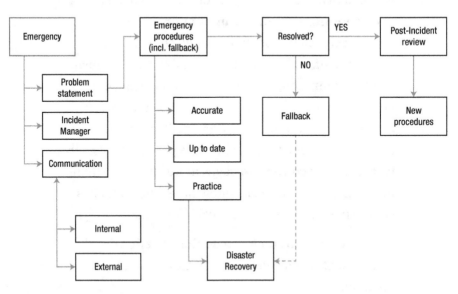

Figure 10-1. *Emergency procedures, from incident start to resolution, including the creation of new "peacetime" procedures*

Ask for Forgiveness

Everyone makes mistakes. How people handle them – both their own and those made by others – defines the ethical background of the entire IT environment. In the long term, this attitude will affect the levels of innovation and risk that people are willing to embrace as part of their work.

If you have made an error in your work, you should "own up." This is not meant to be a humiliating or punishing act. It should be an act of introspection that allows people to understand where they had done wrong and how to avoid such situations in the future. Similarly, you should be accepting of the fact your colleagues will sometimes err. A healthy workplace that allows people to discuss their mistakes and improve them will typically foster a higher level of innovation and cooperation. If people are afraid to speak up, they will avoid doing "risky" tasks, which can lead to intellectual stagnation. Worse, out of fear, they might try to cover up their mishaps, making the handling of emergency situations much more difficult.

Emergencies and Managers

Managers play a critical role in how their teams handle emergencies. Quite often, they do it badly. Naturally, people tasked with leading teams or groups will assume that they had the necessary skills to handle emergency situations. Unfortunately, while many managers have good "peacetime" skills, they may not be best suited for emergencies.

Technical problems can often be very complex, with nonlinear interaction among different components. The symptoms may be vague or obscure, and they will require a high level of expertise to troubleshoot them, so that situations with an unknown state can be brought back under control. Line managers may not necessarily have the right knowledge to act as decision-makers in such scenarios.

System administrators handling emergencies will already have enough stress as it is, without having someone watching over them. The presence of a manager can be distracting or even counterproductive, especially if the person does not have the right skills to fully grasp the problem.

Frustrations with managers: Whenever we had an emergency, the typical procedure would be for the on-duty manager for that week to assemble a group of engineers most likely or most suitable to handle the situation, bring them into a room, start a phone bridge – often with a customer contact on the other end – and then start working on the problem. Usually, the issue would not be well defined, so we would spend time even trying to frame the problem before we could actually do the initial analysis. The noise from the phone bridge and the multiple conversations in parallel were quite distracting and made concentrating on the task rather difficult. The on-duty manager and, sometimes, others (including more senior managers, who would often join as the situation progressed or escalated) would sit in the back of the room, working on unrelated activities on their laptops, and then occasionally raise their heads and ask for a "status update." They would rarely coordinate work, often had no technical expertise or useful advice, and their attitude made people feel as though they were being "monitored." We rarely ever fix things working this way in these emergency sessions, and it felt like an activity for the sake of it.

In an emergency situation, the manager's activities should be limited to coordination and communication. This includes prioritizing the emergency over other work for the technical experts, and scheduling shift teams if necessary. The one manager doing the emergency management should be the only person required to communicate status to other managers. Once the ashes cool down, managers should foster a culture of open dialog, without fear of retribution. It is often the vindictive attitude by team leaders or managers that causes people to "bunker down" in their work.

Conclusion

Emergency situations are a result of two elements – an unknown failure condition not encountered before and, even more importantly, the lack of preparedness by companies and technical teams to handle these conditions. The right approach is the certainty that emergencies will happen. Using the Design for Failure doctrine, the idea is to incorporate emergencies into the everyday operations and then work back from these catastrophic what-if scenarios to effective, robust mitigations.

These mitigations are encapsulated in Break Glass procedures, which need to be complete, up to date, relevant to the risk and probability of the scenarios they address, and universal enough to be applicable under the broadest range of conditions. Break Glass procedures also include effective communications and a detailed information trail so that ethical violations and nonstandard work actions during emergencies can be contained. With accurate data, system administrators can resolve previously unknown problems and incorporate them into everyday work so that the same emergency never needs to happen twice.

In the story, we also saw Mike featured prominently, acting as the incident manager in the crisis situation his team was facing. Indeed, leaders play a critical role in the greater scope of things.

EPILOGUE

Ethics for Managers

Wendell wasn't surprised that Mike suspected him of wrongdoing, but he was still feeling shocked that he was being asked to stay behind after the meeting. With his head sunk low, Wendell pivoted on the ball of his foot and then walked back into the corner by the AC vent. He was feeling hot all of a sudden, and not from the few steps he had taken across the room. Caesar gave him a sideways stare as he exited the room – pointing two fingers right at Wendell and then adding a little wink.

Mike sat down at the table again near Wendell. He had a blank document opened on his laptop, and it looked like he was going to take notes.

Wendell frowned. Somewhat reluctantly, he sat down near the corner, one chair away from Mike. He was thinking that there were so many things that Mike could accuse him of doing, but he knew he hadn't done anything wrong and that he certainly hadn't enabled customer data to be copied through the firewall. At least he couldn't think of any way he might have done that.

"I don't want to blame you. I am just hoping that you can explain things," Mike began in an accusing voice. "From what everyone was saying in the meeting, you were present every time something unethical happened over the past couple of months."

Wendell just sat there with a blank look on his face for a few seconds. "I did see some strange things," Wendell mumbled. "Copying software, disks being shot, and unapproved changes being made – but I didn't

© Igor Ljubuncic, Tom Litterer 2019
I. Ljubuncic and T. Litterer, *System Administration Ethics*,
https://doi.org/10.1007/978-1-4842-4988-8

do any of these things." Wendell didn't want to accuse anyone else, but wanted to make it clear that strange things had been happening independent of himself.

"I guess not, but you were involved. And you had access to administrative accounts, and a copy of the customer database," Mike emphasized.

"Only because you gave them to me," Wendell protested. "I didn't ask for that stuff. I thought it was strange to get administrative access during my first week at work. You were basically setting me up to get blamed for something." Wendell paused, and then continued, a little shaky. "I didn't realize getting a copy of the database was a bad thing – not until Frieda got me thinking about it several weeks later." He shrugged. "What was I to do?"

"I'm not blaming you," Mike reiterated. "But it's like you said, you had administrative rights before you knew what you were doing." He turned the back of the laptop toward Wendell and started typing. "I began wondering what you were up to ever since Frieda pointed out your lack of ethical understanding in the workplace – leaving your desktop unlocked and touching equipment in the data center – what else have you been up to?"

Wendell's apprehension was beginning to turn to anger. His face was still red, but now his neck was getting a little tense too. "Frieda was out of line; you said so yourself. I only stepped away for a minute while the rest of the team was right there." Wendell huffed. "And as far as the customer database goes, *you* asked me to do a project that parsed through customer data. With Belinda's help, I think we did a good job of keeping the data secure and creating the reports *you* asked for!" Wendell was beginning to sweat, so he slid his chair closer to the AC vent. "Didn't you say I got great results and that I should deploy the reports?"

"Well, yes." Mike hesitated a little. "But why were you in the data center – and why were you colluding with Gopal on the database upgrades?" He began to raise his voice a little.

Wendell was starting to feel cornered. "You asked me to!" Wendell cut in. "*You* said I should hang out with Gopal to learn about automation." Pausing, and in a calmer voice, he continued, "As I recall, you also approved that weird but fun team activity, and other strange ..."

Just then, Frieda opened the conference room door. "I have this room now; it's five after."

"Hey, Frieda!" Wendell blurted out just as Mike was about to talk.

"Hold on. Stay in here, and close the door behind you please," Mike spoke up over Wendell.

Frieda stared at them for a second. They could see the anger build on her face as she turned to close the door. "I've already waited 5 minutes for this room. Make it quick."

Mike continued, sounding rather rushed. "Okay. Do you think I approve strange and weird things?" he said in a tone that implied otherwise.

"I've been meaning to talk with you about your home system policy, Michael. You have been approving some high-priced items to go to people's homes." She wagged her index finger at him. "I'm sure that array you approved for Elwood had the customer database on it. Did he wipe that disk?" Frieda was beginning to get on a roll. "And those network changes you approved just to satisfy that one noisy customer, what was their angle anyway? You ..."

The door opened again as people poured in for Frieda's meeting. Mike quickly stood up and headed for the door. He turned around as Wendell took his time weaving through the people coming the other way. Looking at the calendar on his phone, Mike called back, "I'll see you in my office in half an hour."

Wendell spent the next half hour writing down all the things he thought other people had done wrong over the past couple of months: giving out root access, getting access to private information in the database, fudging data for reports, not funding software licenses, pushing through changes without the required info. All of these plus more were approved or instigated by Mike, Wendell thought.

The half hour passed quickly.

Wendell walked into Mike's office holding his list.

Mike startled a little, like he was interrupted from a deep thought. "Oh hi, Wendell. Thanks for coming by my office." After an awkward pause, Mike shook his head, "I can't believe Frieda brought up all of that irrelevant stuff. But she did make me think about a few things I let slide."

"She got me thinking too," Wendell said with impassiveness. "Mostly about the weird stuff I've seen going on that I mentioned to you."

"I don't want to blame you," Mike spoke. His tone was different now. No longer accusing as before. "There does seem to be an underlying problem – and that's probably not just you. What do you have there?" Mike pulled the paper from Wendell's hand. "Huh! Interesting. And you say all of these things happened?"

Wendell nodded.

"Well, people should know better than to do this kind of stuff." Mike slammed the paper on his desk. "We are all professionals here." Mike rose and started pacing around the office. "Well, you are new, and well, Elwood really hasn't had sysadmin training." He walked back behind his chair, staring at the paper on his desk. "And Gopal does his own thing, and from what you have here...David is downloading software!"

Mike continued staring at Wendell's list on the desk. Forgetting that Wendell was still in his office, he fell back into deep thought. *I guess it hasn't been made clear what is expected of professionals. Everyone on my team seems to have their own idea of what is ethical as a sysad. With everyone screwing things up, I really can't blame Wendell now or that will come back to me. It would have been so easy to just fire someone to show that I had found the problem. With Frieda and Wendell's accusations, the only person I could fire now is myself! Now what can I do to take the heat off me from upper management? What can I do to prevent problems from happening again? I wish I had some type of document I could point to. Like a code of ethics, but for system administrators!*

Mike noticed his eye was on the piece of paper on his desk. He picked it up and read Wendell's list again, thinking *these are things not to do*. "*Don't* give out the root password, *don't* access private information, *don't* fudge data ..." He looked up at Wendell shaking the paper in his hand. "Great document!"

Do We Need Managers?

Many managers went through ethics training in business school. They have had years of experience making ethical decisions. Most likely, they have made small mistakes throughout the years and learned from them. Being ethical within your own standards for the things that you do is relatively easy to gauge and contain. Holding yourself to a common ethical standard, and then being an example for a whole team or department is a little overwhelming – especially if you don't have any feedback from those around you on how well you are following the ethical standards.

Getting ethics right within a team might be so difficult because it is a relatively new concept for managers.

The foundation of management started in the military, and is probably best exemplified by the Roman Empire. The hierarchical structure of the Roman legions still exists in our corporate structure today, but the expectations around ethics has completely changed. A Roman centurion was the authority for the legionnaires serving under him. The centurion made every decision for the soldier, from what to eat to where to fight. Ethics was not a concern as long as they followed orders.

In the office place, managers do not have such overarching authority. The manager can assign work and set policies, but employees today have complete autonomy on how to do the work and follow policies.

Beyond the military, throughout the ages, many countries had a nobility class and the common workers. The nobility followed customs and manners when interacting among themselves, but no ethical concerns were paid to the common workers. As long as food was grown and goods were available, the nobility was happy to ignore the masses.

The real changes for management happened in the industrial age. Machined parts and factory assembly required not only precision parts but also predictable and interchangeable workers. To get this precision on the factory floor required military-like efficiency. Every worker doing exactly what the manager told them to do when it needed to be done.

Henry Ford perfected the assembly line using interchangeable parts to produce the Ford Model T in 1908. This mass production worked well to build the same car over and over again. But what if there was a flaw in one of the parts? How could an assembly-line worker, who was busy frantically installing the next part, report a bad component from the assembly work earlier in the line or a new way to do things better? Workers were interchangeable, just like the car parts, and did not deviate from the assigned assembly-line process.

In the 1970s, the auto manufacturers in Japan were trying to get into the American car market. In those days, Americans joked about unreliable and falling-apart Japanese cars. The Japanese managers looked for a way to improve quality and turned to their assembly-line workers. Any worker could stop the line if they found any problems. The problem was then root caused and eliminated before any more cars left the line. This worked so well that it forced Ford and other American manufacturers to introduce their own quality systems that, over a longer period of time, brought the same high-quality standards to American automobiles. Some of the processes introduced during this period, such as the Kanban board, TQM, and Six Sigma, are used by system administrators and their managers today.

Modern ethics started out of revolts to the modern assembly line. Shorter working hours, better pay, safety standards, child labor laws, and eventually unions were standardized in the early 20th century to not only improve the well-being of employees but also to increase productivity. Managers realized that if employees were well rested then they made fewer mistakes on the job. When they did not get sick or injured on the job, they would be available to work a full 40-hour week. Better pay meant job security, which led to experienced healthy and happy workers. Labor unions and government regulations standardized how workers are treated into a code of ethics – ethics about who can work, how many hours, in what conditions, and for how much pay. These ethics were enforced through the threat of strike by the unions, but there was very little consequence to the manager for mistreating an individual worker.

Then came World War II, which in the United States brought lots of competition for workers. Men joined the military and became reacquainted with the hierarchical management style of officers and enlisted men. Women began working traditionally male jobs. Due to the desperation of the situation, the efficiency and pace of work increased, but many shortcuts were taken which didn't incorporate ethics.

The aftermath of World War II brought new ethical standards to both the military and engineering. Atrocities (such as human testing) that happened during the war were found to be perpetuated by workers and soldiers following orders and not questioning authority when what they were being asked to do was clearly not ethical.

> *The duty and responsibility for ascertaining the quality of the consent rests upon each individual who initiates, directs or engages in the experiment. It is a personal duty and responsibility which may not be delegated to another with impunity.*
>
> —*The Nuremberg Code*

These new ethical standards encouraged workers to think for themselves and to question management when work was assigned that did not follow the code of ethics. Enlisted men were expected to learn the rules of engagement and other ethical codes, following them even when in stressful combat situations.

This leads us to today's manager. Not a military leader, not an aristocrat, not an industrial baron, and certainly not a dictator (well, ideally), but a coach who partners with employees to get the work done in the most ethical way possible.

System administrators have more workplace privileges and freedoms than any worker in history, it seems. They dress however they want to, work from anywhere, participate in deciding what work to do, and even purchase their own tools (laptops and phones). There are so many opportunities to make poor ethical decisions: doing personal errands during work hours, downloading movies on their laptops, doing freelance contract work, or not wearing pants during a phone meeting. What is ethical and what isn't? A manager of a system administrator must now also be their protector, setting clear guidelines on what can and cannot be done with their newfound freedom.

Back to the Future

What's next for the manager? Will hierarchical management someday become unnecessary?

Maybe in the future, a manager for system administrators' responsibilities will be split into several jobs done by several different people: program manager, Scrum master, human resources, coach, and ethics protector. The organizational structure might flatten, making the manager's roles equal to the system administrator and other technical players. All of these roles with different areas of ownership but equal ethics responsibility could then work together to create great ethical solutions.

With the coming decades being focused on data mining and artificial intelligence, ethics will be more important than ever. In the past, a system administrator could just stay away from and ignore private and sensitive data. With data mining, they could be involved in line item redacting of individual fields based on the permissions given by the data owner.

Account access was an on/off process in the past. In the future, everyone may just have an account everywhere, and it will be the data that needs to be protected with permissions. Not only permissions for people, but for different AI services, too.

Should AI programs have the same permission criteria as people? Can an AI program get access to genome data to search after a criminal? What about the search for a criminal's relatives? Or for people with the same traits as potential suspects? Hopefully system administrators won't need to make decisions on what is ethical, but they sure will need to be very diligent about following and enforcing the defined ethical commandments. Managers (or ethics protectors, as they may be called when the robots take over) must be there to guide and protect system administrators as ethics evolve.

If anything, the past has taught us that we cannot blindly rely on machines to make hard decisions for us, especially when human life is at risk. During the Cold War, had we fully entrusted our fate in computers and algorithms, we probably wouldn't be writing this book right now. In 1983, a Soviet Union's early warning system near Moscow detected an incoming American ballistic missile strike. Following protocol, the correct response would have been to retaliate in the short span of time available. Fortunately, Lieutenant Colonel Stanislav Petrov decided the warning was a false alarm and did not report the incident up the chain of command. It turned out the incorrect readings were caused by atmospheric reflection from high-altitude clouds, causing the early warning satellite infrared sensors to mistake them for missile launches. Lieutenant Colonel Petrov's logic and ethics and, in turn, his actions that day prevented nuclear war.

Almost four decades ago, our reliance on computers was a fraction of what it is today, and our dependence will only grow. Future managers will not have to face the difficult moral questions of human interaction; they will also have the burden of keeping machines in check.

The importance of ethics has never been greater.

The Ten Commandments of System Administration: A Manager's Perspective

Separate Roles

"Mike's keen on getting you on board as quickly as possible, so we're doing the expedited version."

Managers should set clear **policies** for using computer privileges, provide the right **tools** to make it easy to follow the policies, and then **reinforce** the importance of the policies. Mike, our manager in the story, provided a tool for storing and retrieving passwords, and processes for allocating personal privileged account credentials. This was a good start, but the employees saw the tool as an annoyance and a barrier. Mike allowed employees to work remotely, but he did not update the password tool to enable secure remote work. Because of this, Alex created a workaround that opened up a network vulnerability. Rather than reinforcing the ethical area of the first commandment (Separate Roles), Mike pushed Alex to allocate privileged accounts to Wendell. He should not have done that before Wendell had a business need for the privileges and was properly trained on privileged account usage. Without Mike reinforcing a culture of ethics, the system administrators on his team did not escalate when they had problems following the team's policies. In turn, this snowballed into overuse of privileged access without logging or accountability.

Respect Privacy

"Mike wants me to run a little experiment. He wants me to see if there are any correlations between our customers' home addresses and store locations."

Mike assigned Wendell a project that could not be completed without getting access to private information. Mike was not the data owner and did not have authority to grant access to the customers' home addresses. But since Mike is the manager, Wendell didn't think twice about getting the required data to complete the project. In an ethical culture that protects private data, employees will not access data using privileges unless authorized by the data owner. Managers must not put their team in a compromised position, and should serve as an example when it comes to respecting privacy.

> ***Data privacy: My manager insisted that we restore the accounts receivable database to the disaster recovery servers as part of the annual recovery test. The policies stated that all customer data would be located in the main data center. After bringing the issue to my manager, he agreed that the restore should be done with fake/random data. He also worked to change the policy so that the disaster recovery servers would be a valid recovery location for the database.***

Do Not Change Data

> *"Mike complained that his reports to his management look bad because of these odd glitches."*

Too often, managers create reports that show **the message they want to tell**. Data fields are left out, data sets are ignored, anomalous data is removed, only the mean of the data is displayed, and the scale of the graph chopped: anything to get the desired results. Mike had two possible paths: explain the data anomalies to his management or fix the anomalies at the source. He chose the unethical path of getting his staff to manipulate results.

Do Not Steal (Intellectual Property)

"Since it's not in our planned budget for the year, there's no way we can get funding to purchase it. Mike's never going to approve it."

Budgets, the bane of a system administrator's existence. System administrators often spend a sizable portion of their time writing scripts and configurations to avoid spending money on software that is already available. Managers complain that they spend more money on salaries for writing programs than they would have spent buying the software; and then once the thing is written, the maintenance never stops. It's not all bad though.

Open-source software was spawned from lots of independent programmers wanting to avoid purchasing licensed applications. This led to a community of coordinated development to create great tools while sticking it to the corporate man. While it's all fun and good to create great tools, it's illegal to steal intellectual property that was developed to provide the solution you needed – solutions that were created by people like **you** trying to make a living writing code.

Managers could prevent money conflicts by actively creating a budget for software and discussing the scope and constraints of the budget. When new things come up that will cause cost overruns, managers must then prioritize or consciously cut initiatives. Any cost overrun should be an opportunity to plan a more accurate budget the next year, possibly with a line for unplanned initiatives or, better yet, a budget entry to support the development of open-source tools.

> *Managing intellectual property: I have a couple of examples of when managers quickly reacted and purchased licenses for software that was being used in production. One was for a training class where one copy of the training application had been copied across 20 desktops in the training lab. In that case, the manager had the correct*

software purchased for the next class. Another case was when I installed a database for the accounting department of a small company. After they used it for several months, I remembered to let them know that they were using an evaluation copy. The manager wasn't happy that this new tool was going to cost them money, but seeing how the accounting department was much more efficient, he purchased the software to become compliant.

Do Not Steal (Computers)

"Mike had agreed to let him run this somewhat unconventional team building activity."

In the story, Mike set clear rules about how to track disks and data, including destroying disks before they left the facility. Taking disks to be destroyed in a different manner at an off-site location doesn't seem like a big deal, and at face value, it looks like a *really* fun team building event. But approving disks to be taken off-site for a day snowballs into Daniel taking a few disks home for testing and then Elwood taking home a full disk array that probably contained customer data. When managers define policies around using business equipment outside of work, they need to not only protect the business assets but also protect the employees. In most instances, a fully depreciated computer should be fine for the employee to take home from a business perspective, but releasing it to the employee with unlicensed software or sensitive/confidential data is exposing them to litigation that could get them (and yourself) fired.

Do Not Go Where You Are Not Wanted

"Look," Mike cut in. "Let's keep it down, people are trying to work. Wendell here is a new guy, so you need to give him some slack."

Rules about where you can go and what systems you can log into are mostly there to protect the employee. Elwood should have made sure Wendell signed into the data center log and noted his reason for being there. Of course, Wendell didn't cause any harm, such as plugging a USB device infected with a virus into the database server, but because he was there, if a virus was ever discovered, then he must be investigated. Managers should support their employees' decisions and actions as Mike did, and then they should address ethical concerns, such as taking an unnecessary trip into the data center. We've witnessed many major incidents caused by the wrong people being in the data center, usually relating to the big red Emergency Power Off (EPO) button by the door.

> *Don't hit the red button: I have heard a couple of different stories about someone pushing the big red button, the EPO button that cuts all power in the data center. This button only needs to be pushed if someone is being electrocuted. The first story I heard was about a data center that had a red door release button right next to the EPO button. One day, a student intern hit the wrong button when leaving the data center. After this incident, a flip cover was put on over the button and a sign was posted indicating which button was for the door and which one not to touch. That intern was eventually hired; he now shares this story with every new employee joining the company. The second story was when a security guard smelled a burnt capacitor during a security sweep in the data center. She hit the EPO button thinking it was the right thing to do. Through that experience, she and the security team learned about the smoke detection and fire suppression systems in the data center. They also learned that the EPO should only be used when someone's life is in danger. In both cases, the lessons learned prevented a recurrence at each company.*

Follow Procedures and Get Out

"Mike is fully aware of the request, and he told me to do what I can to get marketing off his back."

Making changes in innovative ways is exciting and fun for the system administrator; following procedures is boring and dull. Mike telling Gopal to do what it takes to meet the customers' needs is like telling Elwood to destroy the disks with his 12-gauge while they are still in the server rack! Managers need to be encouraging system administrators to use known methods for making as few changes as possible when using privileged access. These methods can be reinforced by providing infrastructure as code (IaC) tools that can be used to build and refine the computer environment within a test framework and then replicate it to production once ready. The excitement for the system administrator is then not in inventing a new way to do the same thing over and over again, but in refining, automating, and then building new functionality on top of the existing foundation.

Communicate Change

"I'd like to talk about something that might be urgent. Well, it is urgent. Mike insisted on this getting done right away."

Managers might not understand how to build a server, how to use the software tools, or how to program, but they do know how to communicate. If there is any one area where a manager can add value for the system administrator, it is in communicating – communicating across functional teams, communicating with customers, communicating goals, and communicating change. When Imam mentioned Mike's name in the change control meeting, Henry pushed forward with urgency, not because Mike was offering a carrot or a stick if the change did or did not happen, but because Mike is the conduit between his team and everyone else.

If Mike insisted on the change, then he must have done the hard work of understanding the customers' needs and addressing concerns from other groups. This level of communication is the manager's job, which enables system administrators to do their job efficiently and without interruption. Of course, both managers and system administrators should follow the change procedures, which include communication processes and schedules, but it is up to the manager to refine the communication process and to only augment it when their independent communication warrants.

> *Communication story: As part of my role as the operating system architect, I developed a framework of automated kernel crash collection and analysis for our Linux servers. The tool was distributed globally to tens of thousands of servers, and helped us identify bugs in the kernel, which we would then submit to the operating system vendor for patching. One time, we found a fairly major bug. As soon as we had the patched version available, we rolled it out in the local data center. However, in one of our sister sites abroad, the compute team was reluctant to make any changes, due to pressure from their customers. They were aware of the risks, but decided not to go forward with the patching. As Murphy would have it, they soon experienced major downtime, with hundreds of servers undergoing kernel crashing overnight, prompting emergency patching site-wide, which had a much greater impact and disruption to the customer than a planned, preemptive rollout would have done. Following this outage, the sister site (with newfound cooperation from the customers) established an emergency patch rollout process, which included proactive communication about patch criticality.*

Do No Harm

"All right. Give it half an hour, then do it."

More difficult than communicating is making the hard calls. Even though many managers don't have the expertise to understand all of the trade-offs between technical solutions, they will still be asked to make the final go/no-go decision. Experienced system administrators will present managers with as few choices as possible, ideally two.

Managers should spend a lot of their time training their employees on ways to help them understand the important aspects of the technical work. Managers do this training by asking pertinent high-level questions such as

- Why is this change needed?

- What will happen if you do nothing?

- Is there a better way to do this?

Managers gather knowledge to be ready to answer the crucial question: Should we make this change? Or even more crucially: Should we make this change *even though* this unexpected anomaly happened?

When the manager answers, it should be with the clear intent to do no harm.

Break Glass

"Mike had taken over the keyboard, and now that they had access to the wallet, he was feverishly writing down the privileges passwords for the different system types."

The manager must make themselves available to lead in any Break Glass situation and set a calm, methodical tone. Mike added to the chaos of the emergency by running around and shouting. He also handed off the most delicate task to Wendell without any oversight or follow-up. As leaders in Break Glass situations, managers should do the tasks that keep their employees safe. They "tell everyone" by communicating the status to management and customers through each phase of the situation: expected completion time, next update time, and expected residual issues. Managers coordinate with other teams that need to do validation testing or take the next shift of work. They also "leave a trail" by taking notes, capturing the timeline, and tracking who is involved.

A manager leading a Break Glass situation will document and understand what caused the need for Break Glass, what the current state is, and what needs to be done to complete the need for Break Glass. Finally, when the situation is under control, the manager coordinates plugging the holes and repairing the drapes. The next workday, the manager can use the notes he or she took as the base for the post-incident review meeting.

Create a Culture of Ethics

Constantly checking people's work, running independent audits, and penalizing employees for bad behavior – that is no way to run an organization!

A better way would be employees following procedures and getting their work done on time.

A team set up to have a culture of ethics is one where system administrators:

- Improve procedures.

- Protect themselves with software tools.

- Learn from mistakes.

- Talk about ethical concerns.

A manager who sets up the foundation for a culture of ethics:

- Exemplifies ethical behavior.

- Provides the right tools.

- Accepts mistakes as learning.

- Listens to ethical concerns.

Posting the ten commandments of system administration ethics on the wall is not enough to make sure things are done ethically. Managers must make ethics be an integral part of the daily culture.

In a culture of ethics, workers look out for ethical issues and will quickly fix tasks that are not following ethical procedures. They will create tools to automate those procedures and run internal audits to detect procedures that are not designed for ethics. These audits will not be for spying on people or to find whom to fire, but to detect areas for improvement and refinement as the team strives for a culture of ethics.

> *Ethics in culture: An application user asked the area owner of license management how they could spoof the MAC address on their new server in order to share the license with the old server. The license manager found an under-utilized floating network license that another department had already purchased. They then helped negotiate sharing the floating license, keeping both departments license compliant and also saving the company money.*

In turn, managers need to listen to their employees' complaints about unnecessary rules and procedures. If you want a culture of ethics, the list of ethics must be relevant for the work at hand. If employees continue to work around or violate an ethics commandment, then this might be an indicator that the commandment needs to be changed. Managers who refine their code of ethics based on the assigned work will gain trust from the team; they will in turn continue to work harder to follow the common set of ethics.

Exemplify Ethical Behavior

Everyone has an internal code of ethics. System administrators generally want to do what is ethical, but without specific guidance, they will follow their own internal ethics, ethics displayed by their peers, and, most influential, ethical examples seen from their managers. How does a new system administrator quickly learn ethics? How do experienced system administrators stay motivated and not become complacent? How can managers make sure every employee meets the same ethical expectations?

Managers can define a baseline of ethical behavior by being ethical themselves. They can achieve this by following the ethical policies to the fullest and including ethics in all projects and initiatives. The ten commandments of system administration ethics are not optional for managers. A system administrator should never have the option to escalate to a manager to break a commandment. Managers should be clear that the commandments must be followed at all times, in public and in private, up and down the employee and management chain. Some easy steps managers can take to be a good example for ethics include the following:

- Have the ten commandments of ethics listed in conference rooms and meeting notes.

- Include agenda items in project and staff meetings to talk about ethical dilemmas.

- Listen to concerns about ethics and take immediate action.

- Don't make one-time exceptions – Refine procedures and processes if required.

- Do have a process for adjusting the ethical policies as a whole.

- Even critical projects that must be completed quickly need to include an ethical component. It is important for ethics to be incorporated in the planning of projects and not as an afterthought. For example, what if the wrong person had access to the project data or private information was shared or communication about the project was not sent? Beginning with ethics will prevent a lot of problems in the end.

Let's look back at the assignment Mike gave to Wendell. By not including an expectation of ethics in the project, Wendell relied on his own and Belinda's internal knowledge of ethics. Wendell, being new, did not have examples of ethical behavior from Mike. Belinda, on the other hand, experienced many times where Mike, and those working on behalf of Mike, exemplified ethical behavior. Based on the outcome, the examples she experienced were to protect the production database, but non-production copies were free to use. In some companies, that might be fine, but in our example, private customer data was exposed to someone who did not have the need to know and was copied to a potentially less secure location.

Provide the Right Tools

How can I catch ethics violators in my organization? What can I do to see if private data was accessed or if restricted servers were utilized for unintended purposes?

These are **not** the right questions to ask in a culture built around ethics. The goal is not to catch violators, but to **prevent violations from happening**! Ethics-focused tools protect employees by providing clear boundaries and directions, like guardrails on the highway. System administrators want to protect their customers and data and, if managers provide guidance and tools, will do all that they can to follow the ten commandments of system administration ethics. With the right tools in place, it will be clear to the system administrator where the ethical boundaries are and if the boundaries are breached. Tools, procedures, and culture should self-manage ethics so that reporting ethics violations directly won't be necessary. System administrators will simply report procedural issues where improvement is needed. Continuous improvement over time will close any gaps in the ethical guardrails, creating a much more ethically secure environment than what a manager would get in a culture that is continuously searching for violators.

Since a culture of ethics will improve over time, the initial set of tools does not need to cover every ethical boundary for every situation. Costs, functionality, and reliability are the three main things to consider when selecting tools. Managers should prioritize available funds for the ethical commandments that are most likely to be violated in their organization. A medical facility might prioritize funding for the second commandment (Respect Privacy), a brokerage might focus on the sixth commandment (Don't Go Where You Are Not Wanted), and software developers could decide to spend money primarily on the eighth commandment (Communicate Change). Tools with the most detailed functionality will focus on the highest-priority ethics areas, while lower-priority areas can be covered through procedures. A software development group that uses cloud services and has a stipend for desktop equipment won't have a need for ethics tools focused on the fifth commandment (Do Not Steal (Computers)) since the work procedure eliminates any violation opportunities.

Managers can provision tools by buying them, getting open-source tools, or allocating time to build the tools. Each method has different advantages and disadvantages. This is shown in Table E-1.

Table E-1. *The breakdown of cost, functionality, and reliability*
requirements for different types of software life cycles

	Cost	Functionality	Reliability
Buy	High upfront and licensing costs, but predictable over time	High functionality, but no flexibility to customize for your organization	(Typically) highly reliable with the backing of a company of experts
Open-source	Low upfront and no ongoing licensing costs. Maintenance will need to be done in-house or paid for through a vendor	Usually focused on a point solution. No flexibility unless you provide development resources to contribute back to the open-source development community	Highly dependent on the popularity of the tool and the development community behind the tool. It is best to use open-source tools that have been well proven in similar organizations. Anything that goes wrong will need to be corrected in-house
Build	It's free! No. Building and maintaining custom code requires a lot of development time, which means paying salaries. If done right, the developers should have development and test environments	Low functionality to begin with, but focused on the highest-priority areas for your organization. Over time, more ethical boundaries will be established	Every deployment is the first time the software is ever used in production. Expect problems and gaps in coverage. Since the tool targets the specific needs of the organization, problems are easier to detect and can be fixed in-house

Continuous improvement usually requires tools to be built in-house. This is a fine way to understand and prototype functional needs, but unless you have a development team, the next step should be to identify an open-source tool that meets most of the critical needs. For the highest-priority ethical area, more money will likely need to be spent on software licensing or development time in order to meet all of the requirements that are needed from the tool.

Listen to Ethical Concerns, Especially About YOU

Historical hierarchical management structures are not designed for employees to freely discuss ethical concerns about themselves and especially their manager with management. After all, the manager is the person who hired you, gives you an office, decides work assignments, sets policies, gives raises, and can fire you. What advantage does it give to an employee to question their manager's ethical behavior or policies?

In the modern work environment, managers most often act as a coach rather than a dictator. Managers can provide experiential advice that shows vulnerability and exposes mistakes they made while learning. Being vulnerable as a coach helps the employee feel comfortable about sharing their concerns and eventually mentioning ethical concerns about management behavior and policies. Quickly addressing the concerns, through policy or personal behavior changes, will reinforce that ethics is taken seriously.

To encourage system administrators to tell their manager about ethical concerns, they first need to care about ethics and the consequences to the organization when ethics are violated. The employee might think they were hired to keep their heads down and do their job. One way to get them to look up to see how their behavior affects others is to assign them a clear area of ownership. Having clear responsibility prompts them to look around to see how others, including their manager, are impacting their area. Managers can reinforce this ownership by providing training in the assigned area and providing the tools required for the job.

> *Noticing ethical issues: A recent restore of home directories was discovered by one of our system administrators to be exported to all servers within the firewall. After this discovery, management purchased tools to help detect open shares and changed policies for restore locations. Because management wasn't focused on blame, but on preventing another data exposure incident, the team worked together to identify all possible ways this open export could have been exploited. Many potential security holes were plugged due to one person identifying an ethical concern.*

Since management owns ethics policies, system administrators with an area of responsibility will bring ethical concerns within and affecting their ownership area to their manager. Over time, as trust is gained, the employee will pay more attention to other areas that interact with theirs and, eventually, begin to notice ethical issues across the organization.

Forgive and Refine

Why would you fire someone for making one mistake? What if they made a million-dollar mistake? Well, they just learned a million-dollar lesson about what mistake not to make again. In a culture of ethics, they will then tell everyone they ever work with about the lesson they learned. They will also work hard to get procedures and automation in place to prevent anyone from making the mistake again. Since system administration is not taught in school, many learn from making a series of little mistakes over the years that help them learn. In an environment that encourages sharing mistakes as well as successes, those lessons propagate between system administrators resulting in the next person's mistakes being even smaller.

A manager that reprimands employees for making a mistake will only cause people to hide their mistakes. If people are hiding their mistakes, then no one can learn from them, and they will happen again. Earlier in this chapter, you saw how people learned from mistakenly hitting the red EPO button. Here are a couple of other examples showing how the overall computing environment improved after a mistake.

Learning from mistakes: One time, I wanted to deploy a new test version of a popular source code Software Configuration Management (SCM) client tool on a handful of systems. If this test turned out well, our plan was then to deploy the software in a staggered manner to the entire environment of about 5,000 machines. I added the deployment rule to our configuration management server and went to have lunch. A few minutes later, I got an urgent call from one of our internal customers, complaining that their SCM servers were being unresponsive. I finished my lunch early and went to investigate. I soon learned I had used a wrong classifier (OR instead of AND) in the rule for the test version deployment, which pushed the new software to the ENTIRE environment. The clients then effectively subjected the handful of servers to an accidental Distributed Denial of Service (DDoS-ed), creating a massive queue of registration requests and blocking legitimate work. The load finally ebbed after a while as we cleaned up the environment – accidentally, it did prove that the new version was working and that we had a fairly robust setup in place. The longer-term lesson was to add sanitation rules on the configuration management servers to avoid simple but potentially big errors like mine. The manager of the team was quite understanding and accommodating of the whole situation. She realized this was an easy-to-make mistake, and she emphasized the use of better and more extensive pre-deployment checks.

Conclusion

Technically minded people expect technical challenges when they come to work in an IT environment. They rarely pause to think about the moral implications of their actions or how they may affect the technical elements of their duties. While some people are aware and even mindful of the softer side of relations and communication at their workplace, they don't necessarily ascribe a moral dimension to it, especially not when it comes to their own responsibilities.

Unfortunately, the world of IT is rapidly changing and has become so tightly woven into the fabric of society that it is impossible to separate the ethics from hardware and software. IT is no longer just a heap of machines doing computation; it is a vital part of our lives, embedded in critical urban infrastructure, in our healthcare and private lives. Most system administrators do not expect or believe to have signed up for a complex ethical adventure when they sit down in front of a computer.

Throughout this book, we have discussed many different aspects where ethics cross the technological boundaries. We talked about the principles, methods, and tools that system administrators, data center technicians, engineers, and even programmers can utilize to minimize their exposure to ethical violations. Each chapter reviewed the almost casual ambiguity and the gray-area pitfalls of seemingly innocent, everyday actions that can have immense ramifications on the freedom of work, on morale, on data privacy, on customer relations, and on the overall security of the IT environment.

And then, there are managers. Their conduct and approach to the work done by each of their employees will directly influence the ethical tone across the entire team. Managers play a crucial role in identifying and controlling the subtle work behaviors so that they promote and encourage ethical conduct and minimize violations in a productive, transparent manner. While most managers don't necessarily do hands-on technical work, their actions are just as important in shaping the outcome of commands, scripts, and programs.

For the managers building their career in IT, the future is uncertain. The world of computers from 20 or 30 years ago has changed significantly, and it will most likely change even more profoundly in the decades to come. We are branching into fields of technology and science that did not exist only a few short years ago, and their impact on our lives will trump the introduction of the Internet to the general population. The moral implications of artificial intelligence, deep learning, and an even growing dependency on machines in society will be the kind of challenges that humanity has never faced before. And the brunt of philosophical, ethical, and possibly even criminal responsibility will fall on the shoulders of techies just looking to do some honest scripting or coding. The manager of tomorrow will definitely have a tougher job than their current peers.

Looking to the future, this book does not have all the answers. But it is a solid foundation for finding ethical certainty when faced with complex technological ambiguity. Perhaps we cannot fathom or solve every challenge that is going to rise on the IT horizon. But in the same way, many basic principles of society and democracy as laid down by the Ancient Greeks and Romans still hold true today, thousands of years later. The ten commandments of system administration ethics are a good starting point for finding clear, unequivocal guidelines to technological issues of the present and the future. Hopefully, time will prove us right.

Index

A

Accidental harm, 212, 223
Account management,
      15, 19, 22, 148
Accurate management, 117
Active deterrents, 117
Administrative account, 17
Anscombe's Quartet, 74
Audits and alerts, 20–21
Automation, 22, 24, 149

B

Break glass procedure
    failure, classification, 244
    last resort solution, 245
    risk, mapping, 244
Bring Your Own Device (BYOD), 119
Brute-force solutions, 113
Bugs, 213, 223

C

Change action calculator, 196
Change board process, 190
Changing data
    repercussions, 63
    results

automation and
    filtering, 64–66
documented data access
    process, 68
guidelines, 66
skewed metrics, 67
suspect error
    finding source, 69, 70
    issues, 70, 71
Chief information security
    officer (CISO), 43, 51
Clear processes, 145
Commandments, manager's
    perspective
    Break Glass situation, 271, 272
    communication, 269, 270
    culture of ethics, 272, 273
    data anomalies, 265
    data center, 268
    ethical behavior, 274
        employees mistake, 280
        ethical concerns, 278, 279
        managers, 274
        right tools, 275, 276, 278
        steps, 274, 275
    go/no-go decision, 271
    IaC, 269
    intellectual property, 266

CPSIA information can be obtained
at www.ICGtesting.com
Printed in the USA
LVHW081108210922
728931LV00001B/2